Castles of Gold

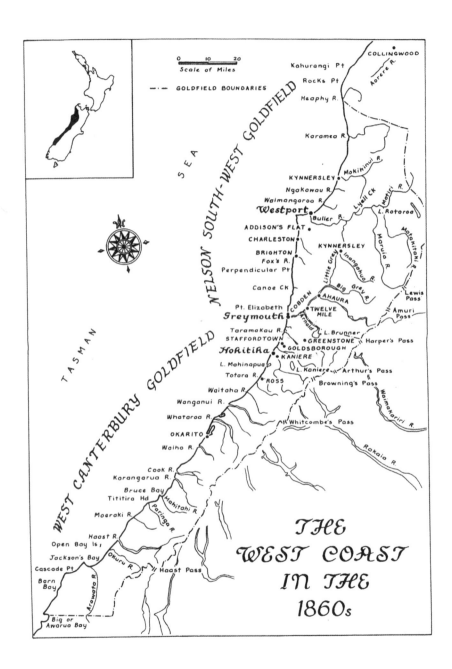

Map of the 'West Coast' of New Zealand

Castles of Gold
A History of New Zealand's West Coast Irish

Lyndon Fraser

OTAGO

For Philip Ross May and Patrick O'Farrell

Published by Otago University Press
PO Box 56/Level 1, 398 Cumberland Street, Dunedin, New Zealand
Fax: 64 3 479 8385. Email: university.press@otago.ac.nz
www.otago.ac.nz/press

First published in 2007
Copyright © Lyndon Fraser 2007
ISBN 978 1 877372 44 5

Printed by Astra Print Ltd, Wellington

Contents

List of Illustrations

Acknowledgements

The gold rushes to the West Coast were, in the words of Philip Ross May, 'as much' an episode 'in Australian as New Zealand history; because of its physical isolation from the remainder of the South Island', the region had 'strong links with the eastern colonies of Australia'. Such were the manifold connections of trade and people, he suggests, that in the mid-1860s the land that stretched north from Awarua to Kahurangi Point was 'an economic dependency of Victoria' and Hokitika 'a trans-Tasman suburb of Melbourne'.[1] It seems appropriate, then, that I should complete *Castles of Gold* as a Visiting Fellow in the Department of History at the University of Melbourne. This position has given me the space to write the final drafts of the manuscipt and provided a stimulating and warmly collegial environment in which to work. I would like to extend my sincere gratitude to Patricia Grimshaw, Elizabeth Malcolm, Charles Zika, Stephen Wheatcroft, Val Noone and Gabrielle Murphy for their assistance and encouragement during my sabbaticals here in 2002 and 2006. I am also very grateful to Rob Hyndman, Suzie Webster, Geoff Richards, Deborah Perrott and all my family and friends.

I have accrued a great many debts to others over the six years it has taken to finish this book. The project received generous financial support from the Ministry for Culture and Heritage, the University of Canterbury and the University of Aberdeen. I would like to give special thanks to Angela McCarthy, Ted Matthews, Nicola Hansen, Rebecca Osbourne, Sarndra Lees, Rochelle-Lee Bailey, Mary Rooney and Sarah Dwyer for their invaluable contribution to the research process. Kevin Clark and Gerard Hogg arranged admission to Roman Catholic repositories in Christchurch and Wellington, Rory Sweetman kindly facilitated extensive photocopying of the *New Zealand Tablet* in Dunedin and Jim Stenhouse gave permission to use the

Registrar-General's death and marriage records in Lower Hutt. My research for *Castles of Gold* was also assisted by the enthusiasm and munificence of staff at the West Coast Historical Museum and Archives New Zealand in Christchurch.

This study would not have been possible without the help of many family historians and local informants who shared their materials and memories with me. I am deeply obliged to Kevin Bourke, Julia Bradshaw, Barrie Lynn Callinan, Ian Cameron, John Coghlan, Peter Ewen, Peter Kerridge, Ted Matthews, Jack Minehan, Donald Murphy, Bill Nolan, Brian Nolan, Bill and Mary O'Connor, Teresa O'Connor, Ron Patterson, Peter Read, Dennis Regan, Mary Rooney, Juann Ryan, John F. Tourelle, Brian Wood and Les Wright. I am also grateful to Donald Harman Akenson, Terry Austrin, Barbara Brookes, Seán Brosnahan, Malcolm Campbell, Bob Hall, Don MacRaild, Brad Patterson, Jock Phillips, Evan Poata-Smith and Katie Pickles. My editor, Wendy Harrex, and staff at Otago University Press have been marvellous. Finally, I want to thank Anna Rogers for her fantastic work as copy editor of the manuscript.

I owe my greatest intellectual debt to the brilliant West Coast historians Philip Ross May (author of my favourite New Zealand book) and Patrick O'Farrell (my PhD examiner). *Castles of Gold* is warmly dedicated to their memory.

LYNDON FRASER
MELBOURNE, NOVEMBER 2006

1   The Prospect

I

When Ellen Walsh of Paulstown, County Kilkenny, sailed to Hokitika from Melbourne in 1870 she entered a landscape quite unlike anything she had encountered in Australia. Beyond the rolling breakers that swept over the treacherous bar at the port's river entrance, Ellen caught her first glimpses of the goldfields' capital and its surrounding hinterland. A glance northwards from the open roadstead outside the mouth revealed the back premises of Revell Street, the town's principal thoroughfare, stretching in an irregular fashion along the beach that had been an unmarked wilderness of sand dunes and driftwood before the gold discoveries six years earlier. A vast expanse of rugged coastline led toward Greymouth, the region's second port, and on past the richly auriferous terraces and pakihi that sustained instant mining townships like Brighton, Addison's Flat and Charleston, to the flourishing commercial centre of Westport, on the north bank of the Buller River. The view from starboard encompassed the grand sweep of South Westland, with its extensive collection of ramshackle towns, abandoned beach workings and tiny encampments hidden behind a dense mantle of scrubland, flax and ancient rain forest. In the background, a magnificent procession of towering mountain ranges zigzagged in both directions up and down the coastline, their majestic silence contrasting vividly with the crashing waves that assaulted vessels approaching the Hokitika bar.

As they rounded the North Spit and reached the sanctuary of the harbour, Ellen and her fellow passengers confronted the brilliant spectacle of Gibson's Quay, the available wharfage tightly jammed with shipping, the riverbank bustling with horses and drays, workmen and messengers, while the shrill cries of scavenging gulls punctuated the incessant clamour from the streets below.[1] Along the winding quayside an array of substantial buildings proclaimed the town's status as a major goldfields emporium and pointed inland toward the Kaniere diggings, clearly visible from the upper reaches of the harbour.

An extraordinary mixture of peoples made up the new society that emerged here during the nineteenth century. On the bush tracks and beach highways connecting the numerous goldfields communities, travellers might encounter French priests, solitary hatters, 'black' tinkers and old hands, together with 'All Nations' parties, domestic servants, prostitutes and small mining gangs from rural villages in China's Upper Panyu. The cosmopolitan nature of the region's population was also readily apparent in rickety townships like Charleston and Brighton, where the distinctive accents of Durham coalminers, Norwegian sawmillers and Shetlanders from Unst mingled with the voices of London dressmakers, Cornish engineers and Limerick housemaids. In the streets of Greymouth, Poutini Ngai Tahu of the Mawhera reserve rubbed shoulders with diggers from Dumfries, North Devon and Cape Breton, as well as the merchants and storekeepers of various nationalities who rented properties on their land. As the gold rushes gained momentum, the entire region from Awarua north to Kahurangi Point became a meeting place of diverse connections, influences and interrelations.

The bewildering cosmopolitanism of the digging population elicited colourful reports from contemporary observers. Julius Haast, the Canterbury Provincial Geologist, described how he heard not only English but 'German, Italian, Greek and French and several other tongues' spoken in the streets of Hokitika. The prospectors he encountered came from a range of social backgrounds and included many 'respectable people', who 'once had a better position in life, and another song sung at [their] cradle'.[2] Writing to his grandniece Ellen in Montana, Cork-born miner John O'Regan drew comparisons between the local and North American environments: 'The colonists [are] all white except a few niggers and Chinese [and] are composed of all races just like your population. The taste and habits of both people are much a like, even the conversation is very near and like the Yankees.' He was impressed by the standard of dress on the goldfields, 'particularly the young girls, who always sport Pompadour colours and rakish "Muslin whiskers"!!! Like the American girls also they have bad teeth and shew age under 30 years, are fond of pleasure and hop Sally dancing.' Yet the exotic strangeness of the landscape created a marked point of contrast for a toughened colonial accustomed to harsh summers in Australia and the wide expanses of the American West: 'Well the surface is as a Countryman said to me one day. "Mr O'R', said he, "Do you know what this country reminds me of?" I had a notion of what was coming but waited for his comparison and it was a good one. "It is like a Troubled Sea".' O'Regan considered the 'many rivers' to be 'deep and rapid, one particularly like the Colorada. It never gives up the dead.' But the unusual fauna compensated for the 'dreary aspect' of the scenery. 'There are very small birds that cannot fly knocking about yet. Some haunt my house and garden. I give them a bit when they come. They have a shrill and slender voice like the devil.'[3]

The cultural complexities noted by visitors to the region were compounded by the rapid expansion of the mining frontier. From Greenstone Creek, where prospectors struck payable gold in 1864, an army of diggers moved across the ground like locusts, drawn by the intoxicating dream of the elusive pile. Crude settlements materialised suddenly on the beaches or riverbanks, fresh strikes caused headlong rushes and the tiny encampments of canvas tents and shanty stores evaporated overnight as restless men swarmed toward new alluvial country. The spectacular discoveries pushed the diggings south to Bruce Bay and along the Buller coastlands as far as the Mokihinui, further accelerating the momentum of the seaborne invasion from Otago and Australia. Even when the region's economy settled into a less frantic rhythm after the boom years of the 1860s, the ebb and flow of people continued, albeit on a much reduced scale. By the early 1880s, Ellen Walsh, now the widowed Ellen Piezzi, reported forlornly from Goldsborough that she 'had a great many losses this year. Pepel gone true the cort turning onsolvent. I lost a fine cow £15 pounds wurt in a hole in the bush. I canot get any of my old accounts in. The pleas is so poor.' The vicissitudes of the local scene encouraged many to seek their livelihoods elsewhere: 'Mrs pozzi is gone to chrst church. That is at the other sids but the famely is here yet. Dont know When they goe. They canot sell the pleas yet. There is Now money here at present in serkleason [*circulation*]. Any one have they are gone away.'[4]

The makeshift character of this strange and turbulent world was vividly portrayed in contemporary photographic images. Plates 1–3 depict an array of vessels crammed along every available wharf at Hokitika, a view looking east up Gibson's Quay toward the faint outlines of the Southern

Alps, and a small section of Revell Street and its adjacent neighbourhood, much as Ellen Walsh saw them in the early 1870s. The buildings pictured here are rough and weathered, the wood and corrugated iron conveying a sense of impermanence, as if the whole townscape might be swept away or abandoned at any moment. This impression is strengthened by Plates 4–6, which show rickety Charleston from atop Nile Hill, the settlement at Goldsborough (near Stafford) and Dillmanstown amid swathes of bush and fluming, with Patrick McGrath's store perched precariously on the edge of the main thoroughfare. These once-crowded places have vanished, along with the frontier mining camps like those of Clare-born Dan Molony and his party at Dirty Mary's Creek (Plate 7). The men and women who first converged on the region did not build to last and left only blackened headstones in deserted cemeteries to mark their presence (Plates 8 and 9).

The very act of viewing these images in the present, from our own vantage point, shows that their meanings are not fixed 'from one moment or period to another'.[5] How can we regard them now without a revisionist's eye for the bleak terrain of tangled tree-stumps, receding terrace faces and discarded tailings? The transition from haphazard fossicking to more elaborate mining techniques such as hydraulic sluicing, deep whim-shafting and tunnelling resulted in several kinds of ecological damage: the silting of river systems and waterways, the arbitrary dumping of debris and the destruction of indigenous vegetation.[6] Francis Redwood, the first Catholic Archbishop of New Zealand, was one of the few contemporary visitors to reflect on the environmental impact of gold fever. From Piper's Hill, above Kumara, he saw 'an admirable picture of the plateau beneath, which was a sea of splendid native verdure, of every tint imaginable. What grand timber trees! lofty, thick and straight, with a profusion of varied vegetation entwining their stems. It was a sight to delight a New Zealander's eye and cling to his memory for ever.' But this idyllic setting had disappeared and 'the present township, shorn of its early importance, shows not a vestige of the forest in its vicinity, but is surrounded with a bleak, bare, treeless scene such as most mining places but too often present. It is desolation after paradise.'[7]

The expansive spirit of the gold rushes – so brilliantly captured in Philip Ross May's writing – was simultaneously a glorious triumph and a colossal tragedy. On the one hand, we can find much to admire in the extraordinary dynamism unleashed by the expansion of capitalism in the region. The sheer scale of human movement, the relentless surge of production and the disturbed, accelerated sense of time were exhilarating aspects of goldfields life. On the other, however, we cannot evade the destruction wrought on the landscape by the waves of energetic fortune-seekers, nor the rapid cultural and material appropriation of land and resources from Poutini Ngai Tahu. John O'Regan hinted at the wider forces at work in his description of local Maori. 'The aboriginal race so nearly black with long and coarse hair, stout and prone to obesity, great warriors with their own weapons. Cannibals in the truest sense', he told his niece, 'but have good sense and are hospitable, particularly to Irishmen more than to others. If they were a million strong, England could never conquer them. They have a war dance which is disgusting to look at.'[8] The events that burst upon the region and its inhabitants with such 'revolutionary violence' cannot be fully understood without reference to its larger imperial dimension.[9]

Several thousand Irish-born migrants and their descendants lived in the richly variegated communities that developed along the West Coast's bush-lined rivers and alluvial terraces. Most newcomers made their way to the region from the Australian colonies – either directly or via Otago – and many belonged to expatriate networks that extended back and forth across the Tasman Sea. As Donald Harman Akenson reminds us, they were also active participants in far-reaching imperial systems, even though few had been directly involved 'with any official imperial apparatus'.[10] My aim in the next section is to place the experiences of men and women like John O'Regan and Ellen Walsh in their wider global context, a task that is fundamental to the writing of Irish migration history. The final sections offer a brief overview of the arguments and approaches that underpin the book's thematic chapters and relate these findings to recent work on the Irish abroad.

II

'Growing up in Ireland', says historian David Fitzpatrick, 'meant preparing oneself to leave it.'[11] Since the opening decades of the eighteenth century more than nine million Irish people have ventured abroad, a number that exceeds the country's population at its historical peak on the eve of the Great Famine (1845–50). During the nineteenth century, emigration became 'a massive, relentless and efficiently managed national enterprise'.[12] Between Waterloo and the Famine an estimated one and a half million people left and an even greater number fled their homes when the potato blight struck.[13] Between 1851 and 1920 more than four million migrants sailed from Irish ports for various overseas destinations, the great majority taking passages directly to the United States.[14] Large contingents went to Canada, Australia and New Zealand, while smaller numbers settled in Latin America and South Africa. As many as a million others migrated to Britain, where many settled in London, Manchester, Liverpool and Glasgow.[15] Overall, then, around five million people left Ireland in the seven decades after the Famine. Such was the magnitude of the diaspora that by the late nineteenth century more Irish-born people and their descendants were living overseas than remained in the old country.[16] In this sense, Dunedin's first Roman Catholic bishop, Patrick Moran, was correct when he reminded an audience in Cashel there were two Irelands: one at 'Home' and the other – 'a greater Ireland' – abroad.[17]

The steady stream of migrants that thronged busy wharves at Queenstown (now Cobh), Moville and Belfast had journeyed from all parts of Ireland.[18] Nonetheless, the surviving evidence shows that the exodus was a *structured* and *selective* phenomenon. Before the 1830s most of the migrants sailing to overseas destinations were Protestants rather than Catholics, and more likely to come from Ulster than elsewhere.[19] During the Famine, the epicentre of migration shifted toward the west of the country and the outflow included higher proportions of family groups, Catholics and rural poor than had previously been the case.[20] By the 1850s and 1860s, when most of the West Coast Irish headed overseas, the profile of this widespread movement of people had been transformed.[21] A striking feature of the post-Famine traffic was that men and women left Ireland in roughly equal numbers, an unusual pattern in the context of European migration.[22] Like Thomas Kelly, a native of Shanoul, County Wexford, who sailed for Melbourne on the *Elizabeth Anne Bright* in 1862 and followed the restless army of fortune-seekers across the Tasman, most were unmarried adults in their early 20s or late teens.[23] Some came from the skilled trades and middle-class backgrounds, but labourers and domestic servants predominated, though these labels more often reflected intention than actual previous experience in paid employment.[24] The religious composition of the post-Famine flight remains hazy, but it seems likely that Protestants sailed to colonial ports at the same rates as their Catholic counterparts, at least until the 1920s.[25] Although far from comprehensive, the available records show that the migrants were not an undifferentiated mass and instead belonged to particular localities, social categories and personal networks. Whatever their origins, few returned home – despite persistent appeals from kinsfolk. Cecilia Coghlan of Foxford, County Mayo, for instance, promised to give her widowed stepdaughter, Ellen Anne Edwards of Hokitika, a 'cead mile failte' – a hundred thousand blessings – if she visited the family again.[26] The possibility of reverse migration, which 'ended only with death', must have softened the pain of separation in a society where mobility was 'part of the expected cycle of life'.[27]

Where did the migrants come from? The official figures compiled by Ireland's Registrar-General for the years 1851 to 1920 show that mass movement was numerically heaviest in the west. Of those people who stated their residence, 29.5 per cent (1,248,172) departed from Ulster, 17.7 per cent (748,651) from Leinster, 35.4 per cent (1,495,460) from Munster and 17.4 per cent (735,177) from Connacht. The bias toward these last two provinces – which together contributed more than 53 per cent of the total outflow – became more pronounced after 1881, when they provided nearly three-fifths (57.4 per cent) of all the migrants. In proportional terms, however, Munster and Connacht had much higher emigration rates than Ulster and Leinster. The most western provinces lost 10 per cent or more of their populations overseas in each decade between 1851 and 1911, while the relative intensity of movement from the north and east of the country slumped dramatically from the 1890s. Altogether, Munster lost 14.9 per cent of its inhabitants to emigration across the entire 1851–1920 period, compared with 13 per cent for Connacht. By contrast, less than one-tenth of Ulster's population (9.8 per cent) joined the exodus, with smaller flows recorded from Leinster (7.6 per cent).

The county level data for original residences at this time reveal how far the geographical pivot of migration had shifted away from the pre-Famine sources in south Ulster and the northern midlands towards the west.[28] Yet the statistical evidence obscures the extent of this transition. David Fitzpatrick and Cormac Ó Gráda have convincingly demonstrated that cohort depletion rates provide a more reliable basis on which to compare regional migration patterns. Their findings indicate, first, that the extant listings badly underestimate the volume of traffic from Connacht, and, second, that large-scale emigration gradually extended down the length of the Atlantic seaboard.[29] Here were found the counties most inclined

to send people abroad – Donegal, Mayo, Galway, Clare, Kerry and Cork
– though departure rates remained high across the southern midlands and
in the Ulster border region. Briefly put, post-Famine migrants were more
likely to come not from the commercialised south- and north-eastern parts
of Ireland but from the most impoverished and least urbanised counties,
which had the worst rural housing conditions, a high proportion of Irish
speakers and a greater dependence on potato cultivation or cottage industry
for survival. Many contained substantial areas designated as wretchedly
poor 'congested districts' by the British government and therefore eligible
for special state assistance.

There were also important local variations within these broader patterns
of movement. In County Mayo, where Cecilia Coghlan contemplated the
return of her stepdaughter, mass migration was initially heaviest in the
fertile lowland corridor that stretched from Killala to Westport, before
extending south and east to the Galway and Roscommon borders. By the
time of Ellen Anne Edwards's departure in the late 1860s, this situation
had reversed and Ireland's poorer eastern and western peripheries sent
people abroad with greater intensity as population pressures, a shortage
of land and the changing demands of the marketplace made emigration an
attractive option.[30]

We may never know completely why so many people left Ireland after
the Famine. Ordinary people had a wide variety of personal reasons for
sailing abroad. Patrick Clune, Robert Keown and David Beatty were
lured by the prospect of sudden wealth and followed the blazing golden
trail to Victoria in the 1850s and from there to the West Coast by way of
Otago.[31] Ulster-born Felix Feran spent the early years of his working life
at London's Kew Gardens; Denis Downey served with the 55th Regiment
of the British Army in the Crimea and imperial troops during the New
Zealand Land Wars.[32] For Ann MacNamara, the spirited daughter of
large farmers in the Glendree district of County Clare, a passage ticket to
Hokitika was 'a great escape' from an unsuitable match.[33] We may surmise
that such migrants shared a fundamental expectation that they would
be better off elsewhere, but there is little direct evidence to show what
they thought about their prospects and the world around them. Global
migration, however, represented more than the sum of personal decisions.
Much larger forces were at work in shaping the magnitude, composition,
timing and direction of migrant flows.

The amazing mobility of Irish men and women formed just one part of a massive population movement – some 55 million people – from Europe to other parts of the world between 1815 and 1930.[34] This phenomenon needs to be understood in relation to the evolution of world capitalism.[35] Like their contemporaries in Galicia, Calabria and Canton Ticino, the inhabitants of places such as Carrowduff, Annaghdown and Grey Abbey confronted sweeping changes outside their immediate control. At one extreme their lives were being transformed by epic developments – the Industrial Revolution, new demographic cycles, the spread of commercialised agriculture and dramatic improvements in transportation – which created local conditions, demands and desires conducive to migration. On another level, however, Irish men and women responded to the new economic order and its rapidly changing imperatives in ways that provided for the collective welfare of their family networks.[36] The decision to venture across the oceans was one way of coming to terms with the enormous pressures that threatened to overwhelm them. But it was rarely based on individual preference alone. As surviving migrant letters reveal, the enterprise 'was expensive, premeditated, calculated, and the outcome of negotiation involving a wide circle of interested relatives and the collection of extensive evidence concerning the available options'.[37] To understand the inner dynamics of Irish mass migration, then, we need to examine the intimate connections between huge structural changes, geographical locations and people's everyday lives.[38]

III

From the end of the Great Famine to the beginning of the First World War, thousands of Irish men and women made their way to New Zealand from Great Britain, the Australian colonies and other places. The recent expansion of Irish migration history in this country has greatly enlarged our knowledge about their everyday lives.[39] Most importantly, this exciting research has spurred recognition of the regional, cultural and religious diversity of migrant streams to this country. Yet there is still much that we do not know about Irish people's understanding of themselves and their rapidly changing social world. Although the origins and composition of the flows are now becoming clearer, substantial work must still be done before we can answer important questions about the responses of these newcomers to their new world. *Castles of Gold* is an attempt to provide some answers for one region that has reputedly been the most Irish part of New Zealand. The chapters that follow explore the experiences of Irish migrants on the West Coast of the South Island from 1864, when the gold rushes began, until the formation of the Irish Free State in 1922. The book is framed around five principal themes – migrant pathways, work conditions, marriage, religion and nationalism – all of which lend themselves to detailed investigation and comparison with other groups and places of settlement.

Castles of Gold focuses squarely on the role of *ethnicity* in the adaptation of migrants to a new environment. Each chapter draws on the substantial insights of scholars working in the field of Irish global history, whose research has shown that ethnic identity 'is both a matter of self-identification and of taxonomies developed by the host society'.[40] This vast international literature serves as a useful corrective to earlier historical writings on the process of group formation among the Irish in the United States, which assumed that newcomers arrived in the New World with a well-developed communal identity that was either pre-destined or remarkably continuous. Although the role of culture in ethnic studies remains contentious, there is broad agreement that ethnicity is a social and cultural *relationship* between two or more groups that assumes political relevance in different times and places.[41] We would do well to remember that ethnicity is defined by people as they live their own history, and not a primordial 'given' of social existence.

The proliferation of international studies provides useful guidance for historians keen to explore the social worlds of Irish men and women in New Zealand. Aside from demonstrating the value of neglected source materials, this expanding literature has led to the emergence of several themes and debates about migrant lives in new communities scattered around the globe. One of the most important questions facing scholars is the degree to which Irish people blended easily into receiving societies or asserted distinctive ethnic identities and constructed ethnic associations as a means of adapting to their new environment. Even a cursory glance at recent scholarship reveals considerable variability in the organisational importance of ethnicity across the diaspora. At one extreme we may place the ethnic defensiveness and urban machine politics manifested in the great Atlantic cities of New York and Liverpool, an experience quite different from those of Irish settlers in Victoria and South Australia, where various factors militated against the formation of cohesive, self-sustaining ethnic communities.[42]

These variations are further complicated by the fact that the same society usually contained several layers of ethnic affiliation.[43] Some scholars have also noted the difficulty faced by researchers where ethnic organisations attracted support only from a small and vocal minority. David Fitzpatrick, for example, has acknowledged the existence of ethnic defensiveness in parts of the United States and Britain, but convincingly argues that this evidence

> obscures the fact that vast numbers of emigrants quickly dropped out of ethnic networks, or exploited them only as a transitory tool for self-advancement. Most Irish-Americans probably did not read Irish newspapers, join Irish clubs, subscribe to Irish causes, or even wear shamrocks on St. Patrick's Day. But the active minority has dominated study of the Irish overseas, partly because evidence of non-involvement in negative, dull and impossible to aggregate. It is fact that most Irish settlers were excluded from the most desirable houses, jobs and clubs; it is supposition that most of those excluded chose ethnic solidarity as their strategy for escaping alienation.[44]

We need to add an important caveat to Fitzpatrick's bold claims: ethnic alignments cannot be reduced simply to numbers and a small cadre of committed activists may indeed play a critical role in facilitating ethnic mobilisation. Yet, in assessing evidence for the formation of self-sustaining Irish communities, we can overstate the social importance of ethnic group boundaries and obscure the non-ethnic dimensions of migrant social worlds.

One of the most fruitful ways to capture the complex layering of Irish ethnicity during the nineteenth and early twentieth centuries is through Don Handelman's typology of ethnic incorporation,[45] which distinguishes between four kinds of ethnic collectivism. At the least incorporated level is the *ethnic category*, where groups are identified by perceived differences, but cohesive networks or organisations based on ethnicity do not exist. The second is the *ethnic network*, in which people regularly interact along ethnic lines and resources are distributed among group members, who also share a strong sense of solidarity. When these members have shared interests and develop overarching political or religious organisations to express them, we may extend the notion of networks to identify an *ethnic association*. Finally, at the highest level of incorporation, we can talk of an *ethnic community*, which possesses more or less permanent boundaries over and above the ethnic networks and shared political organisations described earlier. Although this valuable model may be read in a number of ways, we may follow Alan O'Day in employing it as a *developmental framework* for analysing the emergence from ethnic categories of institutionally complete ethnic groups.[46] It is a useful tool that facilitates historical comparison and offers considerable scope for refining the study of Irish ethnic and diasporic identities.

How might we apply this model to the experiences of Irish men and women on the West Coast of New Zealand's South Island? My central argument in *Castles of Gold* is that these newcomers did not choose ethnic solidarity as a means to pursue their goals and, for most, an ethnic or religious category sufficed in an environment where local communities, churches, trade unions, kinship ties and non-ethnic political parties had far more social relevance. The small-scale structure of West Coast localities, the relative economic homogeneity of its inhabitants and the absence of entrenched anti-Irish élites militated against the rise of sectarian animosities and the maturation of intensified ethnic consciousness.[47] As a consequence, Irish migrants did not construct and sustain informal social networks based on 'principles of ethnic categorisation'.[48] Theirs is a complex story characterised by successful adaptation and the rapid disappearance of ethnic boundaries, rather than by conflict and defensive unity.

IV

The main sources on which this book is based will be familiar to readers with an interest in family history. Since the original household census schedules have been destroyed, the best clues about the origins and social characteristics of migrant populations in colonial New Zealand are to be found in civil registers. I made extensive use of these records in my first book, *To Tara via Holyhead*, and my methods have since been refined and expanded by Terry Hearn and in my own collaborative research with Sarah Dwyer.[49] I was fortunate to be granted limited access to these restricted volumes – now kept by Archives New Zealand – in the cold bunker underneath the Registrar-General's Office in Lower Hutt. The most valuable registers for historians are undoubtedly the bound copies of death certificates, which give 14 pieces of information for the deceased, including age and occupation, place of birth, length of residence in the colony, mother's first and maiden name, father's name and occupation, and the details of the burial. Local officials did not always manage to ascertain these facts – as the Hokitika registers attest – and they depended on the reliability and goodwill of their informants. Nonetheless, these sources provided a crucial foundation for tracing the lives of Irish migrants on the mining frontier. By carrying out record linkages with other nominal materials such as probate files and cemetery transcripts, I overcame some of the worst errors in the extant listings and assembled an impressive body of evidence about the identities and careers 'of those otherwise silenced by death'.[50]

The bare bones revealed by such sources represented a starting point for exploring the human dimension of the goldfields migration. To capture the distinctive textures of people's everyday lives, I have employed several kinds of local and family records. Many of these are widely available to researchers: newspapers, street directories, provincial government correspondence, immigration files, mining and police records, internment registers, photographs and so on. Other valuable materials, however, are held privately. The most abundant manuscript collections have been preserved by church archivists and transferred to various institutions in Christchurch and Wellington. In addition to parish returns and ephemera, these archives contain diaries, memoirs and numerous sequences of correspondence exchanged between church professionals. The collections of the largest denominations are indispensable to historians of migration as they help us to understand how newcomers adapted older cultural traditions to meet the exigencies of the new world.

Aside from church materials and a limited number of contemporary accounts, I have used personal letters sent from Ireland, the West Coast and other places of overseas settlement. This documentary archive allows us to follow the paths of migrants like Michael and Patrick Flanagan from Termonfeckin, County Louth, to the crowded docks at Liverpool and across the oceans to far-flung colonial outposts in eastern Australia, New Zealand and California.[51] We catch fleeting glimpses of others 'buried waist deep in daily routine' aboard emigrant ships and in families, churches and mining camps. Most importantly, we hear the voices of ordinary Irish men and women struggling to make sense of their experiences and the challenges confronting them. Blended together, all these sources help to illuminate the distant realities of human beings who were 'the voluntary agents of [their] own involuntary determinations'.[52]

My research for this book has also drawn upon material artefacts, family memory and other forms of life writing. This approach reflects my own experiences as a museum professional, a contributor to women's history and an historian 'exploring the past' with anthropology students. Yet it also owes much to the people and stories I have encountered in the field. *Castles of Gold* is therefore far more 'ethnographically informed' than any of my previous writing. The past, it seems to me, exists not only in the documentary record, but also in the memories, 'buildings, objects and landscapes of the present day', the observation of which requires 'the working experience of both the field and the archive'.[53] The next chapter moves in this direction as it attempts to shed light on the pathways and backgrounds of those Irish men and women who flocked to the West Coast goldfields after the brilliant discoveries of the 1860s.

2 'Land of Gold': Irish Migration to the Diggings

In the foreword to his magisterial account of the West Coast gold rushes, Philip Ross May observes that the region 'packed a quarter of century of history under the normal process of colonisation' into three years.[1] Even a century and a half after the discovery of payable gold at Greenstone Creek, the events that transformed this distant world seem extraordinary in scale and complexity. We can picture the broad outlines of this vast panorama: the swarming population of miners swagging heavy loads along the beaches and tangled bush trails, clad in their distinctive uniform of moleskin trousers, blue flannel shirts, tight-fitting boots and 'wide-awake' hats of grey or black, 'dented near the top';[2] the sudden appearance of canvas and calico towns and mining camps near fresh ground, along with the apocalyptic landscapes of reworked tailings, retreating terraces and extensive tunnelling; the striking architecture of sailing vessels – screw steamers, brigantines, schooners, cutters and ketches – huddled beside crude wharves at the main river ports; and the commemoration of origins or routes in the names of hotels and grog-shanties such as the Edinburgh Castle and the Brian Boru, the Liverpool Arms and the British Lion, the Café de France and Casino de Venice, the All Nations and the European, the Ballarat and the Old Bendigo.

Beneath the heaving chaos of a world in perpetual motion we can make out the larger aspects of migrant lives: magnitudes, directions, connections and relationships. Using a higher degree of resolution, however, we can also catch glimpses of the finer details. This chapter brings into close view the patterns and dimensions of Irish migration to the West Coast from 1864, when the gold rushes began, until the First World War. The first section establishes the main features of the inflow and the social attributes of its participants, but these characteristics alone cannot convey an adequate understanding of 'its meaning as human experience'.[3] This task requires the imaginative exploitation of scattered and fragmented sources, and the critical interrogation of oral evidence. I focus here on the role of personal networks to show that newcomers relied heavily on relatives and friends for material assistance and companionship in a new environment. Theirs is a complex story involving hardship and suffering, and an amazing capacity for negotiating communication and travel systems.

I

Irish-born migrants were strongly represented in the richly variegated communities that developed along the bush-lined rivers and alluvial terraces of the West Coast. Census figures show that the Irish component of the foreign-born female population was almost one-third for the years 1867 to 1896, a proportion that fell dramatically thereafter in absolute terms and relative to other groups (Table 2.1). Irish expatriates outnumbered their English-born counterparts until late in the century and retained a significant presence in the region until the First World War. By contrast, the proportional representation of Irish men was slightly weaker and their numbers declined much more rapidly than the English- and Scottish-born (Table 2.2). This broad picture is complicated by the fact that a substantial number of the Australian-born recorded by the census enumerators were the second-generation children of Irish home backgrounds, some of whom had accompanied their parents across the Tasman Sea. We can also assume that the New Zealand-born contingent featured a sizeable minority with Irish parentage, and that the published data for England and Scotland contain a small number who were descended from Irish migrants to Britain. The existence of these additional groupings reminds us that the everyday lives of Irish people in goldfields communities were differentiated by generation, as well as by class, religion, age, marital status and parenthood. In total, then, the entire group comprised between a quarter and one-third of the total population in Westland and Nelson South-West in the nineteenth and early twentieth centuries.

Further analysis of the census evidence highlights the gendered pattern of Irish settlement on the West Coast. Although newcomers dispersed widely throughout the region, statistical indices taken from each census enumeration district between 1878 and 1921 show that the urban centres had a much higher proportion of Irish-born and Roman Catholic females

Table 2.1 Birthplaces of West Coast's female population, 1867–1916

	1867	1878		1886		1896		1908		1916	
	%	N	%	N	%	N	%	N	%	N	%
Ireland	32.6	1650	31.7	1503	32.3	1272	30.8	967	25.3	691	17.2
			(17.5)		(13.7)		(10.0)		(6.7)		(4.4)
England	34	1432	27.5	1355	29.1	1285	31.1	1116	29.2	1365	34.0
			(15.2)		(12.4)		(10.1)		(7.8)		(8.7)
Scotland	14.3	585	11.2	653	14.0	604	14.6	516	13.5	755	18.8
			(6.2)		(6.0)		(4.7)		(3.6)		(4.8)
Australia	?	1117	21.4	856	18.4	723	17.5	1000	26.2	939	23.4
			(11.8)		(7.8)		(5.7)		(7.0)		(6.0)
Cont. Europe	?	294	5.6	170	3.7	147	3.6	122	3.2	89	2.2
			(3.1)		(1.6)		(1.2)		(0.9)		(0.6)
Other	?	130	2.5	117	2.5	102	2.5	96	2.5	180	4.5
			(1.4)		(1.1)		(1.1)		(0.7)		(1.1)
Totals											
Foreign-born		5208		4654		4133		3817		4019	
NZ-born		4222		6292		8595		10,525		11,665	

Notes
1. Sources: Census of New Zealand, 1878–1916. The figures for 1867 have been extracted from Murray McCaskill, 'The Historical Geography of Westland before 1914', PhD thesis, University of Canterbury, 1960, pp. 6/17, 6/18, 6/21 and 7/17. McCaskill's estimates are based on a sample of 1600 people whose birthplaces were recorded in the annual reports of the Hokitika, Grey River and Reefton Hospitals, over the years 1866 to 1874. These figures do not distinguish between males and females.
2. The percentages displayed in brackets record the respective proportions of the foreign-born components in relation to the entire population.
3. Although Scottish-born women outnumbered their Irish-born counterparts across the entire region in 1916, this pattern does not hold for the provincial district of Westland. Here, females of Irish birth comprised 25.0 per cent of the foreign-born population compared with a much smaller proportion of Scots (13.0 per cent).

than the more remote goldfields and agricultural areas. In Hokitika, for example, the numerical dominance of women over men was evident for both census categories until the early 1900s, while the counties of Buller, Inangahua, Grey and Westland always contained an overwhelming preponderance of males. In the main towns an imbalance in favour of women reflected the continuous demand for paid domestic servants, an occupation that was particularly attractive to single Irish women in their late teens and early twenties. The rural areas and small mining camps, on the other hand, provided fewer opportunities for paid female employment and required considerable numbers of male workers for the extractive gold, coal and timber industries. Although men dominated the region's Irish-born population in absolute numbers throughout the period under consideration, localised clusters of women and men that had profound implications for the

Table 2.2 Birthplaces of West Coast's male population, 1867–1916

	1867	1878		1886		1896		1906		1916	
	%	N	%	N	%	N	%	N	%	N	%
Ireland	32.6	3216	26.4	2490	23.3	1985	23.8	1534	19.2	901	13.9
			(19.5)		(15.2)		(11.8)		(8.0)		(4.9)
England	34	3345	27.5	2917	27.4	2397	28.7	2214	27.8	2165	33.3
			(20.3)		(17.8)		(14.3)		(11.6)		(11.9)
Scotland	14.3	1611	13.2	1473	13.8	1189	14.2	1117	14.0	1149	17.7
			(9.8)		(9.0)		(7.1)		(5.8)		(6.3)
Australia	?	1057	8.7	743	7.0	661	7.9	1640	20.6	1417	21.8
			(6.4)		(4.5)		(3.9)		(8.6)		(7.8)
China	?	966	7.9	1288	12.1	1059	12.8	477	6.0	180	2.8
			(5.9)		(7.9)		(6.3)		(2.5)		(1.0)
Cont. Europe	?	1460	12.0	1069	10.0	780	9.3	697	8.7	507	7.8
			(8.9)		(6.5)		(4.7)		(3.6)		(2.8)
Other	?	523	4.3	684	6.4	274	3.3	297	3.7	358	5.5
			(3.2)		(4.2)		(1.6)		(1.5)		(2.0)
Totals											
Foreign-born		12.178		10.664		8345		7976		6497	
NZ-born		4292		5687		8419		11,190		11,741	

Notes
1. All data from the same sources as Table 2.1.
2. The percentages displayed in brackets record the respective proportions of the foreign-born components in relation to the entire population.

social character of the various settlements were scattered around the region.[4]

In attempting to gain greater clarity about Irish settlement on the West Coast we are faced with an evidentiary problem: the census manuscripts have not survived and the extant shipping lists for the region lack sufficient detail. Nevertheless, other kinds of historical data can help to build 'windows into the past'.[5] Death certificates, used in conjunction with literary sources, provide an alternative basis for reconstructing migrant populations,[6] and provide invaluable biographical details about individuals. Moreover, they allow for systematic linkages with other materials such as probates, cemetery transcripts, parish registers and family histories, thereby eliminating some of the ambiguities and omissions found in the extant listings. The analysis that follows is based on a study of 735 Irish-born women and 1579 men whose deaths were registered on the West Coast between 1876 and 1915.

As Table 2.3 shows, an overwhelming majority of Irish women made their way to the colony after 1864, with almost two-fifths (36.9 per cent) disembarking at the height of the West Coast gold rushes (1865–9). In contrast to their male counterparts (31.2 per cent), comparatively few

Table 2.3 Demographic characteristics of West Coast Irish at date of arrival in New Zealand, 1864–1915

	PRE-1860	1860-64	1865-69	1870-74	1875-79	POST-1880	NOT KNOWN	TOTAL
			SEX DISTRIBUTION OF IRISH MIGRANTS					
Female								
N	50	130	271	127	76	64	17	735
%	6.8	17.7	36.9	17.3	10.3	8.7	2.3	100.0
Male								
N	96	492	479	138	114	102	140	1579
%	6.1	31.2	31.5	8.7	7.2	6.5	8.9	100.0
			MARITAL STATUS OF ADULT FEMALES					
Single								
N	26	58	141	66	40	40	14	385
%	65.0	50.4	54.4	57.9	57.1	67.8	–	57.8
Married								
N	14	57	118	48	30	19	7	293
%	35.0	49.6	45.6	42.1	42.9	32.2	–	43.2
			MARITAL STATUS OF ADULT MALES					
Single								
N	77	431	415	108	77	79	128	1315
%	91.7	88.1	85.2	80.0	71.3	81.4	–	85.6
Married								
N	7	58	72	27	31	18	8	221
%	8.3	11.9	14.8	20.0	28.7	18.6	–	14.4

Sources: Registry of Births, Deaths and Marriages (Lower Hutt); Probate Files, CH 171, Archives New Zealand, Christchurch; Passenger Lists, IM-CH 4 and IM-15, Archives New Zealand, Wellington. Additional information on individual migrants was obtained from genealogies, newspaper obituaries and cemetery transcripts held at the West Coast Historical Museum.

female migrants voyaged to New Zealand in the early 1860s (17.7 per cent). Differences in the timing of migration for both sexes are also apparent from 1870, when more women arrived in the colonies. This evidence indicates that the region's Irish female population came largely from the eastern Australian colonies. This general trend is hardly surprising, given that the physical isolation of the West Coast from the rest of the South Island helped to turn the region into 'an economic dependency of Victoria' during the 1860s, and made the capital, Hokitika, into 'a trans-Tasman suburb of Melbourne'.[7] Although many Irish men spent time on the Otago goldfields, a temporary sojourn in that province was much less common for women, most of whom sailed directly to the West Coast from Melbourne. The available documentation suggests that they were two- or three-stage migrants who had served extended colonial apprenticeships in Australia.

Table 2.4 Age Distribution of Irish migrants to the West Coast at the date of arrival in New Zealand, 1864–1915

	0-14	15-19	20-24	25-29	30-34	35-54	55+
Median age: 26.6 (21.2)				Women N=568			
N	30	86	166	157	105	119	31
%	4.3	12.0	24.0	22.7	15.2	17.2	4.5
	(14.2)	(20.4)	(35.6)	(18.3)		(9.3)	(1.2)
Median age: 29.1 (22.5)				Men N=1421			
N	26	92	269	350	319	329	36
%	1.8	6.5	18.9	24.6	22.4	23.2	2.5
	(13.7)	(11.7)	(35.5)	(27.0)		(9.9)	(1.1)

Notes
1. All data from the same sources as Table 2.3 except the figures displayed in brackets, which record the total age distribution of emigrants from the whole of Ireland – as listed in *Commission on Emigration and Other Population Problems*, 1948–1954, Dublin, 1954, pp. 122, 320. Ages at departure were unknown for 1.1 per cent of men and 1.0 per cent of women listed by the commission over the period 1852–1921.
2. There are significant differences in the median age of women by denomination: Roman Catholic (26.3), Anglican (28.9), Presbyterian (28.0).

What of the migrants' ages and marital status? Predictably, the ages of Irish migrants reflect the fact that many had migrated to other colonies before they reached the West Coast. As a result, these newcomers were considerably older on arrival than their counterparts who left Ireland for various global destinations during the nineteenth and early twentieth centuries. As Table 2.4 reveals, the median age of the Irish men in the sample (29.1) differed notably from the average recorded by the *Commission on Emigration and Other Population Problems* for the whole of Ireland between 1852 and 1921 (22.5).[8] Among those for whom we have information, it is clear that migrants were particularly concentrated in their late twenties and thirties, with nearly a quarter over 35 years of age (23.2 per cent). This trend is strengthened when we consider that the figures used in this analysis record the age on arrival in New Zealand and do not reflect the local reality, where a considerable minority would have made their way to the West Coast after having arrived elsewhere in the colony. Whatever their migration paths, most Irish men were seasoned colonials who had spent time in Australia and were therefore prepared for the hardships of everyday life on the Coast.

The age distribution and median age (26.6) of Irish women migrants also varies markedly from the *Commission*'s figures (21.2). There were relatively few Irish female children in the inflow compared with the wider exodus and those aged from 15 to 24 were significantly underrepresented.

Migrants in their late thirties and fourties are quite prominent. About three-fifths (61.1 per cent) were aged between 20 and 34, a proportion that is less than that reported in Terry Hearn's study of Irish-born housewives arriving in Otago before 1871 (79.5 per cent).[9] Conversely, the West Coast Irish female population contained a much larger number of migrants over 35 (21.7 per cent) than the southern goldfields (5.1 per cent).[10] Both inflows reflected the distinctive colouration of Irish women's migration to Victoria in the 1850s and the complex linkages of kinship and mobility that tied goldfields communities to eastern Australia.

The question about the marital status of Irish migrants is answered by the information contained in Table 2.3. As we might expect in a goldfields population, the movement featured a preponderance of single males, who comprised almost three-fifths of the total sample (57.8 per cent). Most surprisingly, perhaps, married women and widows comprised a majority of Irish female migrants when they arrived on the West Coast. This contrasts markedly with one of the key features of Ireland's post-Famine exodus: a relatively high outflow of women, in which single females travelling in sibling networks were predominant. Of the 678 migrants to the West Coast for whom we have reliable information, 293 were married at some stage in their lives overseas (43.2 per cent) and a further 50 had married in other New Zealand destinations (7.4 per cent). There are striking parallels here with the proportion of married Irish females sailing to Port Chalmers and Dunedin from Victoria between 1861 and 1864 (47.1 per cent).[11] When we examine the places of marriage for the West Coast sample, we find that almost half of the unions formed outside New Zealand were solemnised in Victoria (46.4 per cent). Smaller numbers took their vows in New South Wales (8.5 per cent), Tasmania (2.0 per cent) and South Australia (1.0 per cent), while a few celebrated marriages in England (2.4 per cent) and the United States (0.7 per cent). Of those who married in New Zealand, an overwhelming majority did so in the province of Otago. The high incidence of marriages in both that province and Victoria further underlines the critical importance of Melbourne in the transfer of Irish-born women to the West Coast, either directly or, in some cases, via Port Chalmers and Dunedin. This impression is reinforced by the experiences of the 95 female migrants in my sample who married in Ireland (32.4 per cent). We may never know the individual circumstances surrounding the departure of these women from their local communities and we can only speculate that, for some, marriage and emigration 'represented an alternative to the traditional Irish match'.[12] But it is clear that many sailed to the Australian colonies with their spouses alone and most arrived on the West Coast with families that included children born in Victoria. These women, and their contemporaries who married in such places as Ballarat and Geelong, were the mothers of a substantial portion of the region's Australian-born population.

The crucial importance of Australian antecedents among migrants to the West Coast is reflected in the pattern of geographical origins and religious affiliations. Figure 2.1 depicts the relative numbers of women from each Irish county who came to the region between 1864 and 1915. Although all 32 counties were involved, the migration was selectively regional in nature and not a random or universal phenomenon. We can see that the migrant streams were centred upon a cluster of southern midland counties with strong Australian connections. Clare, Limerick, Tipperary, King's and Kilkenny accounted for about two-fifths of the inflow (41.5 per cent), a preponderance that greatly exceeded their share of Ireland's total female inhabitants in 1861 (14.5 per cent). Thus a substantial proportion emanated from an area that was relatively prosperous by Irish standards and, after the Famine, had made a particularly rapid transition from labour-intensive cereals to livestock production in response to changing market prices. This rural transformation was certainly evident in counties Clare and Tipperary, which together dominated Victoria's intake and consistently provided the largest share of newcomers in absolute numbers and relative to their respective populations. This marked southern orientation, as shown in Table 2.5, is further accentuated when we consider that Munster's proportional representation (51.3 per cent) was almost twice that for the sending society's population distribution (26.0 per cent). Migrants from Ulster and Connacht were underrepresented, although the western seaboard counties of Donegal and Galway were important exceptions to this wider pattern. The distinctive geographical origins of the West Coast's Irish female population best explain the divergence between the Catholic-Protestant breakdown in the region (80/20) and New Zealand as a whole (55/45), along with its close resemblance to the balance of religious affiliations recorded in 1901 for Victoria (70/30), New South Wales (71/29) and Queensland (72/28).

There are, however, some striking differences between the provincial origins of Irish men and women, as a comparison of Tables 2.5 and 2.6 reveals. Nowhere is this more apparent than in the respective proportions

Counties of Ireland

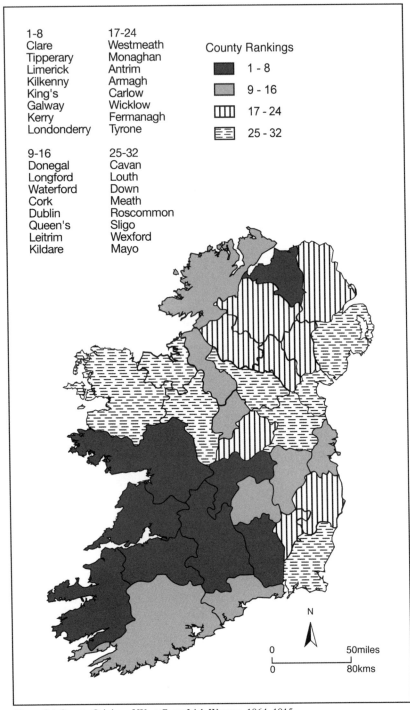

Figure 2.1 County Origins of West Coast Irish Women, 1864–1915

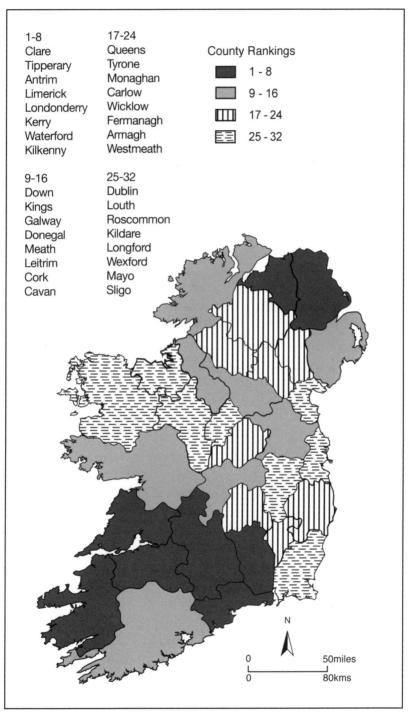

1-8
Clare
Tipperary
Antrim
Limerick
Londonderry
Kerry
Waterford
Kilkenny

9-16
Down
Kings
Galway
Donegal
Meath
Leitrim
Cork
Cavan

17-24
Queens
Tyrone
Monaghan
Carlow
Wicklow
Fermanagh
Armagh
Westmeath

25-32
Dublin
Louth
Roscommon
Kildare
Longford
Wexford
Mayo
Sligo

County Rankings

■ 1 - 8
▨ 9 - 16
▥ 17 - 24
▤ 25 - 32

N

0 ———— 50miles
0 ———— 80kms

Figure 2.2 County Origins of West Coast Irish Men. 1864-1915

Table 2.5 Regional proportions of West Coast Irish female migrants by date of arrival in New Zealand, 1864–1915

	pre-1860	1860-64	1865-69	1870-74	1875-79	Post-1880	Not Known	Total
Ulster								
N	2	20	44	23	17	14	6	126
%	8.3	19.4	19.8	23.2	25.0	26.4	-	21.1
Leinster								
N	3	24	49	9	10	8	5	108
%	12.5	23.3	22.1	9.1	14.7	15.1	-	18.2
Connacht								
N	5	12	23	7	5	4	0	56
%	20.8	11.7	10.4	7.1	7.4	7.5	-	9.4
Munster								
N	14	47	106	60	36	27	15	305
%	58.3	45.6	47.7	60.6	52.6	50.9	-	51.3
Totals								
N	24	103	222	99	68	53	26	595
%	4.0	17.3	37.3	16.6	11.4	8.9	4.4	100.0

Notes
1. All data obtained from the same sources as Table 2.3.
2. The denominational percentages for the West Coast sample were as follows: Roman Catholic (79.6 per cent), Anglican (10.6 per cent), Presbyterian (5.3 per cent) and Wesleyan (1.5 per cent). Data on religious affiliations was unavailable for 3.0 per cent of female migrants.

Table 2.6 Regional proportions of West Coast Irish male migrants by date of arrival in New Zealand, 1864–1915

	pre-1860	1860-64	1865-69	1870-74	1875-79	Post-1880	Not Known	Total
Ulster								
N	2	20	44	23	17	14	6	126
%	8.3	19.4	19.8	23.2	25.0	26.4	-	21.1
Leinster								
N	3	24	49	9	10	8	5	108
%	12.5	23.3	22.1	9.1	14.7	15.1	-	18.2
Connacht								
N	5	12	23	7	5	4	0	56
%	20.8	11.7	10.4	7.1	7.4	7.5	-	9.4
Munster								
N	14	47	106	60	36	27	15	305
%	58.3	45.6	47.7	60.6	52.6	50.9	-	51.3
Totals								
N	24	103	222	99	68	53	26	595
%	4.0	17.3	37.3	16.6	11.4	8.9	4.4	100.0

Notes
1. All data obtained from the same sources as Table 2.3.
2. The denominational percentages for the West Coast sample were as follows: Roman Catholic (75.1 per cent), Anglican (12.5 per cent), Presbyterian (7.8 per cent), Wesleyan (1.3 per cent) and Hebrew (0.1 per cent). Data on religious affiliations was unavailable for 3.2 per cent of male migrants.

of Ulster migrants (32.7 and 22.1 per cent). Although the southern midland counties were strongly represented among both sexes, the region's Irish male population included an important secondary concentration drawn from the highly urbanised north-east Ulster counties of Antrim, Down and Derry, an area that contained Protestant majorities and a rapidly expanding industrial sector (see Figure 2.2). The most convincing explanation for the north-east's prominence is that the West Coast acquired part of its Ulster component through earlier recruitment campaigns undertaken by the provincial governments of Otago and Canterbury. Altogether, migrants from the nine northern counties made up nearly one-third of the male inflow, while Connacht and Leinster were underrepresented. The infusions from Ulster ensured that the male denominational profile more closely resembled the patterns found in Irish society as a whole than the corresponding totals for their female counterparts.

A notable feature of the available documentation is the degree to which Roman Catholics were disproportionately overrepresented among the emigrants from north-east Ulster relative to their share of the area's population. In total, Catholics accounted for almost two-fifths of all those born in counties Antrim and Down, whereas Presbyterians comprised only about a quarter of the inflow, even though this group were the most numerous in both places. In Ulster between 1861 and 1911, the Catholic population declined by about 29 per cent compared with a 16 per cent decrease among Presbyterians and a 6 per cent fall in the number of Church of Ireland (Anglican) adherents.[13] Ulster Anglicans were overrepresented on the West Coast in proportion to the north's non-Catholic population, but the Church of Ireland provided relatively fewer migrants from the southern provinces than might have been expected. Among the Protestant population, the Anglican element was notable for its strong representation in larger urban centres, such as Greymouth and Westport. In addition, more than one-half of all Anglican men and over two-fifths of their Presbyterian brethren had arrived in the colony before 1865, compared with only one-third of Catholic males. This data supports the view that the unrestricted flow of migrants to the West Coast from Australia was dominated by those from the south of Ireland, while the population received substantial numbers of northerners through Otago and Canterbury immigration schemes, which favoured migrants from north-east Ulster.

The migrant streams from the northern counties of Ireland were much more male-dominated than those from the southern provinces. Presumably this configuration owed something to the socio-economic pressures generated in rural Ulster, which favoured the consolidation of holdings into commercial farms and the concentration of the region's linen industry in the factories of Belfast and its adjacent towns at the expense of rural cottage manufacturing. Although the north's urban-industrial growth provided opportunities unavailable elsewhere in post-Famine Ireland, the region could not absorb all the displaced farmers' children, unemployed rural artisans or farm labourers. Moreover, some employment stimulated by economic expansion was more accessible for women, making overseas destinations more attractive for males than short-distance migration to the northern industrial towns. The high rates of male emigration that accompanied the decline of Ulster's population by one-fifth between 1851 and 1911 were unique within the post-Famine exodus. It is significant that most of the Ulster men who made their way to the West Coast chose to leave home during a period of relatively high emigration from the northern province in the 1850s. Emigration from Antrim and Down increased by 114 and 36 per cent throughout the decade, compared with a decrease of 44.5 per cent in total emigration from the whole of Ireland.[14] The prominence of single males was therefore accentuated by the nature and timing of their departure from Ireland, as well as the disparity of the sexes typical of a goldfields population.

What strata of Irish society did the migrants come from? This question cannot be answered conclusively without access to reliable data, but death certificates contain some useful information, especially after 1875 when local registrars were required to list the occupation of the dead person's father. A close analysis of the surviving documentation shows that, although all social levels of Irish society were represented, women migrants came largely from agricultural backgrounds. The farming sector dominated the inflow (65.4 per cent), and a small but significant minority was drawn from families associated with pre-industrial trades. Women from agricultural labouring households, on the other hand, were underrepresented relative to their proportion in the Irish population and compared with the corresponding rates for Irish wives who travelled to the Otago goldfields.[15] The socio-economic backgrounds of Irish male migrants were very similar to those of their female counterparts. Despite its limitations, the evidence allows us to conjecture that newcomers were drawn disproportionately from the ranks of middling tenant farms and the families of an emerging post-Famine élite of prosperous farmers, shopkeepers, merchants and traders. Although better data is needed to confirm this hypothesis, it accords with local fieldwork and the observations of such contemporaries as Father Nicholas Binsfield, who claimed that Catholic miners came from '[the] well-to-do classes at home'.[16]

The most plausible explanation for this pattern turns upon the character of Irish migration to Victoria, which attracted a majority of unsubsidised settlers before 1860.[17] Without state assistance, the poorest or least experienced migrants with few resources would have been unable to afford the passage, which ranged from three to five times the rate for a transatlantic crossing in the 1850s.[18] The fact that substantial fares of this nature were sometimes funded from private sources such as dowry payments underlines the relative affluence that some newcomers had enjoyed within Irish society. This was certainly true for many female workers who participated in the self-financed movement from Melbourne to the Otago and West Coast goldfields during the 1860s and 1870s. We can think here of Ellen Walsh, the daughter of a comfortable Kilkenny artisan-tenant farmer, or 'the Limerick girls', Ann Diamond and her cousin Johanna Weir, whose mossy gravestones in the Notown cemetery obscure moneyed backgrounds in Adare.[19] For women such as these, the decision to leave Ireland was made for family rather than individual reasons and was a logical and practical option in a rural society where opportunities for undowried females were quite limited.[20] Whatever their personal motivations, David Doyle's recent assertion that 'strong and medium farmers' daughters had, at worst, intelligent choices imposed on them' seems a more realistic characterisation of their migration than the fanciful depiction of an independent flight from patriarchal oppression.[21] The complex negotiations that preceded the departure of young people from the households of smallholders, labourers and urban artisans remain inaccessible. Case studies of West Coast migrants from less affluent backgrounds, such as Catherine Bourke, Margaret McGirr and Maria Phelan, suggest that state funding played a part, but we may never know how many newcomers received subsidies or the extent to which their fares were supplemented by private benefactors.[22]

Although some parts of the picture remain hazy, the surviving evidence reveals that Irish movement to the West Coast was highly selective in terms of age, class, county origin, religion, parenthood and marital status. Information contained in the New Zealand census shows that the Irish-born and their descendants comprised about a quarter of the region's population between the mid-1860s and the 1920s. The reports also show that the urban centres contained a stronger proportional representation of women than the outlying goldfields districts. The regional origins of the inflow were quite distinctive, centring upon a cluster of southern rural districts with strong Australian connections. An important secondary concentration in north and north-east Ulster featured a disproportionate number of Roman Catholics, as well as a chronic excess of emigrant males. As we might expect, single men dominated the West Coast's intake in absolute numbers, but more than half of all Irish women had married before arriving on the goldfields. In addition, migrants of both sexes were considerably older than their compatriots who ventured elsewhere and most had served extensive colonial apprenticeships in other countries. Finally, the balance of religious affiliations among the West Coast Irish closely matched that of the eastern Australian colonies and included a similar proportion of newcomers from rural backgrounds.

II

Age, gender, family structure and economic circumstances played an important part in shaping the movement of Irish men and women to the West Coast, but the role of social networks based on friendship or familial ties is less clear. A major study of Catholic Irish migration to nineteenth-century Canterbury suggests one avenue of inquiry.[23] The source materials used in this analysis show that the eastern province's migrants were made up of clusters of people bound together by acquaintance and kinship ties who came to the colony at a critical stage in their lives. Australian historians have documented similar patterns of chain migration and solidarity in several different locations and one scholar has identified personal relationships – along with state paternalism – as a major determinant of Irish emigration.[24]

Regardless of their social origins or marital status, Irish migrants seldom travelled to the region as isolated individuals. The colourful folklore surrounding female miners like 'Sugar Annie' Rankin and Bridget Goodwin, or the shadowy world of prostitutes such as Tipperary Mary, Overland Kate and Leaky Liz, forms an important part of the West Coast's historical landscape, but their stories are unrepresentative.[25] Most newcomers were accompanied on their journey by kinsfolk or followed the paths of relatives and friends who had already settled on the West Coast. Ann Diamond (*née* Gleeson) of County Limerick, for example, spent three years in Dunedin with her husband, Patrick, and friend Mary Maloney, before moving to Red Jacks, a remote Westland mining camp in which they established a substantial hotel and store. According to family tradition, the two women travelled to Victoria in the late 1850s with Ann's cousin, Johanna Shanahan (later Weir), their passages paid for by the Gleesons.[26] Johanna stayed in Melbourne with two of her brothers until 1865, when she agreed to join the others at Diamond's Hotel, a 'carefully furnished' establishment that featured 'coloured prints of Wolfe Tone and Robert Emmet', and corner brackets 'decorated with green velvet plush and hearts and shamrocks'.[27] She assumed responsibility for general management of the hotel and acted as the cook, producing 'excellent meals from an enormous stone fireplace equipped with iron hooks for hanging heavy iron pots and cauldrons, and a spit for roasting'.[28]

The migration pathways of single migrants featured a similar reliance on kinship networks. Typical in this regard was Catherine Minehan of County Clare, who sailed to Sydney aboard the *Spitfire* in 1863, accompanied by two brothers, Patrick and Sylvester. Her departure was part of a much wider movement of family and friends from the parish of Kilcredan to New South Wales that began soon after the Famine and continued unabated until the 1870s. She was reunited in the colony with four elder siblings, Martin, Bridget, Jeremiah and Denis, and later joined by her younger brother, Michael, as well as numerous cousins and Old World neighbours. Catherine Minehan worked as a domestic servant in Sydney before venturing across the Tasman with four of her brothers in the late 1860s. It seems likely that she lived with Patrick and his Kilredan-born wife, Honora White, during the years immediately before her marriage to Patrick Dunn at Ross in 1874. The couple later returned to Australia and settled eventually at Kyabram, Victoria, where they ran a hotel.[29] Such examples highlight the importance of family and neighbourhood networks in Irish migration to the Coast and indicate that these connections often spanned the Tasman Sea in both directions.

The persistent insecurity of goldmining settlements promoted a dependence on friends, siblings and other relatives.[30] In practical terms, Old World social ties provided an important source of companionship, material assistance and information for new arrivals and considerably reduced the risks involved in moving to the West Coast. Johanna Weir, for instance, gave birth to seven children, six of whom were delivered by her cousin, Ann Diamond, at a time when the Notown doctor, John Grattan, suffered from acute alcoholism.[31] At Rimu, a widowed Ellen Piezzi – Kilkenny-born, she had married a Swiss-Italian baker – arranged through her sister Mary for her eldest daughter Helvetia to be educated in Wellington. Ellen managed two hotels with the assistance of male siblings: 'I got my brothes minding the other plase for me and i go home oust Week for cupel of dayes setel up overthing for them and go back again'.[32] In a more abstract way, however, Old World connections could preserve notions of familial duty prescribed by Irish society. Migrants of both sexes constructed complex webs of association, stretching from Nelson Creek to Ballarat, and from South Westland to distant parishes in County Clare. These intimate connections were strongest between adjacent generations, but they also stretched backwards and forwards through time, as shown, for instance, by the letters from Kate Phelan in Limerick City to her Greymouth-born niece, Cecilia Horan:[33]

We were all very glad to get a letter from you. You will be sorry to learn that my Mother whom you wrote to is suffering from loss of memory and forgets all about her relations and at times forgets we are her children. She is healthy and keeps about and never misses Mass every morning and I go with her or she would forget her way home. Sometimes I find her trying to get dressed in the middle of the night to go to Mass and sometimes after dinner she declares she did not get Mass yet but must start off now. I don't know whether you heard that Father died suddenly in May 1914. He went up to bed as well as ever Whitsunday at 10°C and when mother went up in ten minutes after he just drawing his last breath. It was a great shock to us all.[34]

Kate Phelan's unadorned descriptions of family death and decrepitude were combined with reports of further emigration:

My sister Lessie is married in this city and has three girls and one boy all grown up and my sister Matilda died in 1912 leaving ten children twins a fortnight old. The husband is married again and her eldest boy Jack Ryan is starting for N. Zealand on Feb 3rd. He is 26 years old and we reared him since he was two years. He was educated at the Redemptorists college and was in the Bank for a time and has just left it. We are all very fond of him and will be very lonely when he goes.[35]

The enduring significance of personal networks based on ties of kinship and acquaintance is clearly evident in surviving migrant correspondence, which expresses a 'dialogue of moral persuasion' similar to that described by David Fitzpatrick in his widely acclaimed study of Irish-Australian letters, *Oceans of Consolation*.[36] Letter writers were particularly concerned with such major family problems as the dispersion of households, marriage and the support of ageing relatives.[37] Catherine O'Toole of Inagh, County Clare, for instance, penned a moving account of parental vulnerability in an attempt to elicit 'a little gift' from her married daughter, Susan Hogan of Maori Gully:

Your long wished letter of the 30th May last came to hand on yesterday. It was at James Cassidy's some days before I got it. You have no idea how delighted I was when I got it & when it was read for me. I assure you I shed tears of joy when I knew that yourself dear husband & little children being well. If you knew the many anxious days & nights & even months & years I expected to get a letter from you. Picture to yourself if one of your dear children left you & went to a foreign land & that you would not hear from that dear child for a long number of years. Would you not feel sore at heart? I know you would & poor Parents in general would so you see it's no exception in my case. You ought at least to write me a few lines occasionally so that I can know that ye are all right. It would Console me in my old age.[38]

Two other letters survive from the Hogan household, both of which illustrate the diffusion of Irish families abroad. The first, addressed to Susan's husband, Michael, from his brother in New York, defended a decision to go to the United States rather than the West Coast on the grounds that his mate, Michael Ryan, 'who is inseparable from me', did not want to undertake such a long voyage. 'Besides,' he added for good measure, 'Michael Barry my brother-in-law would not have me go to New Zealand.'[39] The second, written by Susan's cousin, whose daughter the Hogans had fostered, further underlines the centrality of trans-Tasman ties among many of the West Coast Irish:

I was very sorry to hear of Mrs Costigan malidy. You said nothing about her Duaghter Catey whether she came back from Melbourne or not. Patt Mulvihill is hear in Sydney. He got marred lately. I was sorry to hear of Miss Crows demise. You said that the others was left Greymouth [*and*] keeping a boarding [*house*] in Wellington. I want to know is Ellen Crow with them or is she still in Hokit*ika*? I was sorry to hear of Malone Demise. Remember me to Frank. I hope he is living in good health. I do not remember this Miss Murray or M^r H/Wall that you say that is dead.

Dear Cousin I showed your letter to Mary Cassidy. She says that she wrote to you on two occations and you have never answered her letters. They are all in good health with the exception of Patt. He has get into Consumption. I don't think he will ever get over it. Mary is married. So is the third of the girls Catey. By all appearrence you*r* son John will be soon married. He is doing well and is a fine sencible young man. I am at loss to know who is this sweethart of mine that is still in the same place as I do not know wh*o* you mane.[40]

Acting as an intercessor for Catherine O'Toole, he encouraged Susan to fulfil her familial responsibilities: 'Now about writing to you mother. I would advise you to write to her in her old adge and I do not think she wants any money from you but she would like to hear from you'. This duty quickly discharged, his thoughts turned to his own economic well-being in Sydney:

Dear Cousin I am going to tell you something about myself. I am in this great city. I have a horse and dray working in the town. I am not doing much more than a livin at it. I had a bit a hard look as usual. I had a grand horse. He gat the favour and it took a lot of money to get him right. When I gat him right and in good working order he hurted his shoulders with heavy pulling and now I have him laid up again for a few days. Bit I hope it won't for long.[41]

Although the migration of people like Susan Hogan (Plate 10) to the West Coast undoubtedly placed additional strains on familial bonds already disrupted by other departures, it is wrong to assume that mobility led inevitably to weak kinship networks. Such connections played a key role in shaping colonial population movements and maintaining social relations across large distances.[42]

The significance of personal correspondence for migrants on the diggings and their relatives elsewhere can be astonishing for modern readers, more attuned to a world of instant email communications and text-messaging. As David Fitzpatrick and Angela McCarthy have shown, letters mattered so much because they provided tokens of reassurance to family members separated by the oceans and allowed them to influence one another's actions.[43] The very act of communication was expensive and time-consuming, its codes and conventions challenging for even the most literate migrants. It also entailed an element of risk: valuable correspondence might be lost or delayed. On the West Coast goldfields, where the population was highly transient, miners anxiously awaited news from aboard and arranged for mail to be sent to local post offices. Louthman Michael Flanagan, for example, writing from Charleston in 1867, described the receipt of a letter from his brother in London as an 'event' and 'the most welcome epistle' he had read 'for a long time': 'It is such a length of time since we saw your handwriting before and as you are the very perfection of a letter writer if anything could throw a little light upon or import a ray of hope to the dreary monotony of a life in this climate it would be a few words of encouragement or an assurance that their were some in the world yet who were anxious to hear from us'.[44] Directing his letters to Charleston as requested, Richard Flanagan told Michael that he had been expecting news from New Zealand 'by the last two or three mails. I suppose in your remote district and in the cares and anxieties of your daily occupation you often miss the oppertunities of writing you had intended availing yourself of.'[45] It seems likely that he had received colonial papers in the mail, a possibility suggested by his forthright warning about recent political events: 'I see by the news that those misguided people, the Fenians, are not without sympathisers in your part of the world. I hope you will have sense enough to hold aloof from mixing up in any way with people who have anything to do with them. They have only brought misery and misfortune on themselves and all who have had anything to do with them and injury on their unfortunate country.'[46]

The exchange of letters between dispersed kinsfolk and friends was usually supplemented by local newspapers, which were much cheaper to send and provided an additional means of contact. In the Australian colonies, the postage of printed papers to and from Britain exceeded the volume of correspondence in weight and absolute numbers throughout the nineteenth century.[47] This phenomenon is neatly illustrated by an intestacy case held at Archives New Zealand in Christchurch. I had been making considerable progress through the West Coast probates when, one afternoon, I was presented with an enormous intestacy file from Hokitika. Dreading the next hour of work and anticipating a 'duffer', I fumbled with the fragile ribbon that had not been opened for over 100 years. To my astonishment, the dusty bundle yielded a rich prospect that included several Australian newspapers and a handful of migrant letters. Household disharmony seemed to be the main agent of emigration in this case, yet the correspondent maintained links with home and in so doing voiced his adherence to a moral code of familial obligations that accompanied many Irish people abroad.

Ulster-born Alexander Mitchell drowned in a remote section of the Waimea River where there were 'no grave yards, no roads and no other means of carriage of [his] remains . . . than on men's shoulders'.[48] The legal documents that support an application by his two surviving brothers for letters of administration to Mitchell's estate shows that he emigrated from the family homestead at Ballinaskeagh, County Down, in 1846. After landing in Quebec, he made his way to Dundas, where he found a job as a clerk in a local foundry. Mitchell disliked this position intensely and told his father that he would rather 'beg for work everyday than be confined the way I have been this summer'.[49] He tried his hand at harvesting in the company of an ex-neighbour and claimed to have earned 'a good deal more money' than from his previous engagement. Yet he complained bitterly that a lack of capital prevented him from purchasing suitable farmland in Canada. Mitchell made repeated appeals for financial assistance from home and his own correspondence combined expressions of filial piety with reproaches about 'odd and disrespectful' letters received from Ireland.[50] These requests became more desperate when he borrowed money to purchase a small farm in Woolwich, Canada West, and faced mounting pressure from creditors. Despite this dispute with his family, Mitchell continued to take part in deliberations about further emigration by relatives and acted as a patron for new arrivals. During the winter of 1850, he employed 'a little daughter of Ann jane [sic] Porters' as a housekeeper and assured his father that he would find work for the son of an old acquaintance: 'I will take an Interest in his welfare so far as in my powers or any person in the neighbourhood. If James wishes to work for me i will give him more than he can get from another and if not where ever he works i will see his pay is sure.'[51] A combination of hard times and bad debts eventually broke his resolve to remain on the land and he joined the exodus of 'new chums' bound for the Victorian goldfields in 1853.

Mitchell did not correspond directly with kin in Ireland during his sojourn in the Australasian colonies but maintained contact by sending newspapers to family members. More importantly, he was able to draw upon a network of expatriate acquaintances who provided much-needed companionship in the New World and sustained connections with home. A former neighbour, Richard Megaffin, for example, wrote to Mitchell's parents from Ballarat and assured them that their son 'was doing well and in Good Health – he wished us to Remember him to his Friends'.[52] Mitchell seems to have relied on old companions after relocating his carting business in Invercargill and extending his operations to the Waimea diggings in South Westland. His family received periodic reports about his progress from returned Australian and New Zealand diggers, whom he had instructed to call on them. Like other historical records such as wills (see Chapter 3), Mitchell's case documents the persistence of Old World social ties and suggests that interaction with expatriates was an essential part of the Irish colonial experience.

The surviving West Coast letters are peppered with news about relatives and friends, as well as advice or encouragement to intending migrants. Writing from Reefton in 1890, Andrew Burns admitted that he could not tell Michael Flanagan much about his old friends:

I think that the only ones that are here so far as I know are Tom McKenna and Pat Brennan. Neither of them have made their fortunes as yet. Tom McKenna is quite poor. Pat Brennan is doing a good business here as Auctioneer and Commission Agent though he's far from making his pile. Most of the other old people you knew are dead or away in some other place. You may well have known Harry McGill. In the old times he used to be boating to the old Twelve-mile. He had a good farm on Totara Flat and sold it a short time ago for over two thousand pounds. He has gone with his family to Ireland where he intends settling down. Tom Clinton left here for Ireland about fifteen years ago. He made about eight hundred pounds in a mining speculation here and like a wise man went home. He married a widow at home shortly afterwards who had a little fortune of her own and he is now I believe in very comfortable circumstances'.[53]

In a different vein, the Monaghan-born hotelier and entrepreneur, Samuel Gilmer, who retained considerable business interests on the West Coast after moving to Wellington in 1879, tried to lure his younger brother, William, back from Mullaghanee with the promise of a remittance: 'As for you going to new south wales is new Zealand not large enough for you? I would have thought it was but I suppose really you have not yet decided which will be your lot. But I can imagine all there is to be done on a few acres of Irish soil is not much after all is said and done. Would you not have been better here only for your health.' If his physical condition improved, he advised William to make for Greymouth, but added '[y]ou should be the best judge off those matters. You are now away more than twelve months. The time soon passeth.'[54] William, however, was hesitant, confiding to another brother, Robert, that Samuel had urged him 'to go out again & live in Greymouth. I w^d be only too glad to accept his offer, only I don't know how to manage being married . . . I'll have to try something else than farming in Ireland, working & spending money for nothing.' Perhaps it was not surprising that William chose to remain in Mullaganhee, even though he described Ireland as 'a very miserable place. We have not had more than 2 or 3 dry days at once all this summer. Harvest is ripe & no dry weather to cut it. The potato crop is a failure. Things are looking very bad indeed.' He complained to Samuel that his 'luck in farming has not been very good as yet. I lost 3 pigs with disease & a horse took founder & don't seem to get better. I think his feet will get old like Dan long ago. I suppose you remember him.' Yet William's reluctance to emigrate is clear, despite his chronicle of misfortunes: 'If I had only middling health I w^d not stop long in Ireland, altho, I've fair health recently. If I thought my wife could get a situation as teacher, I w^d very soon leave. I think she intends writing to you, about using your influence in getting her a school.'[55]

    The letters that eased the pain of separation for Irish writers and readers scattered around the world often contained symbolic tokens, such as locks of hair and small items of clothing, and remittances.[56] For many correspondents, however, photographs were by far the most highly treasured objects, and widely circulated among family and friends. Nothing makes the human story of Irish migration more poignant than appeals for images of grandchildren, nephews or daughters-in-law that writers would never meet, or reciprocal requests for portraits of brothers, sisters and friends. The receipt of photographs could be an unsettling experience for fragmented families, documenting the passage of time and changes in appearance. Andrew Burns, for example, writing to Michael Flanagan, remarked candidly on 'the portraits' he had sent from Reefton: 'I'm afraid that if you received the originals you would not say you could see no difference in our appearance now and twenty years ago'. Yet he seemed much more positive about the comparisons made with another photograph. 'I got the portrait of my sister Mary from home and I would not know her. She looks quite old. I think I stand it better than she does.'[57]

The importance of physical tokens in the communication ritual is also evident in a South Westland family history.[58] Edward O'Connor, the fifth-born child in a large farming household at Killarney, County Kerry, was 18 years old when he sailed from Liverpool to Melbourne on the clipper, *Champion of the Seas*, in 1866. After a brief period in Victoria, he joined the 1867 rushes to the southern districts of the West Coast goldfields, working mainly around the Ross district where ground-sluicing and deep leads dominated the industry. Edward later ventured across the Tasman, mining at Ballarat for several months, before returning to Hokitika on the steamer *Tararua* in 1871. There he remained, earning a living as a miner and contractor, until he had gained sufficient funds to become the licensee of the Imperial Hotel in 1879, the year in which he married Bridget Cashman of County Kerry. The nature of family discussions that preceded a decision to send out three of Edward's younger siblings from Rathcommane in 1882 are not known, but it is clear that his improving financial status made this alternative more viable. Patrick (21), Michael (20) and Kate (23) obtained state-subsidised passages to Hokitika, their application supported by a handwritten reference from their father, James:

I certify that Patrick & Michael & Catherine O'Connor are sober, industrious and of good character. I also believe that they are of sound mind, and free from any bodily or mental defect likely to impair their efficiency as good farm-labourers & dairy-maid. I certify that I have known Patrick & Michael since born, that I have trained them to every sort of farm business and that they now understand thoroughly everything in connexion with such business. I certify that I have trained Catherine to dairy-management since she was able to do so and she now understands everything in connexion with it. I also certify that the statements contained in the Schedule, with reference to age, county, occupation etc are true.[59]

In an amazing twist of fate, the *Crownthorpe*, on which the O'Connors travelled, encountered very bad weather in the Bay of Biscay and retreated to Southhampton. All three returned to the family homestead in Rathcommane to await the next sailing for New Zealand. During the interim, Kate decided not to repeat the hair-raising sea voyage and Michael arranged to join another brother, Jeremiah, in New York. Michael's steerage berth was taken by William (19), who had to assume his brother's identity for the duration of the journey to Sydney on the *Hurunui* and across the Tasman aboard the brigantine *Zephyr*. Patrick and William must have been very relieved to arrive at Hokitika on 16 April 1883, where they stayed with Edward's family in the Imperial Hotel.

While the two brothers settled into the rhythms of everyday life on the goldfields, Jeremiah O'Connor was barely making a living in New York. Writing to Edward from Brooklyn in 1885, he complained that he had endured 'a great deal of disappointments' since receiving his last letter. 'I got hurt twice when at work but thank God it was not serious although it laid me up Idle for some time. This summer i got an attack of intrenitten fervour [*enteric fever*] [*and*] was under the care of a doctor. However this excuse is no good to answer your letter long before this.' The progress of their cousin, Denis Flynn, who was living in Boston, seemed much more satisfactory: '[He] was here to see us a year ago last summer. He was asking about you and all the folks. He looks first rate. He is a very steady man and has a splindad job: 125 dollars a mounth that is equeal to 25 Pounds Brittish money.' Jeremiah expressed delight at the photographs that Edward had sent him and apologised for not reciprocating: 'They were indeed very good and as for the Children they look lovely and espeacelly the little girl. Dear Brother we had our picture taken twice but they were not to our liking. We did not like to send them.' Promising to post more suitable images of his family, he asked Edward to '[t]ell Pat and William that we would like to have their pictures'.[60] The expense of arranging to have portraits taken and posted must have been a burden for struggling migrants such as Jeremiah O'Connor, but the frequency with which these tokens were sent around the worlds attests to their role as potent symbols of contact in the face of separation.

Like many of her Irish contemporaries, Mary O'Connor used an amanuensis to communicate with her children in the United States and New Zealand. The only surviving letter, written by her daughter Johanna O'Leary and addressed to William, is a collective narrative in which the voices of both women can be clearly heard. Mary told her son that he looked well in a recently received photograph and noted with some satisfaction that 'there was no great change' in his appearance after more than a decade in the colonies. She wondered about the reasons behind Patrick's decision to leave goldmining and join the police force, as well as the background of his wife, Mary Ellen Dolan: 'Is it not surprising now Patts courage failed him to leave or has he a better Pay in the Police? Why don't you get him to send his photoes. Is his wife a native? Do you see him often or is he far from you? He never takes any notion to write. I hope he is well.' Her expectations were stated very directly: 'Mother would like him to write and send his photoes to her'. The news that Mary O'Connor reported from home was dominated by the themes of emigration, death and illness. Two daughters of her eldest son, John, were working for an American tea company and he was 'well off' on account of 'getting plenty money' from his children. 'The rest are at home. He buried a splendid girl. Her name was Johanna. She was borne that night your brother Dan was Buried. May their souls rest in peace. Amen.' James was suffering from a lung infection that flared up badly during the spring, while Kate had 'some sort of an Inward pain in her stomack' after the birth of her last child, an ailment that even 'the Cork doctors' could not diagnose. The sorrowful chronicle of death and departure created a gloomy picture of change and decay in Rathcommane:

> You asked about Daniel Kelleher. He is dead and Buried with the past 4 years. James Willie Lizzie Bridget Dannie Maryanne are in America. Jane is married and Mary is married to your uncle neds son dan myers and he can earn more than 1 pound per Day. He is a machine molder the Myers sent 26 pounds to their father at Xmis and often through the year. Your Uncle Jacks Lads are still together. He Buried his wife and so Did your Uncle daniel bury [*Nassie?*] noonen. He has all his Babies together. Yet Billies Is with tade but not as gay But still alking. Your aunt Hanna is well. Maurice is not married. The rest are in America and do not ever think of them. Old Daniel Falvey is married the third time. Jam Piggott Buried his wife and Bidy Kiely was Buried. It would be too much to tell you all the strange things.

The re-emergence of Johanna O'Leary's voice at the end of the letter is a welcome respite from Mary's dark recitations:

So I think it is time for the Writer tell you something about herself. Dear Brother I came a good Distance to write this. I am living in the County Carlow over 200 hundred miles from Killarney by rail. I have only the one little boy. His name is Patrick. Myself and husband are well. I would like you to send myself your Poto and the litt/e one. I would like them taken in a group and myself and Husband will send on ours as soon as I get year [*yours*]. In the summer mother and the rest will send you theirs as there is no Potographer in Killarney until summer. Well done. I have no more to say. We all join with mother is sending yourself and wife and child our fond love. Good by from all of us to your wife. Don't neglect wrighting.[61]

The O'Connor correspondence, like the other sequences used in this chapter, suggests that, for migrants, 'home' was a particular locality and a small group of relatives and friends. To understand the anatomy of migration, therefore, we must focus on places like Inagh, Mullaghanee, Ballinaskeagh and Rathcommane, as well as Clare, Monaghan, Down and Kerry, tracing the influence of personal networks based on ties of kinship and neighbourhood back to these tiny Irish localities.

III

We are now in a position to reach some conclusions about the main features of Irish migration to the West Coast. The movement that followed the discovery of gold at Greenstone Creek in 1864 formed part of a much larger trans-Tasman flow which 'embraced not one but two generations'.[62] It always contained an overwhelming preponderance of males drawn into the extractive industries of gold, coal and timber. The uneven geographical distribution of the migrants, with larger numbers of Irish and Catholic women living in the region's urban centres, shows that, in certain places, their labour was needed more than men's. Most women performed routine tasks within the unwaged household sector, while single females in their late teens and early twenties usually found employment as paid domestic servants in the main towns. The majority of Irish-born people were two- or three-stage migrants who ventured to the region after serving extensive colonial apprenticeships in Victoria, New South Wales and Otago. The regional origins of the inflow reflected this general trend and turned upon the key centres of Australian emigration such as Tipperary, Clare and Limerick in Munster, but also included strong contingents from the northern counties of Londonderry, Antrim and Down. Newcomers were considerably older than their compatriots venturing abroad between the Famine and the First World War, and more than half of the women had married before their arrival, three-fifths forming unions in the Australian colonies. Predictably, the balance of religious affiliations among the migrants matched the patterns found in Victoria and included a similar proportion of men and women drawn from agricultural backgrounds. The strong presence of well-heeled migrants from rural Irish families underlines the fact that newcomers were differentiated by class, as well as generation, religion, parental and marital status. Finally, we may surmise that the Irish were highly visible on the West Coast, given that the entire multi-generational group comprised about a quarter of the total population between the years 1864 and 1915.

The migrant stream that flowed into the region differed in several crucial respects from the corresponding movement of Irish people to other New Zealand destinations. The predominance of Roman Catholics, the high proportion of married females, the critical importance of Australian connections and the relative insignificance of state assistance set the West Coast apart from the provinces of Canterbury and Nelson. Irish men and women were among the earliest arrivals on the goldfields and formed part of a diverse 'charter group' with a powerful role in defining the nature of local community life. The ramshackle towns and mining camps of the Coast presented a greater challenge than those conditions encountered by Irish migrants in Timaru or Christchurch, yet the crucial function of Old World social ties suggests underlying similarities on both sides of the Southern Alps. The selective recreation of kinship and neighbourhood networks provided an important source of companionship, material assistance and information for Irish migrants on the goldfields, and helped to preserve notions of familial duty prescribed by Irish society. Distance may have strained or even broken allegiances anchored in Ireland, as the Mitchell correspondence shows, but the evidence seems to indicate that migrant connections crossed the Tasman in both directions and stretched as far as distant rural homesteads in places like Ballinaskeagh and Rathcommane.

3   'The Elusive Pile':
Working Lives on the Goldfields

The rushes that exploded with such dazzling intensity along the region's sparsely inhabited coastline led to the emergence of a vigorous and distinctive borderland world shaped by the feverish search for gold. An army of restless diggers swarmed through the sodden wilderness, rolling up their swags and moving on quickly at news of fresh strikes, seemingly oblivious to the hazards of swollen rivers, dense bushland, steep mountain ranges and driving rain. A supporting cast of storekeepers and publicans, wardens and bank agents, barmaids and musicians, followed in their wake, their fortunes closely tied to those of the digging population. Behind this relentless advance, settled communities began to evolve from the makeshift canvas and corrugated iron shanties that mushroomed in a spectacular fashion on the beaches and pakihi. By mid-1866, a mere 18 months after its foundation, Hokitika, the goldfields capital, was one of New Zealand's leading ports in terms of customs revenue, shipping and immigration. Travellers marvelled at its impressive buildings and busy civic life, the crowded concert-halls, the annual festivals and the stores overflowing with an abundance of Australian merchandise. Beneath the outward signs of prosperity, however, it was clear that an economy based on 'wasting natural assets' could not continue to expand as it had done throughout the boom years.[1] As the gold began to peter out, large numbers of men and women drifted back to the Australian colonies or travelled elsewhere in search of better opportunities. Few ever intended to stay and most had been attracted by the prospect of making a quick fortune or high wages that might be used to purchase land in the colonies or at home.

This chapter uses a variety of sources to explore how Irish men and women sustained themselves in goldfields communities from the mid-1860s. Historians have shown that the opportunities available to the Irish abroad had a profound influence on the formation of their ethnic identities. Thus, in parts of the United States and Britain, where migrants faced considerable hostility and restricted avenues for social mobility in long established, hierarchical societies, ethnicity assumed far greater historical significance than in the Australian colonies and New Zealand. As William Pember Reeves observed, the Irish here did not 'crowd into the towns, or attempt to capture the municipal machinery, as in America', nor were they 'a source of political unrest or corruption'.[2] Part of the explanation for these differences can be found in the role that newcomers played in the labour markets of host communities, along with other factors such as the timing of migration, the size of the migrant group and the extent of anti-Irish prejudice. As we shall see, the West Coast Irish were at the forefront of colonisation and well represented in all sectors of the region's economy. Although none accumulated wealth on the same scale as their counterparts in North America and eastern Australia, the surviving evidence reveals that they matched wider regional patterns of occupational attainment and general prosperity.

I

The names of localities like Croninville, Callaghan's, Donnelly's Creek, Capleston and Dunganville show that Irish prospectors were prominent among the toughened colonials keen to relive the excitements 'of Castlemaine and Forest Creek and dear old Bendigo'.[3] But we need to find rich leads if we want to recover detailed impressions of their working lives. A voluminous correspondence between the Flanagan brothers, Patrick and Michael, and their associates provides one window into the past. These letters contain revealing commentaries on economic conditions in Australasia and North America, and illuminate the role of social networks in relaying news from one mining camp to another. This personal testimony is rendered all the more important by the fact that the Flanagans reached the West Coast at the height of the gold rushes, so represent a group that is very difficult to trace in the surviving records: the sizeable, roving population of single males that spent time in the region during the early phases of simple creek and gully prospecting.

The Flanagan brothers came from relatively comfortable backgrounds in the parish of Termonfeckin, County Louth.[4] According to the official surveyors, their paternal grandfather, Patrick, occupied 28 acres in Tobertoby worth £31 annually in 1856 and held additional properties in Balfeddock and Beltichburne valued at £107 and £27 10s respectively.[5] Richard Flanagan, who became a customs clerk in London, was among those who left the parish in that year. It is not clear why his brothers departed in 1857, but a farm account book held by the family shows that their grandfather purchased the tickets: 'Paid Patrick and Michael going to Australia £14'.[6] Both men travelled to Liverpool where they boarded the *Oliver Lang* for a three-month voyage in steerage to Melbourne. Twenty-three-year-old Patrick and 17-year-old Michael probably never expected to stay in the southern hemisphere and may have entertained hopes of going home with a tidy pile. In the years that followed, however, only Michael (Plate 11) returned to Ireland, in response to a desperate plea from his ailing father in 1890. 'Instead . . . of the lad of seventeen years you last saw,' he warned him gloomily, 'you will meet a grey old man of fifty.'[7]

These men moved around extensively, in the eastern Australian colonies, New Zealand and California, but the surviving letters affirm the importance of family and neighbourhood networks in structuring the migration process. Michael's enthusiastic account of a reunion with Patrick in Queensland must have provided some consolation to an 'Uncle Priest' in Ireland:

About the end of August last I left Melbourne for this colony to join Pat from whom I had a letter a few days previous to me leaving in which he gave a rather favourable account of the diggings . . . The time passed well enough during our journey the nights being pretty cool compensated us a little for the fatigues of the day under the nearly perpendicular sun. On the thirteenth day from our leaving the coast we got a first glimpse of a curiously made up little township composed of bark and slabs and this was the diggings. I was over a week on the diggings before I found Pat. One day I was wending my way amongst the bark and slabs which compose the township and I saw advancing before one curious looking bushman and as I came close and got a nearer view I found I saw the face before not untill he put out his hand and began laughing did I fully recognise the man I was in search of. Pat was a good deal changed since I last saw him before. His appearance would nearly put one in mind of a Maori. The sun of Queensland browned him very much but the climate did not disagree with him. He was in perfect health, but he looked rather thinner than when I last saw him and although New Zealand seems to have agreed well with him during the three years he was there he did not look three years younger after all. There were two Clougher men along with him when I met him who were his mates one of these was the young man who came out along with Dick Sheridan – Pat Kirk.[8]

Significantly, Michael Flanagan emphasised the importance of companionship as a prerequisite for 'getting on' in Australasia:

The friendship of any true friend and especially one who had influence would certainly be a great benefit to any young man in a strange country but to the friendless and the lonely and to those who do not possess the natural gift of being bold and shameless and who have not plenty of what in the colony is called 'cheek' it is hard, very hard to obtain a footing amongst a class who make money by means which I would live a poor man all my life rather than descend to.[9]

He struggled to adapt to the harsh nature of goldmining, but his older brother relished the 'bracing freedom' of their nomadic existence.[10] On one occasion, after Patrick visited Charleston from a rush north of the town, Michael told Richard that his 'health is the same as ever. He is one of the very few upon whom the climate or the hardships to be endured in this vagabond life seems to have no effect. The prospects of the rush at which he is looked very well some time ago – indeed I had great expectations of it – but it is very wet ground and expensive to work it so that it is growing lower in peoples estimation.'[11]

As payable ground in the region began to dwindle, Patrick led the way again, this time to Grahamstown on the Thames goldfields in the North Island. His perceptive and finely detailed descriptions of the opportunities available in the area dissuaded Michael and his friends from following: 'There are very few claims getting gold but the extraordinary richness of those few keep the excitment up and the large sums invested by capitalists from other colonies is the stream that keeps the mill going. The amount of gold got in the place would not give tucker to half the population . . . Most people have a good opinion of it but I think they are dazled.'[12] To make matters worse, Patrick reported that many of their newly arrived associates were struggling to survive as 'wages-men':

The rush of people here has caused the wages to fall again. There are some working for thirty shillings. Hugh Brown and T McKenna went to work for wages next day after land at 2£. It is not so easy to get wages now as all the newcomers look for work as soon as they come. T Keogh is working for wages, Luke Malloy is here and desires to be kindly reme*mbered* to the boys. He is not long here. He has been in Melbourn Sydney nearly up to Queensland and over to Hobart Town back to Melbourn and down here. Tom Fox has a claim that stands a good show. He has no gold yet. They have been tunnelling on it more than a year. In fact there is no one that you know has done any good.[13]

By the end of 1869, Patrick was 'working hard' for a subcontractor at a daily rate of 6s 6d, desperate to clear his West Coast debts and join his brother, Nicholas, in the United States. 'The worst part of the going to America,' he told Michael, 'is the high rate of fare on the overland. I believe the fare over there after getting down would be more than the sea fare but no matter I believe it is the best thing to be done. If you think there is no chance of getting any of the money we cannot do worse than we have been doeing here.'[14] With Michael's help Patrick managed to settle his affairs in the South Island and sailed for California in 1870, where he penned glowing reports to his connections around the world. These letters were sufficiently persuasive to lure Nicholas west from Ohio and Michael across the Pacific Ocean inside the next twelve months. It was also news that pleased Richard Flanagan in London: 'If he has gone to California with the intention of settling there and has a little Capital I think he has done wisely as it is most undoubtedly a splendid country – far exceeding in many advantages any of our Australian colonies'.[15]

The nature and availability of employment in different places was a dominant theme of the surviving correspondence. Writing from Ohio, Nicholas Flanagan gave an unembellished account of opportunities in the state, making no attempt to hide the persistent insecurity that characterised his working life:

There is very little doing here in winter. In summer lots of work of all kinds. I am in employ for putry near three years. When I first come here I had to take the about the roughest job in the business but after two years I got something better and better pay. Labouring men as a general thing get $1.40 per day and bord will cost them about $18.00 per month. I am getting 50 dollers per month and bord at present but I do not know whether I can manage to hold my present situation long or not. I have kept it for about 13 months. When I first got it I only got $40.00 per mon. After 10 months they raised it to forty five and last month the raised it to forth 50 which is the highest I can get. My hours are long but I have no hard work. I think there is no better country than this for a man that would have a little capitel. Good land is worth from 40 to one hundred dollars per acre in this state but little west of this a man can get better land and purty convenient from 10 to 20 dollars per acre.[16]

The lure of cheap land in the American West compared favourably with Jeremiah O'Connor's miserable assessment of New York (see Chapter 2): 'Dear Brother you wanted to know if i am contented here after spending eight years here now. I ought to be although i have nothing by my time here only a living as i go along. For i need not tell you that a man never raises out of dally labour but a man is well paid for the time he works. But it is not steady and then he has to spend a good deal of it to get work for it is nothing but Bribery on every side here and if there is a study [steady] job offering there are thousands on top of it.'[17]

The intricate system of intelligence that connected wandering miners with busy expatriate networks was vividly illustrated when Louthman Patrick Kirk died in a street brawl during Michael Flanagan's residence in Charleston.[18] After hearing of the tragedy and the arrest of three Irish men on charges of manslaughter, Richard Flanagan offered condolences to his brother on the loss of his mate: 'It is sad and painful at all times to lose a friend, but when one whome we have loved is taken off by the hand of a murderer the blow is hard indeed. I quite agree with you in what you say of our own people. When good there are none better in the world. When bad none worse, if any indeed can equal them in wickedness.'[19] The blow for Patrick Kirk's family in Clogherhead was devastating and his mother appealed to Michael Flanagan for help in retrieving her son's estate. Bridget Kirk's heart-rending petition served as a powerful instrument of moral persuasion:

poor Patt was the quietest child I ever rared it is little I though the day he left Clougher that I would never see him again . . . when Patt father heard he heard it on Monday and he died in 10 days after he died on the 16 of febuary and he never wore in better health he was at mass the Sunday before he heard so you must think that was a trial to lose my husband and son in 3 months there is nothing breaking my heart but to think of him being without the Priest fare from home.[20]

Her explicit instructions to 'get the money' deposited by Patrick in the Bank of New South Wales and the admission that 'it was bad enough to lose him self and not all his Property' were unusual for contemporary Irish-Australian correspondence.[21] This directness suggests that the letters were an act of desperation by a vulnerable and dependent widow rather than a blatant expression of avarice.[22] The impact of her appeal was no doubt enhanced by the collaboration of Michael's 'Uncle Priest', who advised his nephews to 'do your best to have every thing right. Yet do it prudently without making an enemy for yourselves.'[23] The voices that speak in letters like these show that the moral and material obligations prescribed by Irish society 'did not lapse through separation'.[24] The renewal of contact with Old World networks in Westland and the Nelson South-West goldfields consoled migrants and influenced the timing and direction of their mobility.

II

The picture of the colonial mining population that emerges from the Flanagan correspondence suggests that very few succeeded in capturing the elusive pile. Patrick was cash-strapped at the very moment he was planning to purchase a ticket to San Francisco and marry Kate O'Brien, while Michael's estate of £417 3s 1d, which passed to his sister, Judith Garvey, after his death in 1904, was acquired in Tobertoby.[25] There are occasional references to luckier men who had made 'homeward-bounders'. Harry McGill, formerly a boatman at the Old Twelve-Mile, sold his farm at Totara Flat for £2000 with the intention of settling his family back in Ireland; Tom Clinton returned after clearing £800 in 'a mining speculation'.[26] But this was not an experience shared by the other diggers mentioned in the letters. The poorest, however, were those who stayed behind in once-thriving mining townships after the golden years. Writing to Michael in 1884, Philip McCarthy described the declining fortunes of their associates at Charleston: 'The last news I had from the place is that it is very poor & getting worse every day. Bat O Brien, Harry Lavery, Nicholas Sweeny are still on the Township flat getting the Binifit of the Wather! John Woodcock is still on Candlelight flat groundsluicing so is Bill Fox & Jack Gardner.' Brighton was equally miserable, with the local storekeeper, Tom Nevin, supplying only 20 or 30 miners. 'It's surprising how these places holds out and can support a population the length of time it has. No new field has opened since you left except a small flat about half way between Charleston and Addisons Flat which they called Croninville after the prospector Con Cronin.' Their friends with small businesses in prominent West Coast towns or in the North Island seem to have been much more successful: 'Hugh & Pat Brennan are at Reifton. Pat is doing very well as legal manager commission agent & for several of the Meefing companys in that locality. Frank McParland has a store & Bakery at Brunnerton 8 or 10 miles from Greymouth. He is doing a very good business is comfortable & happy with his wife & family a large one of Boy & Girls.' Like many of the old hands, William Bohan had gone to Wellington 'and [was] doing very well at his trade. He has added the wheelwright buisness to the Blacksmithing.'[27]

Although the Flanagans and their friends were not among those who made substantial fortunes on the West Coast goldfields, a small number of Irish men laid the foundations for the accumulation of considerable wealth. The Gilmer brothers, Hamilton, who died in 1919, leaving £300,000, and Samuel, who died in 1925, leaving £150,000, constructed a vast commercial empire that comprised a network of hotels, livery stables, mail services and mining operations stretching from Hokitika to Cobden, east as far as Reefton, and north to Charleston, Westport and Nelson.[28] These business ventures were family affairs that owed some of their success to the participation of various relatives from Mullaghanee, a role that continued after the two men moved to Wellington in the 1880s. The most impressive of their West Coast establishments was Gilmer's Hotel on Mawhera Quay in Greymouth, which featured more than 50 rooms, three large billiard tables, a night watchman and a hall with the capacity to hold 400 people.[29] Like Hamilton Gilmer, Martin Kennedy of Ballymackey, County Tipperary, gained his initial capital on the Otago goldfields after a brief stint in Victoria. He worked as a merchant at Queenstown in partnership with his brother, Cornelius, and relocated to Greymouth at the beginning of 1865. Kennedy was a prominent figure in the region for the next 24 years, with financial interests in coastal shipping, coalmining and general merchandise. By the time of his death in Wellington in 1916, he had amassed a fortune of £150,000, held directorships in several major companies, including

the Bank of New Zealand, and owned sheep runs in the Wairarapa.[30] The
£56,000 estate of Hugh Cassidy, who died in 1922, was worth much less
than Kennedy's, but it still placed him among the very rich in the province
of Canterbury. His migration followed the familiar route from Victoria
to Otago, where he packed goods to the diggings, and onwards with the
'noisy, dirty, drinking, smoking, cursing crowd' to Hokitika.[31] Cassidy's
success as a storekeeper and wagon-driver was such that he was able to
purchase the lucrative coach business known as Cobb & Co. in 1873,
before taking a farm at Springfield some years later. A towering monument
in the Hokitika cemetery, still visible from the beachfront, marks Cassidy's
grave and features an inscription consistent with the stipulation in his will
'to the effect that I arrived in Hokitika in December 1864 and is to have a
facsimile of a man on a saddle horse driving not less than three pack horses
along the beach' (Plate 12).

The careers of men such as the Gilmer brothers, Martin Kennedy and
Hugh Cassidy matched the paths travelled by the colonial wealthy in
Canterbury and Otago. As Jim McAloon has shown, the rich came from
humble origins, arrived early in New Zealand and 'benefited handsomely'
from the use of state power to secure land for colonisation through the
dispossession of Ngai Tahu.[32] At the same time, the labour of family
members was crucial in the creation of substantial wealth: indeed 'the
family was both the reason for accumulating a fortune and a major aid to
doing so'.[33] Not surprisingly, the Gilmers, Kennedy and Cassidy were all
married. Hamilton Gilmer even returned to Monaghan for this purpose,
marrying his cousin, Elizabeth, at Broomfield in 1871.[34] The assistance of
family networks, the timing of migration, access to capital and adherence
to such values as sobriety, thrift and deferred gratification were clearly
critical factors in building wealth.[35] But it is also significant that all four
men worked as miners for only very short periods. With a little capital, they
became carriers, merchants and hoteliers, services that carried fewer risks
than goldmining and quickly 'separated the digger from his profits'.[36]

The success of these men casts doubt on the view that the West Coast
Irish 'were less evident in business circles, except as small storekeepers
and publicans'.[37] It is further undermined when we examine the working
lives of other migrants who left large fortunes. Felix Campbell (d. 1922,
£300,000) of Maghery, County Armagh, for example, spent time in
Melbourne, Invercargill and Dunedin, before moving to the new settlement

at Greymouth, where he set up as a general carrier. By 1866, he had sufficient capital to establish himself as an independent wholesale merchant in the river-port town and his business interests gradually expanded to include mining and brewing, as well as the chair of directors at the Dispatch Foundry. Campbell neatly fitted the profile of the rich in colonial New Zealand, whose commitments were 'concentrated on business and local authority work to the exclusion of most other activities'.[38] He was an active member of the Greymouth Chamber of Commerce, served as the chairman of the Harbour Board and held public office as mayor in the mid-1890s. Most of Campbell's extensive philanthropic work seems to have been aimed at promoting or sustaining local economic growth, his largesse evident in financial assistance that kept the sawmilling industry afloat before the First World War and in private injections of capital to struggling firms and individuals.[39] In his will, however, he bequeathed everything to his three children, naming his son, Thomas Henry, and sons-in-law, Patrick McEvedy and Michael Dennehy, as trustees of his estate. They were instructed to pay Thomas an annual income of £2000 from Campbell's shares in the Dispatch Foundry and transmit the residuary interest in equal shares to his son and daughters, Catherine and Mary.[40]

The involvement of prosperous businessmen in local government suggests that Irish migrants had considerable influence within their own communities. Patrick Michael Griffen (d. 1913, £14,971), a tenant farmer's son from County Waterford, rose to prominence as a wholesale merchant in Greymouth, eventually forming a successful trading partnership with William Cameron Smith (d. 1895, £3082).[41] He served on the town's Borough Council, acted as a justice of the peace and achieved renown as a local 'booster'. His brother-in-law, Daniel Sheedy (d. 1909, £5000), the proprietor of the Brian Boru Hotel on Mawhera Quay, left an estate to his wife, Catherine, that included a large villa on Blake Street with servants' quarters built at the rear.[42] A man of extraordinary energy, he sat on the Greymouth Harbour Board, the Grey River Hospital Board and the Greymouth Borough Council for long periods, as well as continuing a long-standing connection with the Greymouth Jockey Club.[43] There are several similar examples. James Colvin, a Westport merchant with extensive goldmining experience, occupied positions on the Buller County Council, the Westport Harbour Board and the Nelson Education Board, before his election to the House of Representatives in 1899.[44] In Reefton, another veteran digger, Robert Patterson of Killyleagh, County Down (d. 1903,

Table 3.1 Number and value of men's estates on the West Coast, 1876–1915

	£0-1999	£2000-3999	£4000-5999	£6000-7999	£8000-9999	£10000+	TOTAL
Irish-born Estates							
N	341	18	9	2	2	6	378
%	23.0	33.3	42.8	20.0	50.0	30.0	23.8
Total Estates	1482	54	21	10	4	20	1591

Sources: West Coast testamentary registers, CH 383, ANZ–CH; Probate Files, CH 171, ANZ–CH; Registry of Births, Deaths and Marriages (Lower Hutt). Additional information on individuals was obtained from family histories, newspaper obituaries and cemetery transcripts held at the West Coast Historical Museum.

£4900), ran a store and sat on both the Inangahua County Council and the local school committee.[45] The wealthiest migrants were not the only influential people in the main towns and mining districts, as the careers of local notables like Denis Ryall (d. 1904, £162), James Francis Byrne (d. 1913, £100) and Peter Dungan (d. 1906, £193) make apparent.[46] Yet it is clear that 'local government represented the propertied', even though the rich did not form majorities on borough and county councils.[47] The key point here is that Irish men were prominent among those who amassed fortunes on the West Coast and heavily involved in boosting local development. It is also worth stressing that this success depended on a number of factors, including the role played by wives, children, friends and kinsfolk, and seems to have owed little to the support of ethnic networks.

These claims about the economic position of the West Coast Irish are supported by the evidence contained in local death duty registers, which give the value of every estate where probate was granted from 1876 to 1915. A glance at Table 3.1 shows that Irish-born males accounted for one-third of the estates worth more than £2000 (33.9 per cent), easily surpassing their share of the region's population. Most striking, however, is the fact that Irish men left six of the 20 probates involving sums over £10,000, the threshold for membership of the colonial wealthy. James William Fair (d. 1913, £20,882) was a prominent Westport draper, who bequeathed a family business at the corner of Palmerston and Brougham Street to his second wife, Teresa, and three of his sons.[48] By contrast, Thomas McKee (d. 1906, £12,000) and Myles McPadden (d. 1913, £10,485) represented family farming wealth in the South Island, a substantial group that held properties 'too small to create vast fortunes'.[49] The three remaining probates belonged to the Hokitika merchant Patrick Michael Griffen (d. 1913, £14,971), the returned migrant William Glenn (d. 1913, £36,000) and Hubert Dolphin (d. 1907, £14,446) of Loughrea, County Galway.[50] In terms of general prosperity, then, the death duty registers indicate, first, that Irish men did as well as other nationalities on the goldfields and often better, and, second, that the best prospects for advancement on the goldfields were to be found in mercantile activities, farming and small urban businesses such as storekeeping.

Irish-born men were found in various kinds of work, even though the dominance of the mining industry limited the range of employment opportunities.[51] From the figures in Table 3.2 we can see that a significant minority worked as professionals or businessmen, among whom publicans (55) like John Shannahan (d. 1905, £1500) and Richard Cox (d. 1901, £1043) featured prominently.[52] The Irish-born were well represented in the skilled trades, with bootmakers (22), carpenters (21) and blacksmiths (10) reaching double figures. A sizeable contingent ended their lives as general labourers (154) and farmers (109) constituted the third largest occupation. Predictably, Irish men were concentrated in mining (840), an activity that accounted for more than half (55.7 per cent) of the entire sample. We may surmise that, like the Gilmers, Martin Kennedy and Hugh Cassidy, many of those returned as unskilled workers, artisans, shopkeepers and farmers had also spent time as diggers. Despite their limitations, the registrar-general's records suggest that Irish-born men matched wider regional patterns of occupational attainment and did not fit the popular image of 'dispossessed proletarians'.

III

It is clear from the surviving inventories of deceased diggers that single men owned few material possessions other than what they carried on their backs. Aside from their tools and clothing, even the most successful died with little more than a handful of shares in a claim, a modest bank account and some petty cash. Whatever their means, diggers endured terrible discomfort in the damp West Coast bush. Persistent rain made prospecting a dreary undertaking as men laboured 'up to the hips in water, picking away at the slatey, gravely bed, moving large boulders, carrying the clayey-looking earth to the "tom" or "cradle" and working all day without seeing the gold', before returning to sodden camps at night.[53] The wretched living conditions and harsh climate contributed to occasional epidemics of

Table 3.2 Occupations of Irish-born males on the West Coast, 1876–1915

	Roman Catholic	Anglican	Presbyterian	Wesleyan	other
Accountant		1	1	1	
Baker	7		1		
Barman	1				
Blacksmith	6	3	1		
Boatman	1				1
Bookmaker			1		
Bookseller/stationer					1
Bootmaker	20	1	1		
Brewer	1				
Bricklayer			1		
Bushman	2	1	1		
Butcher	7	2			
Cab driver	1				
Carpenter	13	4	2	1	1
Carrier	3				
Carter	8	2	2		1
Cattle dealer	1				
Chainman	1				
Chemist	1	2			
Clerk	5	2			
Coach proprietor	1				
Coachman	1				
Commercial traveller		1			
Commission agent		1			1
Compositor		1			
Constable	3	3	1		1
Contractor	18	2			
Cook	4				
Cooper	1				
Cordialmaker	1				
Customs agent	1				
Draper	5	1	1		1
Dredge owner	1				
Drill instructor	1				
Engineer			1		
Engine driver	2		1		1
Expressman	1				
Farmer	84	12	9	1	3
Fisherman	2		1		
Gardener	5	2	1		
Gentleman	2	2	1	1	
Gourmet chef	1				
Government officer	3		1		
Groom	2				
Gun dealer		1			
Hawker		1			
Horse Trainer		1			
Hotelkeeper	41	11	1	1	1
Insp. Of police	1				
Insurance agent	1				
Journalist	2	2			
Labourer	120	10	16	2	6
Lay preacher				1	
Librarian		1			

	Roman Catholic	Anglican	Presbyterian	Wesleyan	other
Livery stable keeper	2				
Master mariner	1	1	2		
Mechanic	1				
Merchant	5	3	2	2	1
Milkman		1			
Miner	652	90	64	8	26
Mine manager	9	2			
Musician	1				
Newsagent			2		
Newspaper proprietor		1			
Overseer	4				
Painter	3	1			
Pensioner	9	2			
Platelayer	4	1			
Priest	2				
Professor of music					1
Quarryman	3				
Railway ganger		1			
Roadman	1				
Saddler	2				
Sailmaker	1				
Sailor	4	1	1		
Salesman	1				
Sawmiller	1	1			
Sawyer	1				
Sea captain	2				
Sexton		1			
Sgt. Police		2			
Signalman					
Soldier	1				
Stableman	1				
Steward	1	1			
Stockman/driver	1				1
Stonemason	2				
Storekeeper	26	6	2		
Surgeon	1	3			
Surveyor	2	2		1	
Tailor	1				
Teacher	1	1			
Tinsmith	1				
Toll gate keeper	1				
Tram proprietor	1				
Waggoner	1				
Warder	1				
Wheelwright	1				
	1134	189	117	19	47

Sources: Registry of Births, Deaths and Marriages (Lower Hutt).

typhoid and influenza, as well as the prevalence of debilitating respiratory illnesses. Yet the death toll from disease and ill health appears insignificant when compared with 'the appalling loss of life' from other causes.[54]

Gold seeking in such rugged terrain was always a dangerous enterprise, especially when it involved tunnelling and shafting. The fate of Michael Caddigan, smothered by tons of stone and debris when he struck 'a jamb-up' with his pick while clearing an old tunnel, typified the most common kind of mining accident.[55] Badly prepared drives collapsed, terrace faces disintegrated and unsuspecting diggers fell to their deaths down mineshafts. Even simple enterprises proved hazardous. John Nolan was about to begin sluicing his claim at Blue Spur when 'a thin layer of dirt' peeled away suddenly, 'knocking him backwards over the tail race' and pinning his right leg. His 'dividing mate', John Keane, watching in horror, could do nothing to save him. A post-mortem examination conducted at Blue Spur township established 'that he had sustained injuries in many places, on top of the head, temple, jaw, chest and other portions of the body, whilst the leg caught in the falling dirt was crushed from the knee down, the bone being in little splinters'.[56]

The most common cause of death from 'misadventure', however, was drowning. West Coast river crossings were notoriously risky and swept many men to watery graves. Robert Moorhead of Smithborough, County Monaghan, lost his life on the Ahaura; John Kane, prospecting at Rutherglen, drowned 'in the Deep Creek between the Lagoon Township and Diamond Gully'; Michael Clune died at the mouth of the Taramakau, his body recovered from the sea breakers the next day.[57] There were occasional cases of suicide. Patrick Martin, a native of Carleston, County Meath, jumped from the SS *Star of the Evening* as it lay in the roadstead outside the Hokitika River, leaving his worldly possessions on deck. Murder and manslaughter claimed few lives.[58] Limerick-born Jeremiah McGrath, who worked with the Hennessy Party at Welshman's, near Brighton, was one of the exceptions, 'killed by a stroke of a glass decanter at the House of a woman known as Mary Anderson'.[59]

Although nomadic diggers faced hardship and danger, their daily existence was interesting and exciting. The sudden surge of adrenalin as men left to inspect new fields, the enduring appeal of independence and ' the satisfaction of seeing race and wheel, pump and sluice – all fashioned by "the party" – in full work' were some of the most attractive aspects of goldfields life during the 1860s.[60] Above all, diggers seem to have enjoyed the companionship of kinsfolk and old friends, an *espirit de corps* that is plainly evident in the Flanagan correspondence. Their reliance on Old World social connections and notions of 'mateship' are understandable given that mining was a collective endeavour. Men formed small co-operative partnerships of two to six individuals, sometimes amalgamating into larger coalitions or companies to accomplish tasks that required additional capital, technology and labour. As well as retaining their identities for considerable periods, goldmining 'parties' followed the custom of 'dividing mates', whereby any member making a rich strike after they disbanded was obliged to notify the others and re-form the group to work the claim.[61]

The probate file of Croninville miner Patrick Donovan, whose will could not be found after his death in 1891, gives a rare insight into the nature of these arrangements. In a sworn affidavit, his dividing mate, Dennis Collins, claimed he was 'born next door' to the deceased in the townland of Burawn, County Cork, and had 'known him since my early childhood'. The two men never separated during their time in the colonies and used 'a common purse'. Even after Dennis married, Patrick made frequent visits to Charleston and always stayed in the Collins household (Plate 13). On one occasion, he became violently ill and executed a will that was witnessed by Westport's parish priest, Father Thomas Walshe, Charleston journalist Patrick Kittson and Cork-born labourer William Mullins. Dennis's wife, Alice, who nursed Patrick Donovan during his convalescence, carefully related the contents of her former patient's testament. He bequeathed all his mining property at Croninville to her son, James, and devised the residuary interest of the estate upon Dennis Collins. Patrick willed £10 to Reverend Father Walshe 'for the celebration of Masses for the repose of his soul' and asked Alice Collins 'to see that his wishes were carried out'.[62]

How did miners themselves view their chosen vocation? We have seen that Patrick Flanagan was among those who eagerly embraced this distinctive lifestyle and its frenetic pace. David McCullough of County Down, who arrived in the colony much later than Flanagan, seems to have relished his time fossicking at Waimangaroa, Denniston, Charleston and Addison's Flat. He came from a prosperous farming background in Ballycreely, where his father, Samuel, occupied 45 acres of land with an annual valuation of £52, the sixth highest in the townland.[63] Accompanied by one of his friends, Alexander Young, McCullough travelled first class to Dunedin aboard the *Andrew Reid*, arriving on 19 May 1875 'after a very tedeous and long voyage of 123 days from London'.[64] We know very little about his experiences over the next decade, but it is clear that he worked initially at the Albion Brewing & Malting Company for £2.10s per week and boarded privately.[65] By the 1890s he had moved to the Buller region and entered the goldmining industry. In a letter to his parents from Cascade Creek in 1898, McCullough described the nature of his enterprise: 'We are opening up a claim. There are Four of us. We have been over Two years at it now. It will take another six months yet and we may not bottom. The ground is deep and heavy. It is river workings. We hold Four acres. We are going to put on pumping gear. It is rather expensive but we intend to see it out. It is all pay out just now and nothing coming in.'[66] Later in the year the men left their Cascade claim to prospect deep inside 'the Mackley country':

We took a good supply of rations with us. We carried it in stages. There was not a soul there but ourselves. There is neither roads nor horse tracks there. We got alluvial Gold would pay about Four pounds per week but that is not good enough in that country. Too much lost time and expense carrying tucker. You have to carry all you eat on our backs and this is a bit hard work. There are plenty of birds pigeons, Kaka and ducks and also the weka or Wood-hen. It cannot fly. The walk or run along the ground. The dogs can easily catch them. Time goes very quick when you are out prospecting shifting camp so often and carrying Tucker. I have had about Eight months of it this time but at any rate we are back again not a bit better off and very little the worse. There is any amount of men in Newzealand and Australia doing the same. They will go into any Country or through any hardship after Gold.[67]

Based at Waimangaroa, several miles north of Westport, where he had bought into another claim, McCullough contemplated returning to Ireland in response to a plea from his parents who were in poor health. 'It would be very awkward at the present time to get away,' he told them, 'but I will try and be home in the inside of Twelve months.'[68] It was a journey he never made. Samuel McCullough died two months after the letter was written and stated in his will that the family farm was to pass to his wife for life and then to David, provided that he came home within two years of her death. An inheritance in County Down, however, was insufficient to lure 'Old Davey' from Waimangaroa, where he remained until his own death in 1934.[69]

John O'Regan, a miner from County Cork with experience in the United States, Australia and New Zealand, was the only migrant correspondent to attempt a retrospective assessment of his career. Writing to his grand-niece from Barrytown in 1899, he recalled that 'this day 41 year ago, I was within sight of the Australian coast, and only three months before that time I had bade adieu to all I held dear in the world. Then I was young and full of hope and gave myself two years till I would return again but the unexpected always takes place in this life for an ardent hope is rarely fulfilled and my return now is doubtful as that of the Bark of the Styx whose exile was eternal.' Yet, he confessed, 'my hope never dies, and though old in years my heart is quite young'. O'Regan's eloquent summation of his life on the diggings was tinged with sadness and regret:

> You will naturally ask yourself how I fare in this land of gold after my 41 years of work. Well, I got a fair share, that is enough to defray expenses. If I went into a big spec, which I often did, and this failed, it would take a long time to pay back debts. To give you an idea, the last claim I was in before coming to this coast paid the man that worked it $75,000. I sold out for 200 pounds long before the water was on the claim, and being in life's prime I thought I would be able to drop into something good. That was my hope. My father, brother, and sisters being alive, I felt confident that I would see them again but it was not to be. I am alone in the world now. Drunken mates did me no good, but you will ask why not shake them off? This is not easily done, unless you sell out with what result you can judge. I hate drunkards, and the longer I live this aversion will live too. What a curse grog is to a weak mind. What misery to every one about them. I am now making a living but I intend taking some chances in Sweeps and who knows I may be lucky.[70]

We will never know how many of the men who remained on the West Coast shared these sentiments in old age. For most, the quest for the elusive pile 'had become the reality' and 'home' was now a small mining locality like Charleston, Waimangaroa or Barrytown.[71]

IV

As we have already seen, more than half of all migrant Irish women on the West Coast had married before their arrival and most single females chose to marry and establish families soon afterwards. The main problem we face in trying to interpret their motivations, ambitions and strategies is the fragmented nature of the historical sources. Few personal letters have been discovered and their exploits were not as well documented as those of 'wayward women' like Bessie O'Neil, who feature regularly in court records and newspaper reports. Case studies taken from the West Coast death registers suggest that most had been employed as domestic servants in colonial homes before they married in the Australian colonies and New Zealand. But single female domestics such as Honora White, Annie Dougan, Mirah Rooney and Margaret McKeogh were not simply 'prospective wives'.[72] These women formed part of a mobile occupational group that made a substantial economic contribution to colonial societies during the nineteenth and early twentieth centuries. Once married, they continued to play a valuable economic role as full-time workers in the unwaged household sector, taking care of their families, preparing food, doing the laundry, managing resources and mediating between menfolk and children.[73]

Philip Ross May has plausibly argued that the same spirit of independence underpinning the attitudes of male diggers also characterised the outlook of women migrants. In an 'upside-down society' like this, 'where everyone was somebody, servant-girls got the same wages as government clerks, and barmaids were even better off'. The *Hokitika Evening Star*, in a revealing commentary, claimed that 'the colonial virtues flourished too mightily on the diggings':

Were Thackeray living, and on the West Coast, he would certainly pronounce us to be a community of snobs . . . a slipshod, slatternly, stockingless, insolent servant woman demands and obtains from two to three pounds a week as wages besides her keep, while a thoroughly competent lady who opens a school for the education of girls, cannot get a sufficient number of pupils at four shillings a week to support her. Madame, the governess, the educated lady . . . cannot afford a mutton chop to her dinner. Mary, the maid of all work at an hotel has just thrown a dishful to the pigs, and when reprimanded for such waste, gave her mistress twenty-four hours notice to leave.[74]

There was nothing unusual about these complaints in the wider Australasian colonial context. On both sides of the Tasman there were few significant employment openings for single females outside paid domestic work and servants were always in short supply.[75] Some contemporaries lamented the quality of state-assisted domestics and the frequency with which they changed engagements in search of higher pay.[76] Yet the attractions of domestic service for migrant women are easy to understand. Workers received full board and lodging, as well as wages, and were sometimes given clothing and

Table 3.3 Women's occupations at marriage on the West Coast, 1881–1889

	Ireland	England	Scotland	Australian Colonies	NZ	Other	Total
Barmaid	7	–	–	5	–	–	12
Cook	2	–	–	–	–	–	2
Dairywoman	–	–	–	–	1	–	1
Domestic	78 (1)	34 (9)	22 (4)	53 (4)	86 (1)	14 (2)	287 (21)
Dressmaker	6	20 (5)	3	14	12 (1)	1	56 (6)
Farmer	1 (1)	–	–	–	–		1 (1)
Hotelkeeper	6 (5)	2 (2)	–	–	1 (1)		9 (8)
Housekeeper	2 (1)	7 (4)	4 (2)	2 (2)	2		17 (9)
Laundress	–	3 (3)	–	–	–		3 (3)
Milliner	3	3 (2)	–	1	2		9 (2)
Matron	–	1 (1)	–				1 (1)
Nurse	–	2 (2)	1				3 (2)
Pianist	–	1	–				1
Restauranteur	–	1 (1)	–				1 (1)
Storekeeper	1 (1)	1 (1)	–				2 (2)
Teacher	3	5 (1)	3	13	7	1	32 (1)
Waitress	1	1	–	1	1		4
Total	110 (9)	81 (31)	33 (6)	89 (6)	112 (3)	16 (2)	441 (57)

Notes

1. Sources: West Coast testamentary registers, CH 383, ANZ–CH; Probate Files, CH 171, ANZ–CH; Registry of Births, Deaths and Marriages (Lower Hutt). Additional information on individuals was obtained from family histories, newspaper obituaries and cemetery transcripts held at the West Coast Historical Museum.

2. The figures in brackets show the number of widows within the totals. Thus five of the six Irish hotelkeepers in the sample had been married previously. The occupational titles given in the listings lack precision and completeness, but they do match the patterns suggested by newspaper obituaries and family histories

furniture by their employers. Although they were under close supervision in local households or pubs, their position was relatively secure compared with the uncertainties of the male labour market. We do not know how Irish women viewed their experience of service on the West Coast or whether their working relationships involved an element of 'social oppression'.[77] Some barmaids and 'dancing girls' were tied into unyielding contracts by 'greedy employers and unscrupulous agents'.[78] What does seem clear, however, is that the insatiable demand for domestic servants ensured dissatisfied workers such as Catherine Flaherty of County Mayo, denied pay by an Orwell Creek publican, could usually change jobs with little difficulty.[79]

Irish women never dominated paid household labour like their sisters in parts of the United States and Britain, even though a majority of those working for wages did so in domestic capacities (see Table 3.3).[80] West Coast marriage records from the 1880s show that 78 of the 287 brides who listed domestic service as their occupation were Irish-born (27.2 per cent). English-born women, on the other hand, came from a wider range of occupational backgrounds than other nationalities and were less likely to be found in domestic positions. These differences are partly explained by the unusually high number of widows within the group (38.3 per cent): laundering and needlework, for example, could be done at home on a piecemeal basis, an important consideration when women were caring for small children. The extant listings also suggest that a disproportionate number of teachers and barmaids came from across the Tasman, English migrants were overrepresented in dressmaking and Irish widows dominated the hotel trade. But the significance of these trends is impossible to assess given the defective nature of the sources. We are far better placed in relation to the general picture, which reveals that the occupational profile of Irish-born brides largely conformed to wider regional patterns, at least during the 1880s.

How did women's working lives change after they were married? The chronic instability of everyday life in the region's goldfields communities made the paid and unpaid activities of women essential. Whether they lived in isolated mining camps or larger urban centres, the daily realities of female migrants were shaped by housework and the family-centred concerns of child-bearing and child-raising. Like Johanna Weir at Red Jacks, married women kept cows and poultry, cultivated vegetable gardens, made their own butter and jam, cared for the sick or those in trouble, nurtured children and carried out routine household tasks such as cleaning 'by strenuous scrubbing with wood ash on a damp brush'.[81] These activities must have been especially onerous in the wretched living conditions of the mining townships. Bad weather damaged vegetables or saturated crude homes, and sudden blizzards or floods drowned fowls, ruined supplies and temporarily severed communications with other places. The harsh climate, the heavy burden of domestic labour and the constant battle with rats, mosquitoes and bush flies extracted an enormous physical toll on migrant women. And this workload increased dramatically when men were incapacitated or injured, leaving wives responsible for the economic welfare of their families. Such was the case for Ellen Cronin, who milked cows, made butter and worked a small Westland farm after her husband, John, became an invalid. She struggled to bring in an income of £1 per week on land that was slowly being eaten away by the Kokatahi River, a sum that provided their only support during the 10 years leading up to John's death in 1914.[82]

The high mortality rate among adult males on the goldfields ensured that many women spent a portion of their lives as widows, often scratching out marginal existences in remote locations. Catherine Wallace was left with 13 children, including a six-week-old infant, when her husband died in 1896. Coastal steamers arrived at Okarito infrequently with supplies of flour, tea, oatmeal, sugar, salt and syrup, which had to be purchased and then carried around three dangerous bluffs and across two rivers to the family homestead at Waiho Beach. Catherine grew potatoes and onions in a vegetable garden fertilised with seaweed, made bread and used 'an old muzzle-loader gun to good effect when the pigeon stew pot needed replenishing'. The family learned to live from the bush and seashore, catching fish and eels, and dining on edible berries like kiekie, fuschia, miro and supplejack. One of her sons, Mark Wallace, recalled that his mother was '[o]ur house-keeper, our cook, our bread-maker, our seamstress, our nurse, our doctor, our spiritual guide, counsellor and friend . . .When the digestive processes became over-active, there was a flax-root brew to halt the trouble. When nature went into reverse, there was a brew from koromiko leaves. Mum's other names were initiative and resourcefulness.'[83]

Some grief-stricken widows fared very badly. Lucy Searight of Nenagh, County Tipperary (d. 1894, £502), lost her husband, Andrew, in an accident at Reefton's Globe Mine in 1889, when a log hurtled down a steep 'sideling' and struck him on the head with such force that it 'completely smashed the larger portion of the skull and dislodged the brain causing instantaneous death'.[84] She was granted letters of administration to Andrew's estate, securing a bond with the assistance of local businessmen David Harold and Timothy O'Neill. Yet Lucy did not exercise this right and the task of administering the couple's property eventually fell to Joseph Searight, the eldest of their five children.[85] Martha Butler from King's County, on the other hand, witnessed the tragic demise of her husband, Michael, and seven-year-old daughter, who were swept away while crossing the Arnold River when he pulled the reins so tightly that he drowned his horse. Michael's remains were never found, but his daughter's bloated body was washed up on Cobden Beach several days later. Martha managed to identify the child from her prominent teeth and noticed that all her hair had been eaten away by sea lice. On 11 December 1871, three years after the accident, Martha married James Byrne at Totara Flat, a relationship that produced one daughter, Sarah, who died in infancy, and ended acrimoniously when the couple parted.[86]

The close ties that developed between local residents in goldfields settlements like Maori Creek, Addison's and Red Jacks were an important source of support for women in hard times and transcended ethnic barriers. Mary Nolan of Queen's County, for instance, reared 10 children on a property situated alongside the farming families of various nationalities in the South Westland wilderness clearing of Okuru.[87] Yet the limits of frontier pluralism were also clear. Sarah Gillin discovered its outer edges when she nursed a 'Robber Chinaman' ill with pneumonia at Notown Creek and earned the opprobrium of locals alarmed at the actions of a 'Chow lover'.[88] Drunken prostitutes like Barbara Weldon, 'five feet and one inch tall, of stout build and sickly appearance, blind in one eye, and slightly bald on the back of her head', were barely tolerated beyond their dwindling clientele.[89] 'Respectable' widows, however, seem to have received generous community assistance, at least in the smaller towns and mining camps. When several of Catherine Wallace's children became chronically ill with typhoid and required expensive hospital treatment, Kokatahi residents rallied together to pay her debts, even though she had only recently begun leasing a dairy farm in the district.[90] Clare-born Ann O'Donnell (*née* McNamara), who became the well-known proprietor of Waiuta's Empire Hotel, was left to support six children 'in very destitute circumstances' after her husband, Edward, died suddenly at their Kaniere home in 1894. The *West Coast Times* reported that on hearing the news

Mrs Learmont at once sent down to the Woman's Benevolent Society, and a large parcel of clothing etc. was got ready and taken up Saturday afternoon. Their immediate necessities in the way of food and clothing are being attended to, and it is understood that residents on the locality are taking steps to get Mrs. O'Donnell a better house, her present one being scarcely tenantable. It is hoped that a special effort will be made to assist them as they are a very deserving family. Perhaps the Hokitika Garrick Club or the Kaniere Dramatic Society will set in the suggestion.[91]

The concert performances, dances and plays organised by local people raised a substantial amount and helped Ann to set up her first business, a grocery store, at Woodstock.[92] A decade later, in 1905, Hokitika mayor and bank manager Joseph Mandl persuaded her to take over as licensee of the Rose and Thistle Hotel at Blackwater, an astute and timely decision given the development of the Birthday Reef at Waiuta the following year.[93] The success of this venture and the ones that followed owed much to the capital accumulated earlier at Woodstock and the involvement of several of her children in the family business, as well as Ann's own fierce determination and shrewd financial management.

The working lives of Irish-born women who married differed little from those of other nationalities on the West Coast. Most were involved to varying degrees in housework and subsistence-related activities, including the collection of food from the bush, the henhouse and the vegetable garden. Many gave birth for the first time in rough mining townships and shared Isabella Graham's experience of nursing young children afflicted with nasty maladies like diphtheria, watching and praying as they lingered for days between life and death.[94] Less serious afflictions required easier solutions, as Ellen Piezzi noted in a letter to her brother-in-law, 'Victer', in 1881: 'I hope Lucy is getting strong. Give her some worms powders. The worms is at her. Severini past 4 large ones about 10 inses long. I gave him powders. He is all rite again.'[95] Travelling overland to seek medical attention or moving from one place to another was a daunting prospect, especially when children accompanied their parents. Ferry services eased the dangers of crossing the big rivers, but innumerable creeks and streams still had to be forded. The obstacles that confronted diggers' wives were well illustrated by Mary Magee's journey from Greymouth to the Ahaura with her three children in 1869:

> The first day took us to Langdon's Ferry, opposite the Arnold River junction – the second day to Camptown, near the mouth of Redjack's Creek. Next day we went to Nelson Creek on pack horses – I, a six months old baby on the knee of my mother who rode a horse side-saddle. My two sisters were put in gin cases and slung one on each side of a pack horse. The creek was forded about 10 times and in other places the mud was up to the horses girths.[96]

Despite the difficulties of travel and communication, women in goldfields settlements were heavily involved in public work. Some of these activities, like the delivery of cooked food to families in distress, remain hidden from the historian's gaze. But the role played by women in community building projects such as halls, churches, schools and charities is much more obvious in newspaper accounts and institutional records. Ann O'Donnell was among the few to receive public recognition for this kind of voluntary service when she became the first woman to be elected a Life Honorary Member of the Hibernian Australasian Catholic Benefit Society in 1927.

The survival of mining families on the goldfields depended on strong women and the close co-operation of husbands and wives. As a result, female migrants seem to have enjoyed far greater power within marital relationships than in Ireland: for example, they played a major part in the disposition of property in wills. This acknowledgment of Irish women's contribution to their husband's prosperity is evident in the bequests made to widows like Bridget Scanlon of Westport, who received the residuary interest in the estate of her husband, Michael, along with all his coal and goldmining shares and a hotel in Palmerston Street.[97] For the most part, West Coast husbands entrusted their wives with the role of administering their estates and granted them absolute powers of disposal over property.[98] Ellen McInroe, Ann Falvey and Honora Corbett were among those left with full management rights by their spouses, while Catherine Rogers and Ellen Healey shared this responsibility with others; even wives excluded from the roles of trustee or executor were likely to receive absolute shares in residuary property.[99] For these women, emigration was a source of empowerment rather than 'a passive experience to be born stoically'.[100]

Irish-born migrants easily matched other groups in terms of wealth holding. Altogether, they accounted for 105 of the 400 estates handed down by women between the years 1876 and 1915 (26.3 per cent), including six of the 18 inventories valued at more than £2000 (33.3 per cent). The wealthiest, Bridget Scanlon, the Westport publican, was worth £8741 at her death in 1914 (Plate 14).[101] Reefton storekeeper Ellen Harold (d. 1914, £5563) passed on the fourth largest fortune, while Mary Hannan (d. 1914, £2324), Sarah Taylor (d. 1912, £2270) and Mary Enright (d. 1915, £2225) held modest amounts of property.[102] Of the six, only Ellen Kennedy (d. 1902, £2125) of Addison's Flat had not been widowed. She scattered bequests widely among her 11 children and named two married daughters, Mary Peters and Johanna Donohue, as trustees of her estate.[103] Like women of other nationalities, all sought to preserve and transmit property to the next generation, sometimes equally among heirs, but often to give particular children a good start in life. The size of many estates was simply too small to make partible division the best option.

V

What impact did these work patterns have on the formation of Irish ethnic identities in the region? As we have seen, the Irish-born were a numerically strong charter group whose members participated actively in the colonisation process and in building local community life. Most had been 'thoroughly colonialised' by the time they arrived on the diggings and many brought with them an extensive array of skills and resources acquired in Victoria and Otago.[104] The surviving evidence shows that Irish men and women were scattered throughout the region's social structure. Some became very prominent among the wealthy, in local government and within the ranks of local boosters. Others made more modest gains, struggled along in poverty or moved away quickly in search of the elusive pile. Regardless of their motivations, occupations and levels of material prosperity, all migrants encountered an environment where the hardships of daily life were ameliorated by close co-operation between local people, a public spirit that transcended ethnic, religious and linguistic boundaries. The small scale of West Coast communities, the relative economic homogeneity of the region's inhabitants and the absence of entrenched anti-Irish élites militated against the rise of sectarian animosities and the development of a strong ethnic consciousness.[105] These conditions were vastly different from those confronting the Irish in parts of the United States, Canada and Britain, where newcomers provided 'a cheap, expendable labour force for the construction of an emerging industrial and urban infrastructure'.[106] The findings presented here remind us that structural factors played a key role in shaping Irish ethnicity abroad and call into question the idea of a single Irish labour diaspora.

4   Land, Love or Lucre: Irish Migrant Marriages on the West Coast

Matrimony, says Nancy Cott in her panoramic study of the public character of marriage in the United States, is like the sphinx, 'a conspicuous and recognisable monument on the landscape, full of secrets'.[1] This metaphor reverberates with considerable force in Irish history from the time of the eighteenth-century penal code, when the institution's forms and practices were regulated by civil legislation that inhibited denominational intermarriage.[2] The public face of marriage was also shaped decisively by the religious decrees and pastoral denunciations of the Catholic church; hardened clerical attitudes to mixed unions were evident at the synod of Thurles in 1850 and expressed unequivocally in the Irish clergy's strict enforcement of the 1908 papal decree *Ne Temere*. Alongside these canonical laws, Catholic authorities in post-Famine Ireland promoted a particular version of domesticity in which the Virgin Mary assumed a central position and notions of 'proper' womanhood emphasised qualities associated with her life, such as self-sacrifice, purity, married motherhood and hidden sexuality.[3] The iconic status of the conjugal farming family as the foundation stone of society was deeply embedded in the creation of the Irish Free State and enshrined in the constitution of 1937.[4] All the various legal enactments and religious codes that prescribed matrimonial rules in Ireland from the 1700s had profound consequences for ordinary individuals. As in the United States, lawmakers 'set the terms of marriage', creating duties and entitlements, delineating the public roles of husbands and wives and entrenching a Christian model of lifelong, faithful monogamy.[5] There was a major difference, however: the legal apparatus surrounding matrimony in Ireland aligned it closely with the maintenance of denomination-based boundaries rather than a commitment to exclusive intra-racial unions.[6]

The prominent position of marriage in the public order of both the United States and Ireland reminds us that the institution has been much more than 'a matter of private decision-making and domestic arrangements'.[7] In New Zealand, Irish migrants encountered a common law jurisdiction in which marital legislation was based on certain political assumptions about the primacy of lifelong monogamy. Yet, as Nancy Cott has shown, we must also consider that the institution of marriage was shaped by an immediate circle of kinsfolk, friends and neighbours, exercising 'the approval or disapproval a couple feels most intensely'.[8] These less formal aspects of matrimony are crucial in terms of ethnicity, given that they represent a vital means for maintaining and developing group distinctiveness.[9] To explore this possibility on New Zealand's West Coast requires a fine-grained analysis of Irish marital patterns over time. It also demands examination of what marriage, home and family meant for migrant men and women, and the role that Irish culture played in shaping their demographic behaviour.[10] Did newcomers marry later and less frequently than other migrant groups, as they had back home in Ireland? What do these patterns tell us about the motives and aspirations of migrants as they sought to build lives of their own? How many entered 'mixed marriages'? Was emigration and the formation of new households an emancipating experience for Irish women or were they forced to bear the pain of displacement, the weight of traditional family obligations and the claims of new patriarchal structures?

This chapter addresses these critical questions by examining several pieces of surviving evidence that illuminate the marriage patterns of Irish migrants on the West Coast. The first section uses historical data drawn from death certificates and marriage registers to ascertain whether these newcomers married more frequently and at lower ages than their counterparts who remained in Ireland. This analysis suggests that marriage was central to the lives of Irish women in the region, whose marital patterns more closely resembled those of migrants from other parts of Britain than those of their colonial-born daughters or those who stayed in rural Ireland. These findings challenge the assumption that the demographic behaviour of female migrants reflected the peculiarities of Irish culture, and match recent work from the United States, which identifies significant differences between the marriage patterns of Irish men and women.[11] The section that follows seeks to determine the extent of endogamy among the Irish-born and their sons and daughters on the West Coast. Although the available evidence is scattered and fragmented, it suggests that considerably fewer Catholics married outside their faith than most other groups. This broad

Plate 1
View of ships at the Hokitika wharves. *(Alexander Turnbull Library, Wellington, ref. F-27767-1/4)*

Plate 2
Hokitika wharves. *(Alexander Turnbull Library, Wellington, ref. F-127243-1/2)*

Plate 3 (above)
View of the Southern Alps, with Hokitika in the foreground. *(Alexander Turnbull Library, Wellington, ref. F-22856-1/2)*

Plate 4 (below)
View of Charleston from Nile Hill in 1872. *(Alexander Turnbull Library, Wellington, ref. F-25246-1/2)*

Plate 5 (opposite)
View over the gold mining town of Dillmanstown. The business of Patrick McGrath, general storekeeper, is centre right. *(Alexander Turnbull Library, Wellington, ref. F-44217-1/2)*

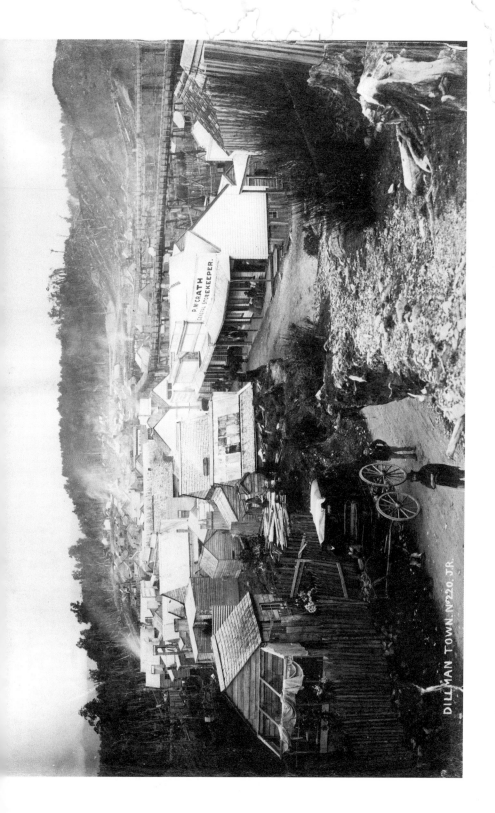

P.McGRATH
GENERAL STOREKEEPER.

DILLMAN TOWN. Nº220. J.R.

Plate 6
Goldsborough (formerly Waimea) township in the late 1860s. *(West Coast Historical Museum, ref. 1128).*

Plate 7
Clare-born Dan Moloney and his party at Dirty Mary's Creek. *(West Coast Historical Museum, ref. 989)*

Plate 8

The Stafford cemetery. *(Photograph by Lyndon Fraser)* The men and women who first came to the West Coast did not build to last and left only blackened headstones in deserted cemeteries to mark their presence.

Plate 9

Gravestones in the Ross cemetery. *(Photograph by Lyndon Fraser)*

Plate 10 (above)
Susan Hogan (née O'Toole) of
Maori Gully with her granddaughter
Molly McCormick. *(Courtesy of Ted
Matthews)*

Plate 11 (right)
Michael Flanagan returned to
Termonfeckin, County Louth, in
response to a desperate plea from his
ailing father in 1890. 'Instead . . . of the
lad of seventeen years you last saw,' he
warned him gloomily, 'you will meet
a grey old man of fifty.' *(Courtesy of
Donald Murphy)*

Plate 12
Hugh Cassidy's (d. 1922, £56,000) grave in the Hokitika cemetery has an inscription consistent with the stipulation in his will 'to the effect that I arrived in Hokitika in December 1864 and is to have a facsimile of a man on a saddle horse driving not less than three pack horses along the beach'. *(Photograph by Lyndon Fraser)*

Plate 13
Dennis Collins of Burawn, County Cork, ran the City Hotel in Charleston with his wife, Alice. *(Alexander Turnbull Library, Wellington, ref. F-3046-1/2).*

Plate 14
The grave of Michael and Bridget Scanlon, Westport cemetery. *(photograph by Lyndon Fraser)*

Plate 15
Patrick Gillin and Sarah Devery were married at Hokitika in 1868. *(Courtesy of Ted Matthews)* Before the wedding, Sarah had to be content with fleeting glimpses of her future husband through the keyhole in a bedroom door of the family's Revell Street hotel.

Plate 16
Bridget Pfahlert (née Quinn) of County Clare married her German-born husband, Ernst, at All Saints Church, Hokitika, in 1868. By the 1880s it was rare for Irish Catholic women to marry in Protestant churches. *(West Coast Historical Museum, ref. 5918)*

Plate 17
Ellen Piezzi (1849–1922) of County Kilkenny. *(Courtesy of Teresa O'Connor)*

Plate 18 (left)
This photograph shows Ellen Maher (formerly Piezzi) in the doorway of the Helvetia Hotel at Goldsborough c. 1895. The three children from Ellen's 1883 marriage to Dennis Maher are standing beside her: (L to R) Ellen, John and Veronica. *(West Coast Historical Museum, ref. 1147)*

Plate 19 (right)
Belfast-born Patrick Gillin and his dog Tweed. *(Courtesy of Ted Matthews)*

Plate 20 (below)
St Michael's Catholic Church, Goldsborough, pictured in the late 1860s, stands on the edge of the township, close to the bush and slopes beyond. *(West Coast Historical Museum, ref. 1139)*

PRESBYTERIAN CHURCH ROSS B.T. 123

Plate 21 (opposite top)
St Patrick's Catholic Church, Addison's
Flat, c. 1900. *(Alexander Turnbull Library,
Wellington, ref. 1/2-084284-F)*

Plate 22 (opposite bottom)
St John's Presbyterian Church, Ross.
(West Coast Historical Museum, ref. 930)

Plate 23 (above)
St Mary's Catholic Church and
Presbytery, Rimu, c. 1905. *(West Coast
Historical Museum, ref. 9296)*

Plate 24 (right)
Jane Ryall of Barrytown walked the
beach each night saying the rosary
'because she believed the breeze blew
straight from Ireland'. She is pictured
here with her husband, Denis, and their
children. *(West Coast Historical Museum,
ref. 997)*

Plate 25
Patrick Lysaght's famous lithograph of the commemorative procession at Hokitika on
8 March 1868. *(Alexander Turnbull Library, Wellington, ref. NON-ATL-0077)*

Plate 26
John Dillon at Kumara, 1889. *(Alexander Turnbull Library, Wellington, ref. F-65471-1/2)*

Plate 27
The grave of Laurence Kirwan, Hokitika cemetery. *(Photograph by Lyndon Fraser)*

Plate 28
Our Lady of the Way, Charleston Roman Catholic cemetery. *(Photograph by Lyndon Fraser)*

picture masks various complexities caused by the impact of such factors as region of origin, socio-economic background, generation and kinship on the selection of marriage partners. Nonetheless, the available data seems to show that, for both sexes, the boundaries of intimacy were framed as much by religious sentiment as by ethnic solidarity.

I

In the aftermath of the Great Famine, rural Ireland experienced a dramatic population decline that American historian Timothy Guinnane has convincingly linked to high rates of emigration, high levels of marital fertility, relatively late ages at first marriage and a large proportion of adults who never married.[12] It seems likely that one of these elements – the increasing rarity of marriage – has been the main reason for interpretations of Irish population history that stress its unique and even pathological character.[13] By 1911 roughly a quarter of all men and women between the ages of 45 and 54 were unmarried, a level of celibacy that greatly exceeded the corresponding rates in England,[14] but still conformed to what John Hajnal termed the Western European marriage pattern.[15] Although there were important variations over time and from region to region, populations matching this model displayed two main characteristics: the postponement of marriage until individuals had sufficient resources to sustain households of their own and the significant incidence of non-marriage, ranging from 10 to as high as 20 per cent in other cases, like seventeenth-century England.[16] Given that each element of Ireland's post-Famine demographic system can be identified elsewhere in Europe, adequate explanations for these patterns must move beyond simple assertions about peculiarly Irish cultural traits.

One striking aspect of the spectacular demographic shift that preceded the Famine and accelerated thereafter was the basic redefinition of Irish family structure. According to the standard picture, before the cataclysmic events of 1845–50 middling and strong farmers had maintained a hold on the land they occupied through a system of arranged marriage, whereby property was transferred intact to a single male heir (impartible inheritance) and his bride furnished a dowry appropriate to the status of her husband. Cash dowries, in these transactions, may be viewed as fines 'distinct from, say, the sale of a heifer, since the bride had to pay for her grazing rights'.[17] The match was a carefully negotiated bargain between two family units, which resulted in the fundamental redistribution of property and social roles. Its essential features were picturesquely delineated in the 1930s by one of Conrad Arensberg and Solon Kimball's Clare informants during fieldwork for their classic rural ethnography, *Family and Community in Ireland*:

> If I wanted to give my farm over to my son and I would be worth, say, two hundred pounds, I would know a fellow up the hill, for instance, that would be worth three hundred pounds. I would send up a neighbour fellow to him and ask him if he would like to join my family in marriage. If the fellow would send back word he would and the girl would say she was willing (and the usual courtesies were exchanged), then on a day they agreed on I and the fellow would meet in Ennistymon (the local market town) and talk over the whole thing as to terms, maybe sitting on it the whole day. Then, before, if it was land I didn't know or the fellow came from afar off, I would walk his land and look at it and the cattle there were on it to make sure of the farm. Then we would go to a solicitor that day and make up the writings in Ennistymon. The money, say three hundred pounds, would be paid over in cash or in promissory notes, and it is usual here to divide it into two parts or sometimes more. One-half is paid at the wedding, and the other is paid a year after.[18]

These arrangements may have been less restrictive before the Famine, but they imposed quite severe constraints on the children of strong tenant farmers and gave parents considerable control over the marriage prospects of their sons and daughters.

The number of families making up this 'critical nation forming class' remained more or less constant during the Famine while the ranks of cottiers and agricultural labourers were decimated, and the survivors were less willing to subdivide their right of occupancy on the land or form reckless marriages. After 1850, the previous demographic diversity was gradually superseded and in rural communities matrimony and the acquisition of land became closely linked. The timing of both events was even more tightly controlled by Irish parents, whose choices reflected the economic advantages of impartible inheritance as the rapid spread of commercialised agriculture affected existing landholding patterns. Arranged marriages and the consolidation of farms, rather than subdivision, emerged as the norm in rural Ireland. For non-inheriting children, however, emigration, funded by the dowry of an incoming sister-in-law, represented a logical and practical option in a society that produced much larger generations than it could possibly feed or employ. Most surplus offspring were consigned to the emigrant ships and other choices were narrowed to working as hired labourers or farm servants (implying social descent), joining a religious order (with the possibility of placement overseas) and, for one daughter, the dubious privilege of entering a loveless match.[19]

The intimate connections between household succession, marriage and the dispersal of non-inheriting siblings are vividly illustrated in the case of one West Coast migrant. John Noonan Callinan left his family homestead at West Gragan, County Clare, for the last time in 1863. The timing of this departure coincided with an agricultural depression, which caused severe financial hardship in many Irish rural communities.[20] Yet the immediate cause of his emigration was his father's death earlier in the year. Michael Callinan (1790–1863) bequeathed the right of occupancy in a large farm of 90 acres to his eldest son, Patrick, making a passage abroad the best option for those who did not inherit.[21] In 1856 John's eldest sister, Catherine, had been sent to join relatives and friends living in the Victorian town of Ballarat. A younger brother followed three years later and settled in west Melbourne, where he developed a substantial contracting business. The emigration of other family members awaited the arrangement of Patrick's marriage in 1860, the payment of their sister-in-law's dowry and his succession to the land. The death of Michael senior opened the way for a further reduction in the size of the family household at West Gragan. John's voyage to Victoria aboard the *Eastern Empire* in mid-1863, and the later arrival of his mother and three younger siblings on the *White Star*, completed a complex process that involved the transfer of land at home and the transplantation of non-inheriting children abroad.[22]

This example contains the key features of the stem-family model of household structure that has dominated historical interpretations of Irish society and culture during the post-Famine period: unitary farm inheritance favouring a male heir, a carefully arranged marriage, the co-residence of three generations and the dispersal of non-inheriting siblings.[23] Yet the Callinans do not adhere completely to the stem pattern. For instance, the fact that Catherine and Michael junior emigrated in the 1850s suggests that the payment of compensation to non-inheriting family members was possible even though the farm was promised to Patrick. Moreover, the Callinan household seems to have contained three lineal generations for only a very brief period, and the provision for John's widowed mother was a berth on an emigrant ship rather than a room in the West Gragan homestead. These minor variations on the standard picture of Ireland's family history have greater significance in the context of recent debates in Irish historical writing about demography, marriage and household structure.[24]

Although it remains highly contentious, the work of historical revisionists has raised important questions about the accuracy of older interpretations based on the rigid stem-family model.[25] These scholars do not dispute the existence of high rates of celibacy and late marriages in post-Famine Ireland, but they argue, first, that few households contained more than two generations, and, second, that there was considerable variability in household composition over time and space. This diversity is clearly evident in Donna Birdwell-Pheasant's longitudinal data from Ballyduff, County Kerry, where Irish farmers sought to balance the integrity of their land with the need to provide for their children in ways that did not 'extrud[e] them permanently from the extended family network'.[26] On this view, the Irish stem-family system appears far more flexible and resilient than the 'doom-and-gloom' characterisations of an older scholarship: 'it is an adaptive pattern that can emerge whenever and wherever economic and demographic circumstances are right and the cultural setting is congenial'.[27]

The broad thrust of recent historical revisionism is extremely useful for scholars exploring the marriage patterns of Irish migrants abroad. First and foremost, it casts doubt on explanations that attribute their demographic behaviour to the operation of peculiarly Irish cultural traits, including a repressive view of sexuality that was expressed in a reluctance to marry. This view was an important subterranean influence in Hasia Diner's *Erin's Daughters in America*, a path-breaking study of Irish women migrants in the nineteenth century.[28] According to Diner, both men and women retained Irish family forms in the United States and showed a marked propensity to marry later and less frequently than other groups. A distinctive post-Famine pattern persisted, she suggests, because it provided much-needed stability and cultural continuity for women in a new land and indicated the primacy of economic motives in their migration. Subsequent research has not supported Diner's appealing hypothesis.[29] In a painstaking quantitative analysis of large samples drawn from the American manuscript censuses of 1880, 1900, 1910 and 1920, Mark Foley and Timothy Guinnane found that any differences in marriage patterns between native white Americans and

Irish-Americans in the late nineteenth century were best explained by the latter group's urban residence and socio-economic status.[30] Their statistical results for 1910 and 1920 revealed a clear trend toward non-marriage, but they argued that even this change could not be attributed to cultural variables. 'Irish-American distinctiveness in marriage patterns,' they concluded, 'is a regional phenomenon.'[31] The complexities of the United States evidence show that adequate explanations of Irish demographic behaviour must move beyond static notions of 'cultural baggage' and take account of the dynamic interaction of Old World cultural resources with colonial settings.

II

Were Irish migrants on the West Coast unusually likely to remain unmarried? If so, did this marriage pattern reflect distinctive cultural traits brought with them from Ireland, as some scholars have maintained? The main difficulty in answering these questions with any degree of precision is the lack of source materials such as census manuscripts that would allow systematic comparisons with the work of scholars in Great Britain and North America. Nevertheless, other kinds of historical data can help to build 'windows into the past'.[32] Death certificates, used in conjunction with literary sources, provide an alternative basis for reconstructing migrant populations,[33] and provide invaluable biographical details about individuals. Moreover, they allow for systematic linkages with other materials such as probates, cemetery transcripts, parish registers and family histories, thereby eliminating some of the ambiguities and omissions found in the extant listings. The analysis presented below is based on a study of 589 Irish-born women and 1374 men aged 45 and over, whose deaths were registered on the West Coast between 1876 and 1915.

Generally speaking, the matrimonial behaviour of these newcomers conformed to the wider colonial marriage pattern that developed in New Zealand between the 1840s and 1880s. This pattern was characterised by major differences in the proportion of women (more than three-quarters) and men (less than one half) who married; a younger age at first marriage for migrant females (23) than typically found in north-western Europe, but a comparatively higher age for males (27); and relatively small numbers of people who married very young.[34] Table 4.1 reports the relevant data for Irish-born men. As we might expect, a substantial proportion on the goldfields chose to remain unmarried (57.1 per cent), a phenomenon probably related

Table 4.1 Marital status of Irish-born men aged 45 and over, 1876–1915

Number of Marriages	1	2	3	4	single	Unknown
	Religious Affiliation (N = 1374)					
Catholic						
N	424	11	0	0	588	6
%	41.2	1.1	0	0	57.1	0.6
Non-Catholic						
N	137	5	2	0	198	3
%	39.7	1.4	0.6	0	57.4	0.9
TOTAL						
N	561	16	2	0	786	9
%	40.8	1.2	0.1	0	57.2	0.7

Notes
1. All data obtained from death registers held at the Central Registry of Births, Deaths and Marriages, Lower Hutt, for the following districts: Jackson's Bay, Okarito, Ross, Hokitika, Kumara, Waimea, Greymouth, Cobden, Brunnerton, Ahaura, Reefton, Charleston, Lyell and Buller. Additional information was taken from probate files, shipping lists, newspaper obituaries, family histories and cemetery lists held at the West Coast Historical Museum.
2. The category 'non-Catholic' contains data from the death certificates of 345 men, among whom the denominational split was as follows: Anglican (170), Presbyterian (112), Wesleyan (21), Jewish (1) and unknown (41).

Table 4.2 Marital status of Irish-born women aged 45 and over, 1876–1915

Number of Marriages	1	2	3	4	single	Unknown
	Religious Affiliation (N = 1374)					
Catholic						
N	398	35	3	0	12	19
%	85.2	7.5	0.6	0	2.6	4.1
Non-Catholic						
N	100	5	4	1	2	10
%	82.0	4.1	3.3	0.8	1.6	4.1
TOTAL						
N	498	40	7	1	14	29
%	84.6	6.8	1.2	0.2	2.4	4.9

Notes
1. All data obtained from the same sources as Table 4.1.
2. The category 'non-Catholic' contains data from the death certificates of 122 women, among whom the denominational split was as follows: Anglican (67), Presbyterian (29), Wesleyan (9) and unknown (17).

as much to the shared values that developed among itinerant miners as to the availability of suitable partners (see Chapter 3). There were few variations in Irish male celibacy rates across the four main denominations, and those men whose religious affiliations cannot be ascertained were least likely to marry. The remarriage of widowers, however, was extremely rare and occurred much less frequently than it did for their widowed female compatriots. As we shall see below, the large age differential between husbands and wives, together with the hazards of mining, considerably increased the chances of widowhood on the goldfields. The outlook for younger widows with dependent children must have been very bleak, even with the support of kinsfolk, and remarriage was always a viable survival strategy in a society with a surplus male population.

Table 4.2 details the incidence of marriage among Irish female migrants and shows that 546 (92.6 per cent) had married at some stage in their lives, while only 14 (2.4 per cent) remained single; in a further 29 cases (4.9 per cent) the available sources do not permit us to determine marital status with any confidence. There are striking parallels here with the proportion of Irish-born women who died in Victoria in the 1890s and had been married at some time (90 per cent).[35] The prevalence of celibacy is also considerably less than that recorded for women aged 45–54 in the Irish census of 1881 (17 per cent), and almost certainly lower than the comparable rates for Irish-born females reaching this age in the United States between the censuses of 1880 and 1910.[36] Like their counterparts in Victoria, some women remarried after the death of their partners (8.2 per cent), a pattern typified by the proprietor of the National Hotel at Kumara, Johanna Moretti, formerly the widow of John Dillacosta, and Tipperary-born Johanna Noonan of Dobson.[37] There is also evidence to suggest that a small minority chose to establish 'colonial' or *de facto* marriages, devoid of legal or religious recognition, just as they did on the Victorian goldfields.[38] One thinks here of the feisty and independent Whataroa farmer, Mary Francis Deehan, who bequeathed a sizeable estate to her two children and provided clear instructions to the executors about her worldly affairs: 'It will be against my wish that John Bridgeman Angela's father should be allowed to interfere with her in any way or with the property I am leaving her . . . And in bidding my son and daughter farewell it is my earnest wish that they endeavour while they are together to live lovingly and happily.'[39] For most women, however, marriage was a central feature of everyday life on the West Coast. Even some of the region's most notorious Irish prostitutes found husbands. Overland Kate of Notown, for example, was delivered by wheelbarrow to the door of a devout Catholic, Thomas Hillier, in a prank by local youths that led unexpectedly to the altar.[40] The well-documented cases of Bridget Goodwin and 'Sugar Annie' Rankin, both of whom worked claims and lived with more than one male companion, are much less representative of Irish women's experiences in local mining communities.[41]

Although the available evidence underlines the near-universality of marriage among Irish female migrants and high rates of male celibacy on the West Coast, it provides the historian with few references to courtship or love. We do know that some single women married almost immediately after landing in the region. Mary Dempsey of Ballinasloe, County Galway, met her future husband, Patrick Morrissey, when she visited his Greymouth cobbler's shop to replace some shoes lost at the end of a voyage from Sydney.[42] Eighteen-year-old Annie Houlihan, on the other hand, was rescued from a Victorian orphanage by Catholic friends and brought to Hokitika, where, within two weeks of coming ashore, she formed a lasting union with Patrick Quinn, a wealthy miner from County Tipperary.[43] In other cases, like those of Maria Phelan and Margaret McGirr, the selection of a marriage partner seems to have been the outcome of a shipboard romance.[44] The temptation to marry in haste always carried risks, as 15-year-old Mary Wiltshire and her sister, Ellen, discovered when they wed two men from Magherafelt who had adopted fictitious names and presented themselves as English migrants.[45] Each of these case studies implies a degree of independence denied to women in rural Ireland after the Famine, where the increasing prevalence of the dowry system restricted their marital choices by strengthening the link between the acquisition of land and a marriage partner.[46] Without the kinds of social and economic pressures that existed in rural Irish communities, migrants were free to marry at younger ages and at much higher rates than their sisters at home. But their actions were not based solely on individual decisions. As we shall see, informal social networks played an important role in shaping the marriage alliances of Irish women on the West Coast.

The small fragments of evidence that survive in family traditions, local histories and personal correspondence suggest that intermediaries actively facilitated some local marriages. Mary Ann Williams's wedding to 'Peter the Greek' Mangos, for example, was arranged by her matchmaking grandfather and took place in Nelson, where she had been sent to board at the convent school.[47] The go-betweens included sisters, brothers, kinsfolk, priests and, in other cases, a combination of friends and relations. Presumably young single people were sometimes 'put in each other's way', thereby ensuring that they formed socially approved unions. Yet intermediaries may have also been involved in more complex negotiations. The marriage of Sarah Devery and Patrick Gillin at Hokitika in 1868 provides the best-documented illustration of these interpositions. Devery was the youngest daughter of a financially ruined King's County landowner, educated at an exclusive Ursuline convent in Dublin and forced, in 1861, to exchange the opulence of Belmont House, Ferbane, for the confines of an emigrant ship to Melbourne. She travelled with her parents and eight siblings. In a double tragedy, Sarah's father, James, and a sister, Ellen, died on the voyage and were buried at sea. Although her widowed mother, Mary Anne, arrived in the Victorian capital with several dependants and few resources, she was reunited with the couple's two adult children who had emigrated there in the late 1850s. Sarah's eldest brother, Arthur, made most of the financial decisions for the household immediately after his father's death, arranging a hotel licence for his mother and moving this enterprise to Hokitika in 1866. According to family tradition, Arthur first met Patrick Gillin, a prosperous farmer and ex-miner, during a trip to the Grey Valley. Impressed by Gillin's personality and business acumen, as well as his handsome two-storey homestead at Kamaka, he encouraged the 37-year-old bachelor to ask his mother for his 18-year-old sister's hand in marriage. An agreement between the parties was eventually concluded, but Sarah herself had little say in the negotiations and was not allowed to speak with Gillin until the morning of the wedding (Plate 15). Before then, she had to be content with fleeting glimpses of her future husband through the keyhole in a bedroom door of the family's Revell Street hotel.[48]

The involvement of relations and friends in arranging marriages shows that West Coast unions were usually much more than a matter for the two individuals concerned. Of course, there were exceptions to this wider community pattern. Mary Jane Diamond, the 17-year-old daughter of a Red Jacks hotelier, eloped with a 40-year-old wheelwright, John McLaughlin, after a ball at Notown in 1880 and rode with him through the darkness to Kumara, where their marriage was witnessed by the parish priest's housekeeper and gardener.[49] Yet even here it seems significant that the nuptials took place before a Catholic priest, a decision that must have dampened some of the anger expressed by Mary Jane's kinsfolk. The extended courtship of Mary Catherine Devery and Thomas Tymons, however, was more representative. We do not know where the couple first met, but it is clear that they exchanged letters on a number of occasions. Writing from Red Jacks in 1868, Tymons confessed that

the last week [*has been*] the longest of my life. Still I have one great comforter and that is the remembrance of the last evening I have spent in the Ahaura.

Oh that happy evening. When will another like it come? It only wanted your consent to have me to crown my greatest ambition. My Dearest Mary when will you say Yes? Every person says we are going to be married. Why should we disapoint them?[50]

His thoughts then turned to the rival attractions of another suitor and the dreadful consequences that he feared would follow Mary's refusal of his proposal:

Your old 'sweetheart' Jeff was on to me today [*about it* crossed out] of course. I denied all about it but could he only have seen the real truth of my heart what a discovery he would make. It is really believed we are going to do it and to tell you the truth I have made myself believe it also. So if you disappoint me, oh God, the consequence will be something awful. I don't think I could ever bear such disappointed hopes and blithed affections. My Dearest Mary, when will you take pity on me and set my mind at rest? I oft ask myself the question Can Mary Devery care anything for me in such an unsettled state of mind? I will leave yourself to answer the question in your next and remember Mary to me will this answer be either life or death.[51]

Fortunately Tymons did not have to act on these dark threats. Mary Devery eventually agreed to marry the Notown storekeeper, a decision supported in a letter sent to him by his future mother-in-law: 'It gave me great pleasure to hear realised in your letter of this morning that which I have heard from my sons including Pat Gillin and the Rev^d Fr Larkin namely that my daughter Mary had in her prudence selected for her partner in this life and also in the next one so worthy as yourself. I am proud to say you have my entire consent and blessing.'[52] We have no means of knowing whether men were expected to take the initiative in courtship, as this case seems to suggest. But we can say that the events leading up to Thomas and Mary's marriage were typical in terms of local community interest, the use of confidants and the strong presence of kinsfolk and friends at the wedding in Greymouth.

In most of the cases detailed above, Irish women married relatively young and chose spouses who were much older than themselves. This impressionistic observation is reinforced by the only systematic data from the West Coast that has been made available to historians: the extant registers of marriages covering the years between 1881 and 1889. As Table 4.3 reveals, the median age at first marriage for Irish-born females in the region (23.6) was more than those of the

Table 4.3 Age distribution at first marriage by birthplace, West Coast, 1881–9

	15-19	20-24	25-29	30-34	35-39	40-54	55+	Total	Medi
				Women					
Ireland									
N	10	83	40	15	3	4	0	155	23.6
%	6.5	53.5	25.8	9.7	1.9	2.6	–		
Scotland									
N	18	26	4	2	3	4	0	57	21.6
%	31.6	45.6	7.0	3.5	5.3	7.0	–		
England									
N	20	54	14	12	3	4	0	107	22.6
%	18.7	50.5	13.1	11.2	2.8	3.7	–		
Victoria									
N	48	107	15	2	1	0	0	173	21.3
%	27.7	61.8	8.7	1.2	0.6	–	–		
New Zealand									
N	124	180	9	3	0	0	0	316	20.5
%	39.2	57.0	2.8	0.9	–	–	–		
				Men					
Ireland									
N	0	10	43	44	39	36	0	172	33.3
%	–	5.8	25.0	25.6	22.7	20.9	–		
Scotland									
N	2	20	30	21	19	27	6	125	32.1
%	1.6	16.0	24.0	16.8	15.2	21.6	4.8		
England									
N	2	49	72	43	26	51	3	246	29.6
%	0.8	19.9	29.3	17.5	10.6	20.7	1.2		
Victoria									
N	1	42	64	9	2	0	0	118	25.8
%	0.8	35.6	54.2	7.6	1.7	–	–		
New Zealand									
N	4	76	42	13	1	0	0	136	23.7
%	2.9	55.9	30.9	9.6	0.7	–	–		

Source: All data were obtained from the Registers of Marriages, 1881–1889, Central Registry of Births, Deaths and Marriages, Lower Hutt.

other main groups, but the difference is only slight, especially when compared with the English-born (22.6), and cannot support an interpretation that stresses Irish distinctiveness. Moreover, the timing and frequency with which they married closely matched the wider colonial pattern that one historian has plausibly linked to an imbalance in the numbers of women and men in the settler population, the willingness of single women migrants to depart from 'traditional expectations' and the absence of parental intervention.[53] The weaknesses of the cultural argument are further highlighted by the fact that the second-generation daughters of Irish Catholic people married at the same ages as their colonial-born sisters from Victoria and New Zealand.

When Irish-born men formed unions, however, they were most likely to have been over 30, at least during the 1880s, as were their Scottish-born counterparts and a large proportion of the English-born group.[54] This pattern is hardly surprising given that most potential husbands were in their late 20s when they arrived in the region and would have taken time to establish themselves economically before searching for a suitable mate. Edward Phelan from Gowran, County Kilkenny, for example, was 28 when he first came to New Zealand, and 41 when he married 24-year-old Ellen Walshe at St Patrick's, Charleston, in 1882.[55] Father James O'Donnell officiated at the Notown wedding of Clare-born James Thornton, aged 40, and his 19-year-old bride, Mary Anne Ruane, while Father Rolland did the same at Boatman's for Timothy Minehan (34) and Bridget Sullivan (22).[56] Few could ever hope to emulate Samuel Beatty, a 70-year-old widower, who married a domestic servant 20 years his junior in Hokitika.[57] The age gap between Irish-born husbands and their wives ensured many women spent a portion of their lives as widows, even without the perennial dangers that so often claimed the lives of male workers in goldfields communities.

The surviving documents provide valuable clues about aspects of courtship and ages at marriage during the nineteenth and early twentieth centuries. They are much less satisfactory for exploring sexuality, separation and the emotions surrounding marriage and childbirth. Some useful evidence can be extracted from court records, but this information is seldom representative of the wider migrant group. Transgressions of state legislation and local custom led to various combinations of rough justice, police intervention and court proceedings, but in theory the whole machinery of betrothal and marital behaviour was governed by Catholic theology and therefore the proper concern of clergy. West Coast priests attended several diocesan synods at which the canon law relating to matrimonial practices was discussed and elaborated in detail.[58] Although the most pressing issues facing religious practitioners involved intermarriage, there were other important questions to consider. Where should the marriage ceremony take place if the betrothed were not of the same parish? How should the honorarium be divided? Was an absolute moral certainty of death required before a spouse could contract another marriage? Perhaps the most intriguing problem, which arose at the 1892 Diocesan Synod, concerned the status of relationships where the promise of marriage was followed by sexual intercourse based on 'libidinous, but not conjugal, feeling'. Did this union constitute a valid marriage in a colony where the Council of Trent (1563) had not been promulgated? The synod report's answer to this 'common difficulty' was quite equivocal:

According to the declaration of Gregory IX, the promise of marriage, if sexual intercourse follows, effects a valid marriage. If a subsequent marriage is contracted, and contracted according to all regulations of the Church and the Civil Power, that new marriage is void, and the partners ought to return to their first marriage.

It is objected by a great many missionaries that the faithful are in many cases wholly ignorant of this declaration of Gregory IX. The Irish, in accordance with their own wishes, believe contrary to the laws of the Church, that no marriage has been contracted. This is now the established practice in Ireland and is approved by their bishops. Others consider the observance of civil law can in no case be put aside. What then should be done, if intercourse follows the promise of marriage but without conjugal feeling and afterwards marriage is contracted with another person?

The answer of the Sacred Congress is that it cannot be accepted that all are ignorant of the law of the church, although some can be found who are ignorant of it. Where the Council of Trent has not been promulgated, for practical purposes pastors of souls ought to consider intercourse that takes place after the promise of marriage as valid marriage, even if the partners affirm that in intercourse they had no intention of marrying. For the purposes of the confessional, generally speaking, sexual intercourse after the promise of marriage is a sign of marital intent; nevertheless, if the partners declare that they did not have this intention, it must be deemed that no marriage has been contracted. If there has been intercourse with conjugal feeling and it has taken place after marriage, a separation must be advised, and there is an obligation if possible to live with the first wife, who is the only legitimate wife.[59]

How the abstractions of clerical discourse were played out in everyday life on the goldfields remains hidden from the historian's gaze. There is no additional evidence available to corroborate the tantalising statement about pre-marital sexual activity and Irish opinion. Did the assembled priests cite an example from Ireland or one that they encountered from time to time among their own flocks? Does this brief reference tell us something about the transposition of cultural resources by migrants to the New World? Silences in the historical record make it hazardous to speculate any further on these questions, but we can say with some confidence that the region's clergy, when confronted by cases of pre-nuptial pregnancy, illegitimacy or temporary 'colonial' unions, acted decisively where possible to solemnise the relationship. This pragmatic stance was particularly well suited to a goldfields environment and, as we shall see, found its clearest expression in clerical dealings with 'mixed marriages'.

III

The gendered character of Irish settlement, outlined in Chapter 2, greatly influenced the likelihood of intermarriage and the formation of religiously mixed households on the West Coast. In towns like Greymouth or Kumara, for example, first- and second-generation Irish Catholic women had a more limited choice of marriage partners within their own denomination than their counterparts in the far reaches of South Westland. Presumably 'mixed marriages' in migrant households had less impact in the larger urban areas where newcomers constructed a wide array of formal structures such as churches, schools, confraternities and welfare networks. For men and women living in remote locations, however, the struggle to fulfil their own spiritual duties and ensure the religious adherence of their children must have presented a far greater challenge. Such was the case for Ellen Piezzi, the daughter of a Kilkenny artisan-farmer, who married a Swiss-Italian baker and sent her eldest daughter, Helvetia, to St Mary's Convent in Wellington '[to] be taugh[t] her fathers langus and musick and brought up better than be[ing] around the publick house door'.[60]

Given the deficiencies of local parish records and the limited access to marriage registers, we may never know fully whether Irish migrants to the West Coast were inclined to form endogamous unions. Nevertheless, information gathered from marriage certificates for the period 1881 to 1889 provides important clues about the factors that predisposed migrant women to marry men from the same religious denomination. A close examination of the 221 extant marriages involving Irish-born women shows that nearly three-fifths married Irish-born men (58.8 per cent), while a large minority selected husbands from outside the boundaries of their own nationality. This significant finding suggests that Irish women were not always confined by ethnicity in their choice of marriage partners. But this analysis treats female migrants as an undifferentiated whole and obscures as much as it explains. A much more revealing picture emerges when we consider the influence of religious affiliations. Of the 169 marriages involving Roman Catholic women, more than two-thirds (69.2 per cent) married Irish-born husbands, while one-tenth were united with partners outside the faith

(10.7 per cent). The remainder formed unions with second- and third-generation men from Irish backgrounds (11.8 per cent) or wed Catholic males of various nationalities (8.3 per cent). The evidence suggests that relatively few Catholic female migrants on the West Coast in the 1880s crossed the religious divide and married Protestants. Where these lines were transgressed, Irish women tended to marry in local registry offices or private homes rather than Protestant churches, a pattern typified by Annie Mahoney of Kilcommon, who married an English-born miner, Samuel Furness, at the Reefton home of her brother-in-law, Stewart Montieth.[61]

There are, however, striking differences between the marriage alliances of Catholic and Protestant females. Although the number of cases is very small, Protestants were overwhelmingly inclined to take spouses from the non-Irish male population (71.4 per cent). Most, though, still chose husbands professing the same religious affiliations. Put another way, the evidence reveals that 162 marriages involving Irish women during the 1880s took place before a Catholic priest (73.3 per cent), a further 20 before Anglican clergy (9.0 per cent), and another 15 before Presbyterian ministers (6.8 per cent); 23 were held in registry offices (10.4 per cent).[62] These figures are remarkably similar to the balance of religious affiliations for the group during the period under consideration. Overall, we can conclude, tentatively, that Irish women migrants on the West Coast overwhelmingly married men of the same religious denomination as themselves, and that Catholics showed by far the greatest propensity to select Irish husbands.

Did second-generation women from Irish home backgrounds also tend to marry men of their own faith? The limitations of the available evidence mean that we can only establish the marital patterns of Roman Catholics with sufficient accuracy. Of the 65 women born in New Zealand to Irish parents and marrying during the 1880s, 41 formed unions with Irish-born migrants or their second-generation male counterparts (63.1 per cent), while 16 celebrated marriages with men of various nationalities in Catholic churches (24.6 per cent). Most surprising, however, is the remarkably low proportion of weddings that took place in Protestant churches (7.7 per cent) or local registry offices (4.6 per cent). As Table 4.4 shows, an almost identical pattern was evident among the Victorian-born. In summary, then, it seems clear that, during the 1880s, most second-generation women selected spouses who were also Roman Catholics or obtained dispensations and celebrated weddings before a Catholic priest.

Table 4.4 Marital patterns of second-generation Catholic women, West Coast, 1881–9

NEW ZEALAND-BORN	
HUSBANDS BORN	N=65

To Irish parent(s): Australian colonies 14, England 1, Ireland (Catholic) 21, Ireland (Protestant) 2, New Zealand 6, Scotland 1 | Other: At sea 1, Dalmatia 2, England 5, France 1, Germany 2, Italy 1, New Zealand 6, Norway 1, Scotland 1

VICTORIAN-BORN

HUSBANDS BORN   N=59

To Irish parent(s): Australian colonies 11, England 4, Ireland (Catholic) 18, Ireland (Protestant) 2, New Zealand 3, Scotland 1   Other: Australian colonies 3, Dalmatia 3, Denmark 1, England 6, Italy 2, New Zealand 3, Scotland 2

Source: All data were obtained from the same sources as Table 4.3.

The marital choices of Irish-born men closely resembled those of their female counterparts over the same period. Almost three-fifths formed endogamous unions (59.1 per cent), a finding that disguises important differences between the main religious denominations. Protestant males were unusually willing to take non-Irish wives (72.2 per cent) and far more likely than Roman Catholics to marry in local registry offices. These trends seem to have been very similar to the English- and Scottish-born groups: most married out (35.0 per cent and 75.3 per cent) and a significant minority eschewed religious ceremonies altogether (see Table 4.5). By contrast, more than two-thirds of Catholic men selected Irish-born spouses (68.9 per cent), a quarter chose second- or third-generation women with Irish ancestry (24.4 per cent) and a mere handful married non-Irish Catholics. Of the seven cases involving intermarriage, three weddings took place before a Roman Catholic priest, two before a civil registrar, another before an Anglican minister and one in a Wesleyan chapel. The wider pattern of religious endogamy is even more emphatic for colonial-born Catholic males

Table 4.5 Marriages in registry offices by birthplace, West Coast, 1881–9

BIRTHPLACE	WOMEN		MEN	
	N	%	N	%
IRELAND (CATHOLIC)	14 (183)	7.7	7 (176)	4.0
IRELAND (NON-CATHOLIC)	9 (38)	23.7	13 (54)	24.1
ENGLAND	64 (183)	35.0	92 (309)	29.8
SCOTLAND	27 (78)	34.6	41 (151)	27.2

Source: All data were obtained from the same sources as Table 4.3. The raw figures in brackets represent the total number of marriages.

Table 4.6 Marital patterns of second-generation Catholic men, West Coast, 1881–9

NEW ZEALAND-BORN

WIVES BORN

N=18

To Irish parent(s): Australian colonies 4, Ireland (Catholic) 7, New Zealand   Other: Germany 1, New Zealand 2

VICTORIAN-BORN

WIVES BORN

N=37

To Irish parent(s): Australian colonies 10, Ireland (Catholic) 11, New Zealand 9   Other: Denmark 1, England 1, New Zealand 2, Scotland 1, Wales 1, Unknown 1

Source: All data were obtained from the same sources as Table 4.3.

with at least one Irish parent. As we can see in Table 4.6, these men contracted only two 'mixed marriages', both of which took place in local registry offices.

It would be wrong to view the continuity of these patterns across two generations as evidence for the existence and maintenance of ethnic solidarity. Rather than forming a remote outpost of an Irish spiritual empire, local Catholicism was a 'curious amalgam' of Irish, French, English and Australian influences.[63] Catholic clergy in the region used the weight of their spiritual authority to discourage migrants and their sons and daughters from entering into mixed marriages. But the main source of their hostility to unions between Protestants and Catholics was religious and they were reluctant to act as the border guards of Irish ethnicity. The pragmatic tone of clerical discourse and its emphasis on faith is neatly captured in a letter from Denis O'Hallahan, the parish priest at Kumara, to the Bishop of Christchurch, John Joseph Grimes. Writing in 1892, O'Hallahan made a strong case for granting a dispensation to one of his parishioners, Miss McDermott, who had been 'keeping company' with a German-born Lutheran 'for nearly five years'. The couple were engaged and McDermott's prospective husband had supported her financially in the house of fellow Catholics at Goldsborough.

> Besides she is very close on thirty five years of age, and certainly cannot get the same chance of a suitable marriage again if she should miss this present one. Of course you know my Lord how hard it is for girls to get married on these gold fields. And also how difficult it is for them to get Catholic men amongst the miners to marry them, and especially so when they are more or less advanced in years.

O'Hallahan reminded his bishop that the marriage would take place regardless of whether a dispensation was obtained and if this happened outside the church there was a strong likelihood that the couple 'may turn away': 'I am anxious that they should be married, for this reason that it will prevent many uncharitable people from talking very, very lightly of them, as they have been & are doing at present'.[64] The requirement to seek a dispensation for mixed marriages before a Catholic priest, along with the decision not to publish the banns and to celebrate weddings in the church sacristy, acted as powerful disincentives to marrying outside the faith. This fact was well understood by clergymen like Tipperary-born Denis Carew of Greymouth, who saw any wavering in these practices as 'an additional inducement for other Catholic girls to look for Protestant husbands since permission is granted for such marriages and that they are called out in the church equally as Catholics'.[65]

A hardening of clerical policy on interfaith marriages is evident from the late nineteenth century, with increasingly strident and frequent denunciations of the practice by the colony's Catholic bishops. In a wide-ranging discussion of Christian life in New Zealand, the pastoral letter of the First Provincial Council (1899) affirmed the sanctity of lifelong monogamous marriage contracted with worthy motives and the blessings of religion. It expressed disappointment that some laity wrongly believed that they were free to follow 'their whims and fancies' in the choice of a spouse, including unions with those without any particular faith or from other denominations:

> Under certain conditions, which ought to be loyally promised and fulfilled, the Church reluctantly permits the contracting of such marriages; but she regards them as unchristian, she consents to them as a mother, who despairs of offering effective opposition, consents to the marriage of a daughter with one, whom she knows is more likely to break her child's heart than to secure her lifelong happiness.[66]

The council held that the 'greatest evil' of these matches was not the imperfect union of heart and lack of sympathy, which together undermine the core elements of a successful marriage. Rather, 'it is found in this fact, that

> in such wedlock deep religion and earnest piety are almost impossible, while the children of these religiously divided families too often grow up in indifference, and sooner or later fall away from the faith. The Fathers of this

Council, therefore, reiterate their most earnest and solemn warnings against the prevalence of mixed marriages, and exhort their clergy to frequently remind their people, particularly parents and guardians, of their duty in this regard, so that, if not all, at least a great number of these objectionable marriages may be avoided.[67]

The general tone of this letter seems relatively tolerant when compared with Archbishop Redwood's instructions to Catholic clergy concerning the papal decree *Ne Temere*, promulgated by Pius X to take effect on 19 April 1908.[68] Before the decree, mixed marriages, though condemned, were accepted as valid in the eyes of God and the church. According to this new directive, however, no marriage of any type was canonically valid unless contracted in the presence of a Roman Catholic priest and two witnesses. Furthermore, non-Catholic parties to these marriages had to sign contracts in which they undertook, *inter alia*, to respect the faith of their Catholic spouses and bring up their children as Catholics. The decree reflected a more aggressive stance by Vatican authorities that had gathered momentum since the mid-nineteenth century and outraged Protestant opinion, just as it did in Australia.[69] Yet its translation to the lives of ordinary people on the West Coast did not lead to the total religious segregation envisioned by some Irish bishops. The proportion of interfaith marriages within the region's Catholic churches remained much the same and the existence of these mixed households in small communities may have contributed to greater understanding between Catholics and Protestants.

Along with the proactive stance of local clergy, the role of informal social networks based on ties of kinship, neighbourhood and religion was critical in shaping the marriage alliances of Irish migrants. Female witnesses at weddings were generally drawn from the same locality as the bride, as were the grooms and their male witnesses. In cases where family members signed the registers, the brothers and sisters of couples usually assumed this responsibility. Jane Clohessy of Addison's Flat, for example, witnessed the marriage of her sister, Catherine, who wed a Galway-born miner, Patrick Kane, at the township's Roman Catholic chapel in 1881.[70] Other migrants like Mary Walsh, Margaret Kiernan and Ellen McMahon called on Irish-born friends at their weddings, a pattern that is also found among their male counterparts.[71] The selection of marriage partners inevitably redefined and extended local social networks and their trans-national connections, even though most Irish migrants selected companions with similar religious values. For Protestants, existing ties seem to have been rapidly supplemented through intermarriage into local social networks. Among Catholics, on the other hand, immediate kinship groups were less easily diluted. Because so many Catholic men and women married within their church, they were bound together in complex webs that were further complicated by the ties of neighbourhood, residential bonding, friendship and baptismal sponsorship.

The choice of marriage partners by migrants presented a formidable challenge to the unity of family networks that stretched from Greymouth to Melbourne, and from South Westland to distant parishes in Munster. Writing from Killarney, County Kerry, around 1900, Mary O'Connor bluntly reminded her son, William, that the 'affection you have for you[r] child ought to make you think of your mother that nursed yourself'. Yet she seemed pleased with the photograph of her new daughter-in-law, Theresa Knowles: 'She is a fine looking Woman and a nice Handsome Woman. All of us are proud to be able to show it to [our] friends.' After asking for further information about Theresa's family, Mary hinted at certain omissions in the retrospective announcement of her son's wedding: 'I suppose she was not an empty girl'.[72] These bonds of reciprocity were most likely to fracture on the West Coast when migrants married across religious lines and turned away from, or were ostracised by, their own families. Catherine Markey of County Meath, for example, sailed to Melbourne in 1872 and later to Five Mile, an isolated frontier settlement near Okarito, where she went to live with one of her sisters, Mary Fitzsimmons. There she fell passionately in love with a Presbyterian miner, James Wallace, a tenant farmer's son from County Antrim. The couple's marriage at Okarito outraged Catherine's family and she was shunned thereafter by most of her kinsfolk, with the notable exception of an older sister, Ellen.[73] Yet the Catholic/Protestant divide was often permeable, as shown by the socially approved union of Limerick-born Johanna Shanahan and William Weir, the son of an Ulster Presbyterian minister.[74] The acceptance of religiously mixed marriages depended on a number of factors, including local attitudes, the strength of migrant social networks and the 'institutional completeness' of religious denominations.[75] Viewing the evidence, it seems reasonable to suggest that Irish West Coasters did marry for love, but that most still chose brides and grooms from the same religious background as themselves (Plate 16).

The letters of Ellen Piezzi, sent to relatives of her late husband between

1878 and 1881, are unique in providing the only first-hand testimony from an Irish woman about the nature of marriage and family on the West Coast (Plates 17 and 18). Born in the Parish of Paulstown, County Kilkenny, during the Great Famine, Ellen worked as a domestic servant in Melbourne before venturing across the Tasman in 1870 to join two of her brothers. We do not know where she met her first husband, Guiglio Piezzi, but it is clear that the couple were married at St Mary's Church, Hokitika, on 11 May 1872. The sorrowful tone that pervades Ellen's correspondence was shaped by Guiglio's tragic death four years later, when flooded rivers made access to emergency treatment for his infected hernia impossible. This cruel blow shattered the domestic harmony that she later described in a letter to her sister-in-law: 'He was a good husband to me and respected his Wife in all his duties to her and Litlones [*little ones*] and kind to them and to his Wife'.[76] Pregnant with the couple's third child, Ellen Piezzi found her misfortunes compounded by bouts of ill health and declining returns on the bush-clad Waimea diggings. The daunting task of running a substantial hotel, keeping long trading hours and caring for young dependent children weighed heavily on the young widow. Although her 'buoyant spirit' languished temporarily, she found the strength to open the Swiss Mountain Hotel at Rimu with the assistance of her brothers.

Ellen's letters contain valuable insights into domestic life on the goldfields, notwithstanding her harsh self-deprecation: 'I am a bad riter. Only for that i would often rite.'[77] On several occasions, Ellen provided personal advice to her sister-in-law about the key ingredients to a successful marriage.

I take the liberty [*of saying a*] fue words to you. Love yor husband as you love yor one flesh. Respect him tentimes beter than yourself. Obey him in everything he tell you to doo No mater What he tell you too doo it for he Nose best What is the bes to bdone and he Never Will tell yto doo rong. Be kind to him and regoice At his fur step coming home to you for it is Like a bell too yor Ere.[78]

This view of the essential prerequisites for blissful domesticity depended on the strict maintenance of familial privacy:

Keep in yor one house and good distand with yor Naberes and don't Let them No anything About yor husband or yor one bisnes. Never tell anything about him to any one. Keep yor one sakret and you Will be come a good Wife.[79]

Ellen reported frequently on the progress of her three children. As we have already seen, the eldest daughter, Helvetia, had been sent to a Wellington convent school where it was hoped she would learn 'her fathers langus and musick'.[80] Ellen's son, Severini, was a 'fine little fellow' who seems to have been a great source of comfort to his mother during her darkest moments: '[*he came*] to mama and say don't crie mama, dident god take my papa frome us? Such a dear little boy he is.'[81] But Severini's close physical resemblance to 'his papa' must have intensified her sadness: 'He wake like and his shape is very like him'.[82] The couple's youngest child, Julia, was 'the pritest of all. I Would be quite lost only having her. When vetia is Way severini is in chool she is With me. She is Dear little girl spake Italia and Engles butfull.'[83]

IV

Despite its limitations, the surviving evidence allows us to draw some tentative conclusions about the marital decisions of Irish migrants on the West Coast. First, there were few significant differences between the marriage patterns of these newcomers and women of other nationalities, a finding which undermines the view that the peculiarities of Irish culture played an important role in matrimony. Irish women married at ages comparable with their English-born counterparts, while the colonial-born daughters of Irish home backgrounds formed unions in their late teens or early twenties. There are striking contrasts, however, between the demographic behaviour of Irish-born women and their male compatriots. Whereas marriage was almost a universal experience for female migrants, almost three-fifths of the Irish-born men had never married. This finding was not unexpected, given the disparity of the sexes typical of a goldfields population, but it is worth emphasising that this pattern was found throughout the colony and may have also reflected the development of a fiercely independent masculine culture among the region's miners. When these men did choose to marry they were usually well settled, financially secure and in their prime; Irish brides, on the other hand, tended to be relatively young and inexperienced. For both sexes, local clergy and informal social networks based on ties of kinship and neighbourhood were crucial in shaping marriage alliances. The available evidence also makes it clear that Irish migrants were not confined by ethnicity in their choice of marriage partners, even though they seemed reluctant to establish religiously mixed unions. As far as we can tell, the demographic choices made by Irish men and women during the nineteenth century helped to define a religious pluralism in the region and allowed the latter to meet their aspirations for economic security, 'respectable' marriages and the establishment of their own families.

5 Old Beliefs in a New World: Religion on the Mining Frontier

In two important essays, British scholar Sheridan Gilley has argued that the Roman Catholic Church in the United States and across the British Empire was an Irish one 'both in its leadership and its following, and was part of the Irish ecclesiastical empire' fashioned by Paul Cullen, the Cardinal Archbishop of Dublin (1849–1878).[1] This process, he suggests, led to the fusion of religious, national and ethnic identity in the '*international consciousness*' of ordinary migrants, who were well aware 'through their newspapers, parochial organisations and political parties of what was happening in Ireland and throughout the Irish Diaspora'.[2] Roman Catholicism, then, along with the various nationalist movements agitating on behalf of the homeland, provided the chief means for constructing diasporic communities wherever they settled. The Irish worldwide, Gilley claims, were an enormously devout people 'who live[d] not only for this life but for another'.[3] We need to consider the place of religion in migrant lives 'with a sense of its importance and a properly critical sympathy'.[4]

How were aspects of an inherited culture handled by Irish men and women in the rough-hewn settlements scattered between Mokihinui and Jackson's Bay? Did parish churches foster a sense of ethnic solidarity among the expatriate population? What role did Irish nationalist movements play in shaping their identities and political allegiances? The evidence presented in this chapter and the next shows that no single idea of 'Irishness' triumphed on the mining frontier. Many newcomers preserved and adapted older religious traditions as they struggled to make sense of their new world. Some maintained a keen interest in Irish political affairs and supported a range of nationalist networks that criss-crossed the globe; others were ambivalent about or indifferent to these kinds of movements and their goals. All migrants shared the need to gain some measure of control over their destinies by drawing on the cultural resources available to them. As we shall see, however, the diggings were not conducive to the kinds of ethnic alignments that characterised Irish settlement in parts of Britain and North America. On New Zealand's West Coast, widespread enthusiasm for Irish causes soon faded and 'diasporic sensibilities', where they existed, held limited appeal for generations born and raised in the colonies.[5]

I

Late on a wet spring morning in 1878, the SS *Tararua* dropped anchor in the open roadstead outside the Hokitika River mouth. News of its approach travelled quickly through the town and a large crowd gathered along Gibson's Quay to await the arrival of Mother Mary Clare Molony and a small contingent of nuns from the Convent of Mercy in Ennis, County Clare. Amid the excited scenes, two prominent Catholics, Edward Burke and Matthew Cleary, set out aboard the tender *Waipara* to greet the Sisters at sea. It would be some time before they returned. The gale that had blown from the north since earlier in the day continued to rage into the afternoon and both vessels awaited high tide to cross 'the dreaded Bar'.[6] As evening descended, a lone horseman galloped down the waterlogged quay and lit gas lamps that swung precariously on the street corners. In the flickering play of light and shadows, observers could make out a sizeable welcome party huddled together, its long vigil broken just before midnight when the *Waipara* sailed triumphantly into port. Despite the lateness of the hour, the Sisters were warmly received on the wharf and escorted to waiting carriages that drove them to temporary quarters at Mulligan's Cottage.[7]

The arrival of eight nuns and two postulants in Hokitika marked the end of an epic journey lasting 85 days. Mother Molony's account of the voyage from Plymouth to Australia via the Cape of Good Hope captures the excitement that they experienced aboard the SS *Garonne*: 'August 11 Beautiful evening, moonlight on the dark waters like diamonds on a velvet robe, scene bewitching, exquisite mackeral-sky. No sound save the voice of the "Great Creator".'[8] Below decks the nuns distributed 'large pieces of sweet cake' to the steerage passengers and heard a mixture of German, French, Scottish and Irish regional accents.[9] The rhythm of daily life in the 'little village' was broken momentarily at Cape Town, where a request for the services of a priest led the Sisters ashore for a visit to the Dominican convent and 'an Irish welcome' from Father Carboy, formerly of the Diocese

of Cashel. An emotional farewell to their compatriots made them feel as
though they 'were again parting from Ennis'.[10] It was with some relief that
Kangaroo Island was sighted on 14 September, after a long run east through
the rough seas of the southern ocean. The *Garonne* steamed slowly along
the coastline – 'so near that it is almost frightening' – and cast anchor at Port
Phillip four days later. The Mercy Sisters spent one week in Melbourne,
where they enjoyed the company of several priests and the nuns of St Kilda
and Abbotsford, as well as 'many old friends who seem[ed] delighted to do
something for us'.[11] This pattern was repeated on their voyage around the
lower half of New Zealand, with similar receptions in Dunedin, Wellington
and Nelson. At Lyttelton '[s]everal people, Irish, and old inhabitants of
Hokitika' came to see the sisters, including 'a most amiable' and enthusiastic
Catholic family: 'Mrs Mulligan, before leaving, presented Reverend Mother
with an exquisite valenciennes lace for the Altar of our future Chapel, which
concealed in its folds a £10 note, the good lady thinking it the most delicate
way of giving a donation'.[12]

From an imagined imperial centre at Dublin, the various places visited by
the Sisters of Mercy on their journey to Hokitika might be seen as part of 'an
indisputably Irish Catholic Church' that stretched out from Cape Province to
Boston, and from Liverpool to Sydney.[13] This view undoubtedly shaped the
activities of many Irish secular clerics in Australia and New Zealand, whose
polemical and authoritarian style was deeply influenced by Old World historical
analogies, traditions and emphases. Yet there is no evidence to show that Mother
Molony envisioned the foundation at St. Columbkille's as the distant outpost
of an Irish spiritual empire. By the time of her arrival, the Irish component of
the region's Catholic population was declining relative to the numbers of those
born in the colonies, and churches also contained parishioners from southern
Europe, France, Germany and Britain. Moreover, local Catholicism was itself
an amalgam of French, English and Australian, as well as Irish influences, an
outcome epitomised by the popularity of French Marist priests like Father
Philippe Martin, who played a key role in bringing the Sisters of Mercy to
Hokitika. It seems appropriate, therefore, that Molony's first public speech in
the town emphasised the centrality of Rome, her veneration for His Holiness,
Pius IX, and the fact that the Sisters had come to New Zealand to promote 'the
Glory of God'.[14] This terminology was ideally suited to an environment with
little sectarian tension and many different local networks and the 'powerful
global histories' of British imperialism and colonisation.[15]

The spiritual landscape that Mother Molony discovered on the West Coast goldfields was markedly different from the one she had left behind. By the late 1870s significant sectors of Ireland's Catholic population had undergone a transformation that Emmet Larkin labelled the 'devotional revolution'.[16] The foundations for this shift had been laid before the Famine, as several historians have shown,[17] but the term still captures the depth and intensity of change, as well as its modern legacy: high levels of formal religious practice, a professional and disciplined clergy, a centralised episcopal administration, direct control of Catholic education and a fervent allegiance to Rome. This remarkable process, which made the Irish people practising Catholics 'within a generation',[18] was a local manifestation of the global offensive orchestrated by a resurgent papacy against the rival ideologies of liberalism, rationalism and scientism. 'The essence of their creed,' writes Hugh McLeod, 'was the combination of a highly dogmatic and anti-rationalist theology with a warmly emotional piety, and a preference for life within a Catholic ghetto, where the faith of the masses could be preserved from Protestant or rationalist contamination.'[19]

The new piety and devotionalism that swept across the wider Catholic world during the nineteenth century involved a decisive shift in religiosity from 'one of non-practice (in the Tridentine sense) to one, not only of habitual practice, but of a showy and flowery expression of Catholicism'.[20] In post-Famine Ireland it found its most visible expression in almost universal attendance at Sunday mass, something that had been characteristic only of the well-to-do, better-educated, urban and Anglicised parts of Irish society.[21] More Catholics regularly received communion and went to confession, while religious societies multiplied in numbers and membership. The clergy, meanwhile, established a much stronger influence over the Catholic populace, their role as 'holy men' vividly symbolised by the introduction of a distinctive clerical garb complete with Roman collar. More numerous and better trained, they were the core troops of Catholicism's civilising mission, intervening to curb the excesses of popular custom and tradition.[22] Priests captured and legitimised folk practices such as holy wells, pilgrimages and wakes, introduced new public rituals and encouraged lay participation in a range of newly popular Roman devotional cults: the *Quarant'ore* (or Forty Hours' Devotion), the recitation of the rosary, the Stations of the Cross (*via crucis*), reparations to the Sacred Heart, making novenas, blessed altars, benediction, vespers, shrines and retreats. These extra-liturgical exercises were reinforced by the promotion of such devotional aids as beads, holy pictures, prayer books, catechisms and scapulars; they were further enhanced by the reinvigoration of worship, which explored the senses through candles, flowers, music, embroidered vestments and the odours of beeswax and incense.[23] Yet clerical authority had its limits. Some unorthodox supernatural beliefs survived in rural areas well into the twentieth century; others like cures, visions and miracles were creatively woven into official Catholic teaching.[24] Older forms co-existed with newer practices, as is so often the case, and the Irish countryside was never entirely disenchanted, as the survival of fairy-lore illustrates.[25]

The growing effectiveness of Catholicism in Ireland owed much to the seismic shifts that altered the socio-cultural landscape after the Famine years: the cataclysmic population losses from disease and starvation, which decimated the rural poor and left intact a stronger devotional nucleus of respectable tenant farmers; the continuation of mass emigration; the confessional framework of local politics; changing work patterns and material circumstances; and, lastly, the models of Victorian middle-class morality and respectability adopted by an increasingly dominant post-Famine élite.[26] The role of Paul Cullen, the influential Archbishop of Armagh (1849–52) and Dublin (1852–78), was also crucial in stamping the new discipline and devotion of the wider Catholic world on the Irish church. Nor should we underestimate the renewed importance of sectional rivalries. In some respects, the 'devotional revolution' represented 'Catholicism's equivalent of the Second Reformation'.[27] Marianne Elliot has argued persuasively that religious change was partly driven by 'fears of proselytising' and tended to focus on the kinds of behaviour 'most criticised by Protestant reformers' and those that reinforced negative stereotypes of Catholics.[28] The increasing polarisation of faith and political life, which grew apace in the late nineteenth century, was expressed in a new kind of ecclesiastical building. Before the Famine, the Catholic church's arrival as a powerful force in the landscape had been foreshadowed by a great surge in church-building and an explosion in the number of convents, schools and monasteries.[29] The churches built after 1850, however, were often larger and more lavishly decorated affairs; their towering Gothic spires, rich ornamentation and continental references symbolised the new Catholic triumphalism and heightened Protestant anxieties.[30] In *Occasions of Faith*, an anthropological study of Irish Catholicism in south-west Donegal, Lawrence Taylor relates this process to the centralising initiatives of an ultramontane clergy and the wider international interests of the church. Hence in this region, and elsewhere on the island, 'two "regimes", Catholic and colonial, were engaged, to some extent, in the same geographical project'.[31]

The dramatic transformation of Catholic religious practice in the nineteenth century was mirrored by changes across the great sectarian divide. Irish Protestants, too, underwent a fundamental shift in religious experience, which was characterised by higher rates of church-going, the spread of new models of 'civility', the decline of certain older folk practices, an emphasis on the conversion of individual believers and an investment in new material resources and personnel. The Church of Ireland, for example, underwent 'a three-stage evolution' that eventually created a more efficient organisational structure, a richer devotional life and a far greater role for laity in the management of its institutions.[32] Methodism made rapid strides in the late eighteenth and early nineteenth centuries, especially in areas like south-west Ulster, which had relatively large Anglican populations. Presbyterian congregations, on the other hand, were energised by a series of internal disputes and reunions, alongside the electrifying impact of evangelicalism.[33] The powerful appeal of this brand of religious expression was dramatically revealed in the Great Revival of 1859, sparked by reports from the United States, which spread quickly through parts of eastern Ulster.[34] Many of the new converts in the towns and rural areas were ordinary workers, who responded to the fiery oratory of the street preachers and their prophetic visions 'with prostrations, cries, groans, weeping and speaking in tongues'.[35] This extraordinary outburst of religious enthusiasm may later have subsided, but it illustrates some of the most important developments within Irish Protestantism and draws attention to its wider international influences. The demand for exciting open-air evangelism, the 'gripping emotionalism', the mass experience of conversion and the appealing combination of 'transcendental mysticism' and the new puritanism were all part of the rise and spread of popular Protestantism in many parts of Europe.[36] Unlike Irish Catholics, however, Irish Protestants did not become 'increasingly homogeneous' and remained 'a complex coalition of disparate elements: gentry and professional Church of Irelandism, respectable evangelicalism, fierce popular revivalism, and much else besides'.[37] Nonetheless, the greater assertiveness of the post-Famine Catholic church accelerated the emergence of a defensive pan-Protestant identity, especially in Ulster, where these developments fuelled existing tensions and reinforced patterns of religious segregation.[38]

The broad picture of religious change sketched above obscures the uneven spread of reform across a society in which conditions varied markedly, often over short distances. In Belfast, for example, the reorganisation of the Catholic church along ultramontane lines was not fully accomplished until the episcopacy of Patrick Dorrian, the Bishop of Down and Connor (1865–85).[39] Some western dioceses like Raphoe meandered slowly toward ecclesiastical modernity. At parish level, however, there were important variations. The reorientation of the spiritual sphere in Killybegs, in south-west Donegal, took place before the Famine;[40] nearly 20 years later, in neighbouring Carrick, the 'powerful and hot tempered' Father Charles MacNeely led the church's 'civilising offensive', on one occasion demolishing a pub with his bare hands.[41] Differences in the timing and completeness of changes in religious practice and pastoral activity were also evident within Protestantism. The impact of Methodist itinerants, as we have seen, was minimal outside the strongly Church of Ireland areas of Ulster such as northern Armagh. There was significant devotional change among Ulster Presbyterians in the nineteenth century, but even here the wider tendencies should not obscure divisions of class: weekly worship better matched 'the schedules, wardrobes and residential patterns' of well-to-do than working-class adherents, some of whom defected to smaller sects or became 'careless'.[42]

So migrants were not an undifferentiated whole, and, in fact, brought with them a wide array of religious experiences. As we saw in Chapter 2, most people moving to the West Coast goldfields were seasoned colonials who had confronted a new and unfamiliar spiritual landscape in Australia. These men and women left distant parishes during the first decade after the Famine; they were a mobile, literate and experienced group, drawn predominantly, though not exclusively, from the 'critical nation-forming class' at home.[43] Their families were likely to have espoused the kinds of religious practices and devotions associated with the Cullenite church and its civilising efforts. Many had probably witnessed the excitement and emotional power of parochial missions, participated in local pilgrimages or heard the incendiary millenarianism of lay preachers at open-air meetings. Others, like the Notown identity Patrick Gillin (Plate 19), recalled the sound of Orange drumbeats during the marching season in Belfast and the nasty sectarian feuds that raged across parts of the town.[44] On a personal level, all migrants, regardless of denomination, needed to adapt these beliefs, practices and memories to the changing conditions they encountered along the ocean fringes of the mining frontier.

As we shall see in the next section, there were striking contrasts between religious life in Ireland and on the West Coast goldfields, even though they shared wider international influences. The strength and distribution of the principal denominations, the physical circumstances of worship, the mixture of nationalities in congregations and among church professionals, the novelty of irreligion and the benign nature of communal relations: all these were key areas of difference in the colouration of faith.

II

A quick glance at the census information presented in Table 5.1 shows that Roman Catholics always had a strong presence on the West Coast, even though their share of the population fell from one-third in the 1860s to a quarter by 1916. The corresponding percentages for Presbyterians, who constituted about one-sixth of local residents, displayed a far greater consistency over time. There were small numbers of Wesleyan Methodists in the goldfields community, as well as a significant minority not attached to any of the main denominations. Predictably, Anglicans were the largest religious category, but they made up less than two-fifths of the region's inhabitants during the entire period under consideration. These general figures obscure localised concentrations – we can find small clusters of Wesleyan Methodists at Brunnerton and Jews in Hokitika and Kumara – yet the overall picture seems clear. The mining frontier was a religiously plural world in which adherents of the major denominations were widely dispersed across the settled districts of Buller and Westland.

Table 5.1 Religious affiliations of West Coast's female population, 1867–1916

	1867	1878		1886		1896		1906		1916	
	%	N	%	N	%	N	%	N	%	N	%
Roman Catholic	32.6	3460	36.7	3887	35.5	4102	32.2	4454	31.1	4160	26.5
Episcopalian	34.0	3490	37.0	3737	34.1	4692	36.9	5835	40.7	5876	37.5
Presbyterian	14.3	1308	13.9	1813	16.6	2014	15.8	2297	16.0	2678	17.1
Wesleyan	?	546	5.8	774	7.1	1027	8.1	918	6.4	1241	7.9
Baptists	?									1729	
Other	?	626	6.6	735	6.7	893	7.0	838	5.8		11.0
Totals		9430		10,946		12,728		14,342		15,684	

Sources: *Census of New Zealand*, 1878–1916.

The sudden arrival of a large and restless population on the diggings created new pastoral problems for colonial churches, which moved early to establish nomadic ministries, build places of worship and organise formal institutional structures. In one sense, these efforts were further instances of a 'civilising offensive', this time against the unruly behaviour of the 'noisy, dirty, drinking, smoking, cursing crowd',[45] whose 'lamentable spiritual destitution' so vexed the *Lyttelton Times*.[46] The effectiveness of missionary endeavour, however, owed a great deal to the initiatives of lay individuals and local building committees.[47] Henry William Harper, the Archdeacon of Westland and first resident Anglican clergyman, neatly captured the flavour of these activities after his arrival at Hokitika in 1866:

I found an energetic committee established; a small, four-roomed cottage ready for me; a large rough wooden church, just completed, both standing in amongst huge stumps of pine trees lately fallen, a most picturesque scene, with tents and miners' huts wherever there was a little clear space; all encircled by a background of magnificent forest . . . To your eyes All Saints would seem an ecclesiastical barn, with its rough open roof, unlined wooden walls, and no chancel. But it is spacious and well-cared for, and well attended.[48]

The erection of 'barn chapels' along these lines was repeated across the West Coast by the main denominations: we can think here of the Wesleyan churches at Hokitika and Kaniere (1865), or St Patrick's Church (1865) and school (1866) in Greymouth.[49] Few lay men and women matched the resourcefulness of Patrick Gillin. According to local memory, he was given permission to finance and build a church for Notown and its outlying districts by the French Marist Bishop of Wellington, Philippe Viard.[50] The timber, iron and other materials were shipped from Auckland, barged 12 miles up the Grey River to Kamaka, and delivered to their final destination by horse and sleigh at a total cost of £254.[51] The old wooden church, first assembled in 1866, has been beautifully restored at Shantytown, where it gives visitors a strong sense of the physical circumstances of worship on the diggings.[52]

The distinctive architecture of local religion is also powerfully conveyed by contemporary photographs. Plate 20, taken in the late 1860s, shows the newly constructed Catholic church in Goldsborough. St Michael's stands on the edge of the township, close to the bush and the slopes beyond, yet it matches the personality of its rickety surroundings. The makeshift appearance, the kitset joinery, the wooden piles and corrugated iron roofing were all typical features of goldfields churches. This wide pattern made for some degree of outward uniformity, regardless of denomination, as we can see in Plates 21 to 23, which depict, respectively, the barn chapels at Addison's (St Patrick's, Catholic), Ross (St John's, Presbyterian) and Rimu (St Mary's, Catholic). Some churches, like the Catholic All Saints in Barrytown, toppled in a storm,[53] needed to be replaced or fell into disrepair as congregations dwindled. Others defied the ravages of time and weather to survive. St Patrick's Catholic Church at Kumara, for example, still stands on the site that Archbishop Francis Redwood celebrated in his published memoirs:

> The Catholic acre-section was pointed out to me. It was just after Christmas, and I said to the Catholics: 'If you will hurry up some sort of church, fit for service, I will come on the next St. Patrick's day to bless and open it.' 'We will, we will,' shouted Mick Houlahan; 'we will, your Lordship, you shall have it without fail.' Next St. Patrick's Day I was there, and so was the church, that is, the shell of a building unlined, which was afterwards lined and finished interiorly, and is the identical church of this day. Under the enthusiastic influence of Mick Houlahan – a brewer whose excellent beer I had tasted at Stafford Town, and who had transferred his business in whole or in part to Kumara – the people contrived to have the trees felled and sawn on the spot, and had a magnificent space cleared and prepared for the church, away from all the danger of falling trees.[54]

The grand church buildings in the three main port towns came much later and left a mixed legacy, from the splendid and highly visible St Mary's Catholic Church in Hokitika to the outworn imperial grandeur of the old parish properties around Greymouth.[55]

The internal decoration of most local churches was lacking in ostentation, as we might expect, but the evidence from Catholic parish returns show that they held a modest range of devotional artefacts. The chapel at Brunnerton, for example, built for £630 and opened in 1886, contained confession boxes, pews, one set of vestments of each colour, one monstrance (for the Exposition of the Blessed Sacrament), a chalice, two statues – the Virgin Mary and St Joseph – and a portable altar.[56] Congregants at Addison's Flat, Charleston and Westport were confronted by the powerful imagery of the Crucifixion,[57] while those attending St Patrick's in Greymouth carried out their devotions under the gaze of the Irish patron saint and the Sacred Heart.[58] The role of this devotional paraphernalia was promoted through the symbolic performance of sacramental power in the mass, the theatre of the Benediction and the emotional recitation of the Public Rosary. It was also reinforced by the establishment of formal lay organisations. The Confraternity of the Living Rosary became widespread on the West Coast, no doubt reflecting the popularity of 'an ultramontane and Irish devotion *par excellence*'.[59] Aside from the Hibernians, there were a number of Catholic societies active in the region, including the Children of Mary, the Apostleship of Prayer, the Holy Family, the Sacred Heart of Jesus, altar guilds and the Holy Angels.[60] The parish returns are not sufficiently detailed to assess their significance in local religious life or to explore tantalising questions about the connections between gender and piety,[61] but they do reveal the institutional development of ultramontane Catholicism: the devotional revolution, it seems, continued along the mining frontier.

The civilising mission of colonial churches was complicated by the isolation of many settlements and the habitual mobility of the diggers. Writing from Reefton, Father Michael Cummins lamented that all around his parish

> there are little digging townships with a Catholic population – but too far and the way too difficult for them to meet in one place for mass – as Boatmans & Larrys – neither of them have chapel or school as yet – Lyell – central place, second in importance . . . is a fearful place both naturally and supernaturally speaking – the people are drunken, immoral and boisterous, no proper hotel, no chapel, no school and nothing done towards either . . . it is full of nominal Catholics of all nations and deserves no other name than little hel [*sic*]. There is much good to be done, but the large and dangerous rivers and frost and snow melting, where with two and three feet wide tracks, we have to ride 1700 feet above a river or precipice, render it difficult for me to attend to all alone.[62]

The novelty of mixed congregations and 'irreligion', real or imagined, only added to the troubles of newly arrived priests unaccustomed to life in the colonies. The ebb and flow of people, the demanding nature of travel and the vicissitudes of the local economy created further obstacles, even after the heady rushes of the 1860s. By the late 1890s, Father Denis O'Hallahan reported that many Kumara residents had chosen to abandon a district 'going down headforemost' for Western Australia, Auckland and other places:

All the young and single men are nearly left for the simple reason that they can get 'nothing to do' here so they have to go and look for something elsewhere. Then again young girls can get no situation, as those in business have to do their work for themselves and the consequence is that they also have to leave for Greymouth, Reefton, Nelson and Wellington.[63]

Small wonder, then, that Catholic clergy struggled to bring adequate levels of pious instruction to the region. Substantial progress was made in providing parochial education, which received no state funding and depended on the munificence of local congregants. Despite hard times, teachers at Kumara were paid through seat rents, the proceeds of annual concerts, weekly church offertories and 'a big donation from the priest to make up any deficit'.[64] Similar strategies were adopted elsewhere. Writing from Greymouth in 1889, Father Denis Carew told John Grimes, the first Bishop of Christchurch (which included the West Coast), that schools had been supported 'for about twelve years by rents for Church seats. And after many other ways have been tried this has been the Easiest and Most Efficacious way to maintain them.'[65] The available evidence does not allow reliable estimates of the number of children attending these institutions, but priests and bishops seemed generally satisfied with their quality and attendance.[66] The enormous investment in private schooling, however, added credence to their complaint that the 1877 Education Act had forced Catholics to subsidise the 'godless' education of others through state taxation while they received no subsidies for themselves or their children.[67]

The men and women on the mining frontier encountered an array of church professionals and preachers. Like the diggers and their entourage, most early missionaries were seasoned colonials with many years of service in parts of Australia and New Zealand. Thus Philippe Aime Martin, the long-serving Rector of Hokitika (1868–1905), spent time on both sides of the Tasman before his transfer to St Mary's Church in 1868.[68] The same was true for his predecessor, Father John McGirr, formerly a chaplain with the 18th Royal Irish in India, while his colourful assistants, Stephen McDonough and William Larkin, arrived from Brisbane.[69] Even the well-heeled Archdeacon Harper, educated at Eton and Merton College (Oxford), and eldest son of the first Anglican Bishop of Christchurch, had lived in Canterbury since 1856. These colonial experiences promoted tolerant views of the diggers and their 'upside-down world'. Harper observed that the mining community was 'remarkable for a generous spirit of comradeship, ever ready to help each other'. His pastoral work forced him to revise some of the ideas acquired from his readings of the Californian and Australian rushes. The miners, he remarked, were educated and well travelled, 'lusty, powerful fellows, given to occasional sprees . . . rowdy, but honest and free from crime'.[70] Father Nicholas Binsfeld, a Marist priest from Luxembourg, echoed these sentiments in his handwritten memoirs: 'Though they were a gathering of all nationalities they lived together in harmony, and entertained fellow feelings toward one another. The Russian Charley, the Norwegian Jensen and the German Michael felt themselves at home as much as Pat or Tommy Atkinson.'[71] In a cosmopolitan environment, with no established church, the profession of faith was considered a private matter, beyond external interference and religious suspicions of the Old World.

The curious amalgam of church professionals and people was visible within local Catholicism, where the Society of Mary, a French religious order, exercised episcopal control. In 1849 *Congregatio de propaganda fide*, the Vatican department with administrative responsibility for missionary areas, ended a long dispute between Bishop Jean-Baptiste François Pompallier and the Marist General, Father Jean-Claude Colin, by dividing authority in New Zealand at the 39th degree of latitude.[72] The Marists were sent to the newly created diocese of Wellington, encompassing half of the North Island and the whole of the South Island, while Pompallier was established in the diocese of Auckland with responsibility for the Maori mission. This instruction placed his former assistant, Philippe Viard, in charge of an extensive southern pastorate with a rapidly expanding population.[73] Despite a shortage of clerical manpower, he lost no time in dispatching priests to the diggings and recruited widely – though not always wisely – for his diocesan regime. Like his successors, Redwood in Wellington and Grimes in Christchurch, Viard considered a pervasive 'Irishness' incidental to the pastoral work of the Church. The Society of Mary did bring a stream of Irish Marists to New Zealand from its seminaries in Dundalk and Dublin in the 1860s.[74] But all three Marist bishops envisioned a thriving *local* religion fashioned along ultramontane lines, an aspiration that led them to resist attempts to impose Irish definitions on the colonial scene. This approach did little to ease tensions between Marist and secular priests (mainly from All Hallows College in Dublin) over the control and direction of the New Zealand church. Unlike the English Benedictines in Australia, however, the Society of Mary was not easily superseded by a rival tradition of Roman-Irish bishops and ultra-Irish clerics.[75]

This state of affairs had profound implications for the kind of Catholicism that developed on the West Coast. The Marist order had set out to build a church that was well adapted to its immediate surroundings and part of a much wider spiritual empire than the one seen from Dublin. Their critics, led by Patrick Moran, the confrontational Bishop of Dunedin (1871–95), accused them of negligence in their administration of the colonial mission. They decried what they saw as the disarray of religious practice, the scarcity of institutional structures and the pastoral efforts of 'foreign' priests, who 'satisfied themselves with saying their prayers'.[76] These harsh judgments depended as much upon faith as evidence: a church ruled by Irish bishops and clergy would be a powerful entity capable of rescuing neglected migrant souls. Yet we should resist the superficially appealing view that French Marist churchmen were unable to achieve the degree of sympathy and reverence that laity reserved for Irish priests.[77] The saintly Jean Baptiste Rolland, for example, attained the status of 'heroic priest' in Reefton and its outlying districts on account of his curing activities and extensive travels with a 'Mass Kit' strapped to his saddle-front.[78] Others, like Emmanuel Royer, John Peter Chareyre and Eugene Pertius generated fierce loyalties among local parishioners. Even when tensions between Irish and French clergy led to discord, as they did at Ahaura in 1899 over the question of Irish nationalism, many congregants supported the latter.[79] The French clerical presence and its high standard of spiritual care and personal conduct were fondly recalled into the twentieth century. Writing from Greymouth in 1921, Patrick O'Farrell's father noted that 'some of the old veterans' wept at mass as 'the Marist Fathers were making their last farewell' and he 'darned near' cried himself. But their departure also had its lighter moments: 'While communion was on Jack Murphy who was standing longside me, was looking out the door with his back turned to the altar. One of the Horans sang out "You are looking the wrong way Jack" & everyone in the porch nearly exploded. It sounded so funny & Jack did a right about turn in double quick time & looked a fool to be sure.'[80]

The 'selfless missionary dedication' of the French priests, epitomised by the image of Father Paul Aubrey, 'his coat off & over his shoulder . . . hitting the track great', contrasted with the swaggering arrogance of the Irish seculars.[81] Most of the latter were All Hallows men, products of a missionary institution energised by Irish nationalism and a charismatic education.[82] The problem, however, was that many were unsuited, by background, training and temperament, to the colonial scene. Drink was the most frequent cause for complaint. Father Matthias McManus was 'not safe to be at large' and said mass at Nelson Creek 'with a face as scratched as if ten cats operated on it for some minutes'. After a spree in Greymouth, he tried to break into the bedroom of Denis Carew's young domestic servant; on another he was rolling drunk at the altar of the Marsden church.[83] Some of his secular colleagues had reputations as heavy-handed bullies; others aired grievances against their bishops from the pulpit or drank so much that they could not say mass. Various incidents and escapades had disciplinary consequences: John McGirr appeared in court charged with assaulting a Catholic school teacher in Hokitika;[84] Michael O'Laverty was accused of indecencies with 'a girl in Maori Gully Church' and given his *exeat*;[85] the 'troublesome' Finnerty, a curate at Greymouth, brought liquor back to his room 'almost every day, and whilst under the influence howls, shouts and sings, [*and*] also has performed semilunatic acts such as lighting very large fires in his bedroom [*and*] leaving them in full blaze when going'.[86] There were, of course, exceptions to this pattern. Monsignor James ('the Mons') Long, born in Limerick and educated at Minchin's College and the Thurles Seminary, County Tipperary, won deep and enduring affection as the parish priest of Greymouth from 1921 to 1963.[87] The same was true in an earlier time for Thomas Walshe, a Mooncoin-born graduate of All Hallows College, who gave five decades of service to Westport from 1867 to 1920. Yet these men were not entirely representative of a wider group that included far too many of those described by Father Denis Carew as 'broken down drunken clergymen'.[88]

There were, too, failures of imagination that sometimes blighted Irish pastoral activities. In his widely acclaimed study *Vanished Kingdoms* (1990), Patrick O'Farrell convincingly argues that many Irish clerics sent to colonies assumed 'that Irish birth, even Irish descent, meant shared attitudes in everything. A common religion to them implied, unthinkingly, a common attitude to Ireland and things Irish.' But this 'paralysing delusion' was based on a fundamental misunderstanding of colonial realities:

A very little thought might have discerned that beneath the green trappings and clichés and docility and the apparent deference, this was not an Irish laity. These were people who had left Ireland for something Ireland could not give. Not just for prosperity – that was to see skin-deep. But for what went with that: freedom, security, confidence, independence, a whole range of attitudes, styles and outlooks the clergy did not encounter in Ireland, and

simply did not recognise in what they automatically presumed was Ireland
once again – because, arrogance of arrogances, they were there. Wherever
they were, was Ireland: the English had taught the insolence of imperialism
better than they knew.[89]

The Sisters of Mercy never succumbed to this 'imaginative blindness' in
Westland, rapidly adapting their foundations to staff parochial schools, visit
the sick and take an active role in local community life. Nor did it blunt
the work of Irish Marists like Denis Carew, the respected parish priest of
Greymouth (1884–1917) and 'forthright scourge' of the region's wayward
seculars.[90] Some of his countrymen, however, were less tolerant, even
toward their co-religionists. Denis O'Hallahan made disparaging remarks
in his parish returns about the Italian-speaking Catholics from Canton
Ticino and the Poschiavino Valley in Switzerland who clustered together
at Kumara and Waimea. 'Those "foreigners"', he told Bishop Grimes,
'are only nominal Catholics, and more a disgrace than an acquisition to
Catholicity here.'[91] Michael Cummins sought prayers for the 'unfortunate
Souls' he encountered at 'the wretched Lyell', contrasting them with the
farming families of the Matakitaki that had not been 'tainted by Colonial
ways'.[92] The formidable Father James O'Donnell of Ahaura, on the other
hand, fought battles on several fronts, including a personal one with alcohol,
organising a petition for a secular bishop at Christchurch which resulted in
his removal and demotion.[93] Whatever their reaction to these machinations,
many Catholics had little enthusiasm for 'distant replicas' of Ireland on
the goldfields; they complained frequently about the conduct of drunken
priests, made efforts to minimise the consequences of scandal and, above
all, appreciated good spiritual care when it was given.

The fluid social structure, the absence of hostile native-born élites, the
rough egalitarianism of the digging population and the small size of mining
localities blurred the lines of social distinction and created an atmosphere of
religious toleration. This was apparent in the way that friendships, mining
parties and business ventures transcended the boundaries of religion and
nationality. The cosmopolitan environment made for alliances scarcely
imaginable within the 'completely separate worlds' of religion, ideology
and social practice in Irish society.[94] We can think here of the proprietors
of the Union Hotel at Notown, who came from different sides of the great
divide: Samuel Haisty was a Presbyterian from Kildare, County Antrim,

married to a Catholic, Susan Hanlon; his partner, John Flynn, born in Ballyvaughan, County Galway, and educated in England, received a private income from a wealthy uncle. According to oral tradition, Flynn was rescued from destitution after the death of his parents during the Famine, a loss he commemorated by lighting a single candle each evening. He achieved the status of local notable, prominent in Catholic affairs, a member of the Westland Education Board and secretary of the Grey Valley Miners' Benefit Society.[95] Flynn's low-key 'Irishness', his willingness to embrace a plural environment and his attachment to a particular locality were typical of the responses that migrants made to their rapidly changing social world.

The nature of communal relations on the West Coast has been subjected to a thorough analysis by Neil Vaney, who paints a cheerful portrait of the local scene. His research shows that although religious tensions led to conflict in a small number of cases, we should take care not to overstate their extent and importance. It is significant that when controversies arose, as they did over Catholic teachings on intermarriage during the visit of the transient Irish missionary Patrick Hennebery of the Society of the Precious Blood, the outcome was vigorous debate rather than violence, with both sides appealing to notions of fairness and tolerance.[96] Vaney's most telling example of cultural pluralism, however, was to be found in death: the great funeral processions for church professionals like Father John Colomb or Reefton's Sister Gertrude were public occasions attended by 'people and ministers of all denominations'.[97] But this was also the wider regional pattern. The 'mournful cortege' which accompanied Bridget Mitchell (née Hannan) from Goldsborough to the Stafford Cemetery in 1880 'was one of the largest' in the district 'as nearly every man and women in the two places and a large number from town followed the remains of the deceased'.[98] A big crowd formed behind Patrick Doody's coffin as it was carried out of St Patrick's Church and 'passed down Third Street, Seddon Street, and Main Street, still keeping the Zigzag Road to the Teremakau punt, where three boats were in readiness to convey people across the River to the Westbrooke Road'. His body lay for a short period at a private residence before continuing its journey by hearse, the long march 'joined by other friends with numerous horsemen included, on it's [sic] way to Marsden, where a large contingent of men coming from Maori Gully, Maori Creek, and the New River District (where the deceased was well known) would meet the funeral'. Doody's obituary described him as a 'notable figure' in the mining community and a man of 'wide acquaintance': 'and to the old land gave in birth, he lived and died a worthy son'. The 'old land' here implied more than 'former'.[99] There was affection for Doody's 'warm heart' 'generous nature' and 'powerful agile frame', all of which the writer attributed to his Celtic origins.[100] Yet he was a loss to his immediate locality, to the here and now, to a dynamic new world free of the 'old' hatreds and walled stockades.

The ecumenical flavour suggested by the funerary evidence is reinforced in the writings of travelling clergy. Nicholas Binsfeld recalled that 'at times non-Catholics would vie with my own in offering gratuitous hospitality'. The arrangement could sometimes lead to embarrassment, as it did on one occasion at Moonlight Creek: 'I solved the difficulty by giving my horse to the Catholic party, whilst I took up my abode with the kind-hearted Protestant host'.[101] This easy acceptance found expression in the local custom of providing free accommodation to clergy as they rode from place to place.[102] It was also revealed by the tradition of giving visiting churchmen 'a show' on the diggings and the way in which their visits turned into major community events.[103] Such was the case when Archbishop Redwood's coach arrived at Piper's Hill, a place so named 'because an Irish piper, an artist in his way, used to play for the pleasure of the passengers as they partook of some refreshments'. A large crowd gathered there to meet him. To his eyes, they were 'as fine a body of men' as he had ever seen – 'tall, well-set, stalwart fellows of all classes and denominations, to the number of about 800, marching in double file. It was one of the heartiest and grandest receptions I ever had in my life, and none did I appreciate and remember with greater satisfaction.'[104]

The pattern of relative harmony continued into the twentieth century, as Patrick O'Farrell has attested in his recollections of Catholic Greymouth:

> I can recall the closeness of this world, but I do not see it as a ghetto. I was never conscious of sectarianism, nor do I think there was much. The economic realities and the community structures were against it. The town was small and everyone knew each other. It was economically homogeneous, with very few if any residents who were really rich, or even affluent. So it was not so much the church which provided social cement, as the town itself.[105]

A number of competing loyalties and influences militated against the formation of ethnic alignments or religious exclusiveness:

The Labour Party and the trade unions cut across any religious divisions. Many of our closest friends were non-Catholics. These were mostly friends from proximity, neighbours, but there were also friends from the Labour Party, or from my father's work. If there was any hostility from Catholics towards other religions, it had a personal direction: I recall one Anglican vicar who was actively disliked, as being a bigot.[106]

In a society which placed such a strong ideological emphasis on harmony and co-operation, the actions of those who inflamed prejudice or old grievances received wide condemnation and marked them as outsiders. It was a lesson that the Catholic church learned during the Fenian controversies of the nineteenth century, when an Irish priest, Father William Larkin, was imprisoned for sedition (see Chapter 6).

III

Historians have analysed attendance at church services to ascertain levels of religious adherence in the past. On the basis of the New Zealand census returns, Hugh Jackson has estimated that about one-quarter of the adult population were regular churchgoers during the late nineteenth century. There were some regional and urban-rural differences in rates of attendance, but the margins were much less than in Britain. When he turned his attention to the denominational statistics, however, Jackson uncovered more striking variations. Of the main religious bodies in the colony, Anglicans had the lowest levels of churchgoing (24.5 per cent in 1891), compared with a larger proportion of Presbyterians (48.0 per cent) and Catholics (58.3 per cent); the adherents of Methodism, on the other hand, led the way in their attendance at public worship (93.5 per cent). The overall percentage of those who went to church in New Zealand on Sunday (28.0 per cent) lagged behind the figures recorded for Victoria (66.0 per cent in 1890) and New South Wales (45.0 per cent). It also fell short of the rates revealed by the enumerators' returns for England and Wales in 1851 (35.0 per cent). 'The churchgoing of New Zealanders,' Jackson concluded, 'was mediocre by the standards of the British at home.'[107]

The census statistics for Westland show that church attendance was at the higher end of the provincial scale (28.0 per cent in 1891) and equal to the levels in Otago and Southland.[108] But the Registrar-General's figures are silent on denominational rates below the national summaries. We can glean some information about local Catholicism from the available parish returns, which suggest that many were not scrupulous in fulfilling their obligation to go to weekly mass. Nonetheless, most Catholics carried out the minimum canonical requirement to confess and receive communion at least once a year. In Hokitika, Father Martin reported 2200 communicants from the Catholic population of 650, with only '12 refraining from the sacraments'.[109] Few 'remained away' when they could attend church in Ross, while the parish priest at Ahaura attributed the small numbers who did not perform their Easter duty 'more to the isolated position of some of the districts than to sheer neglect'.[110] The proportion of non-communicants was greater in Westport and Greymouth than elsewhere, a pattern that is easier to establish than explain.[111] Presumably distance prevented some diggers from attending Sunday mass; others simply ignored the obligation 'except in years of missions when very few stayed away'.[112]

The historical evidence on churchgoing in Buller and Westland gives, at best, a loose approximation of religious adherence. We are no closer to understanding the beliefs and motives of the migrant folk who went to church regularly or their counterparts who did not. Some intimate aspects of faith are found in surviving migrant correspondence, which invariably employed 'the idiom of religion'.[113] In a letter to his grandniece in Montana, John O'Regan of Barrytown explained how the living were tied to the dead through their ability to influence the amount of time souls spent wandering in 'the third place':

Attend to your religious duties regular as you can and if you have a spare fifty cents give it to a priest to say a Mass for the poor forsaken souls in Purgatory. This is the greatest charity you can do. Assist those who can't help themselves. And this act of mercy is put down to your credit and more, your name is known in Heaven. Even one Hail Mary said for this purpose draws upon your head blessings and gives comfort and consoles where nothing else will. As for my poor self, hard hearted as I am, I never forget this act, particularly remembering those who are gone before me. Bear in mind that Purgatory may last to the end of the world.[114]

The themes of charitable giving and devotionalism also featured in the correspondence of the Flanagan brothers and their circle (see Chapter 3). Writing from Big Hill in Victoria, a deeply troubled Charles Fleming expressed gratitude for Michael Flanagan's munificence in language that owed much to the rhetoric of the pulpit: 'My Dearest, my only Friend, How shall I thank you – how shall I attempt to thank you – I will not attempt it. My head and heart are too full. But may God bless you from my heart of hearts. May God bless you. May the Lord of Heaven guied and save you, and may the Ever blessed Virgin Mary take you under her especial protection and watch over you through life.' His vulnerability to destitution prompted a moving jeremiad about the pitfalls of colonial marriage:

This is the prayer of your poor Broken friend. It is one Brother in fifty that would do for another Brother what you have done for me and my poor unfortunate little family. Before I go farther let me beg and beseech of you never under any circumstances to entertain for one moment the Idea of marying in these Colonies until you are in an independent position. Let me tell you – what sad, sad experience has taught me that all the grief, anguish and misery, that could be endured by a single man is as nothing compared to the excruciating anguish of seeing your loved little children in want. Oh may you or your family never experience any thing of the sort.[115]

The positive tone of Fleming's next surviving letter suggests that these difficulties had eased and its enclosures reveal much about the transfer of material resources from the region to distant parishes in Ireland:

The other day I happened to see The Nation Newspaper of the 11th January it contained an advertisement from 'The Rev Patrick Mackey of Glenarm Co Antrim thankfully acknowledging the receipt of 120.15.0 from 'Fox diggings new Zealand'. The money was said to have been collected by a Mr David McAuley and was for the purpose of Building a New Church in Glenarm. Amongst the names of subscribers there appears that of 'Michael Flanagan' and I suppose you are the charitable individual.[116]

The same preoccupations that David Fitzpatrick discovered in Irish-Australian letters were evident on the West Coast: injunctions of piety as a 'symbol of community' for separated kinsfolk; the representation of Catholicism as a 'visible institution' rather than an 'abstract faith', few hints of sectarian tension; and a concern with the virtues of sobriety, industriousness, honesty and fidelity. We cannot begin to understand the ways that migrants made sense of their world unless we grasp its larger trans-Tasman dimensions.

The affirmation of faith expressed in migrant correspondence was echoed in the extant probate records. As we have seen, most estates left by married or widowed decedents were too small to spread widely (see Chapter 3). William Glenn (d. 1913, £36,000), a Greymouth merchant who returned to Ulster, was a notable exception to the wider pattern. After providing for his immediate family and kinsfolk, he left £5 per annum to the Presbyterian Londonderry City Mission, the Londonderry District Nursing Society and the Presbyterian Sustentation fund, in addition to the £10 a year set aside for the Presbyterian Orphan Society.[117] At the other end of the scale, the Nine Mile farmer and miner Daniel Danahy (d. 1904, £99), willed his earthly property to his wife Catherine for life and then to their son or sons 'she may then think best entitled to receive it', the inheritor paying 8s to the parish priest at Charleston for Peter's Pence.[118] Some Catholics made bequests to their local churches, but the overriding testamentary concern seems to have been the welfare of spouses, the preservation of property and the future education of children.

Single men were much more likely to leave money for religious or charitable purposes. Nelson Creek miner Thomas O'Rourke (d. 1902, £600) stipulated that all his property was to be sold and no more than £80 used 'in connection with my wake and funeral and the erection of a suitable tombstone and railing around my grave'.[119] He gave £20 for masses and left his residual estate to his three siblings in Gurtduff. James Quillinan (d. 1902, £341) left £15 to procure masses 'for me and my distant relatives' and £10 each to the Sisters of Mercy and the Grey River and Reefton Hospitals.[120] After making bequests to his sisters and mother, Edward Ryan of Gillespie's Beach (d. 1910, £2892) willed £3 to Mother Gabriel at St Columbkille's in Hokitika, £3 to the Mercy Convent in Ross and £2 10s to Father James O'Connor for a new chalice.[121] Few could match the generosity of John Tyrell (d. 1892, over £1000), the Dublin-born founder of the *Westport Times*, who left an annuity of £5 to 'the Female Orphan House in North Circular Road', £70 to various churches and an endowment of £600 'for the establishment of a Home to be erected in Westport for the succour, relief and comfort of the aged and needy of all or any denominations or creed'.[122] Yet the mixture of charities apparent here is also found in other wills. John Cummins (d. 1914, £600), for instance, left one-third of his estate to St Canice's School in Westport and one-third for masses, but granted the Mother Superior at St Mary's Convent the discretion to use the remainder to support 'any institution' in the town which had as 'any of its objects the maintenance or education of orphans or poor and needy children or the care and maintenance or relief of aged or helpless persons'.[123]

Although modest in number and value, the wills of migrant women contained a range of religious bequests. Ann Parsons of Greymouth (d. 1914, £200) willed £5 to the parish priest of Greymouth 'for masses for the repose of my soul and my late husband's', £5 for a 'new suit of clothes' to her son James and the remainder equally to her four daughters and 'Mary McGrath my granddaughter at present staying with me'.[124] By contrast, Cork-born Maria Anderson Pearce (d. 1909, £640) named a sister living in New South Wales as her residuary legatee and left £50 to John Robert Dart, the Anglican minister at Westport.[125] Other childless widows like Elizabeth Biel (d. 1901, £80), Ellen Doherty (d. 1895, £408) and Mary Rollini (d. 1896, £43) set aside substantial portions of their estates for various religious purposes.[126] The only single Catholic women who prepared wills were sisters Mary (d. 1909, £495) and Margaret Roche (d. 1912, £554) of Greymouth. Margaret instructed her executors, Father Denis Carew and John Deere, to convert her boarding house property into cash and pay £20 each to the priests of six parishes for masses for her sister. She left a sum of £50 to Mother Mary Aubert of Wellington's Home of Compassion, £10 to Mary Barry and the residuary estate to her cousin in Carrick-on-Suir, County Tipperary.[127]

Local churches presided over some of the most significant events in Irish women's lives. As in the United States, Canada, the Australian colonies and other parts of the British Empire, Catholic females were active participants in the globe-circling matrix of Catholic educational and religious networks that stretched out 'infinitely and in all directions'.[128] The development of parish churches, chapels, parochial schools and convents on the Coast after 1865, along with the growth of confraternities and mutual aid organisations, enveloped them in a powerful institutional structure. The reach of these networks of association was extraordinary, given the isolation of many mining communities. Parish returns show that poor communications prevented priests from regularly administering the sacraments to Catholics in remote districts and forced them to construct a series of stations in private households.[129] The supporting role played by women such as Mrs Warren at her residence in Barrytown, where Father Denis Carew celebrated mass for a number of 'forlorn diggers' from the mountains and beaches, was crucial in perpetuating Catholic religious practices in the region.[130] In some places, female parishioners competed with one another to provide accommodation for roving clergy, their success celebrated in names like 'The Bishop's Room' at Frances Sullivan's home in Stafford or 'His Grace's tea-set' in the possession of Ann Diamond's descendants.[131] Others gained considerable status by raising sons who became priests, while most ensured that their children were baptised, even though births were not always registered with the agencies of the state. On the other side of the religious divide, Protestant Irish women constituted a small but significant minority within the mixed congregations of the region's Anglican and Presbyterian churches. Although these migrants left behind far fewer records than their Catholic counterparts, we can still recover fragments of their life stories through family histories and the surviving registers of baptisms, marriages and burials. The extant materials are fragmented and difficult to interpret, but they do suggest that many Protestant women transposed from the Old World religious practices that connected them with various strands of British Protestantism and its global institutions.

A sympathetic understanding of the religious dimension to Irish women's lives on the West Coast does not obviate the need for proper critical scrutiny of power relations within local denominations. Among Catholics, for example, the religious experience was sharply divided on male/female lines, a pattern that found symbolic expression in the seating arrangements at mass in Greymouth as late as the 1940s: 'men on one side of the church, women on the other, men crowded in the church porch'.[132] But Irish women migrants were not merely passive ciphers manipulated by rigidly patriarchal churches or blind followers of tracts on blissful domesticity. When they arrived on the West Coast goldfields, Irish women confronted a volatile society marked by incessant social change, public drunkenness, high mobility and frequent isolation. Yet they exerted some degree of control over their circumstances and made sense of their lives through the selective appropriation and re-creation of religious practices, traditions and institutional connections from the Old World. These women resisted clerical bullies, protected the reputations of drunken priests and valued the high standard of spiritual care given by other clergy, as well as nuns and teaching brothers. They participated in wakes, baked for church fairs, assisted the poor and the sick, enrolled their children in an extensive system of parochial schools and helped to curb the worst excesses of the region's male drinking culture. On a more intimate level, however, personal faith enabled female migrants to cope with isolation and the pain of displacement. Perhaps the most enduring image of this deep religious sentiment is that provided by Mrs Jane Ryall of Barrytown, who walked the beach each night saying the rosary 'because she believed the breeze blew straight from Ireland' (Plate 24).[133]

A close look at the careers of two women underlines the centrality of religion in the lives of many migrants and illustrates the fluidity of social identities on the West Coast. Harriette Coates (*née* Trotter), a prominent Greymouth Anglican and philanthropist, was one of the first Irish women to settle in the region. Born in the parish of Mullingar, County Westmeath, Harriette married William James Coates of Abbeyshrule in 1850 and the couple embarked for the United States soon afterwards. We know very little about their experiences in New York, where they lived for two years. Presumably, the decision to carve out a new life in the colonies turned upon the powerful attractions of the Victorian goldfields. The prospect of freedom, adventure and independence in Australia may have also promised deliverance from the fierce sectarian rivalries, devastating epidemics and widespread pauperism that plagued Irish migrants in New York during the mid-nineteenth century. Whatever the reasons for their departure, the opportunities for personal and family advancement were far greater in Australia and New Zealand than along the eastern seaboard of the United States. William and Harriette spent the next nine years in Melbourne, where they made enough money to set up a small-scale mercantile operation servicing the needs of miners at Bendigo and Castlemaine. The couple sailed for the Otago goldfields in 1861 and followed the rush from there to the Grey River three years later. According to family tradition, they stayed under a tree during their first night in Westland, the discomfort partially ameliorated by a delicious meal of whitebait provided by storekeepers Reuben Waite and Isaac Blake. It was an inauspicious beginning to a long and eventful residence in Greymouth. Although the family continued its involvement in mercantile activities from the port-town, their ultimate ambition was to purchase good farmland. This aim was finally realised in the 1870s, when they took up property on the partly cleared flats at Blackwater, Omoto and Haupiri.[134]

No letters or other first-hand testimony survive to reveal what Harriette Coates thought about life in the colonies. We do know that she played an active role in building up the family business and reared several children, one of whom attended Christ's College and went on to become the mayor of Greymouth. The surviving evidence also shows that Harriette was deeply involved in church and community affairs. After arriving in the river-port, for example, she canvassed local residents and raised £500 for the erection of a small building that would serve as an interdenominational hall and an alternative refuge for sailors to the hotels and grog shanties that lined Richmond and Mawhera Quay. Harriette's voluntary work, her leadership in organising the combined churches' annual picnic and an episode where she lent silver candles to a French Marist priest, Stephen Hallum, for the first mass in the town, support the claim that she was 'an ecumenist ahead of her time'. Yet there was also something distinctly colonial about the enlightened Protestantism – 'politically liberal, religiously tolerant, socially inclusive' – that she espoused.[135] Like other migrant women, Harriette Coates embraced and reshaped this tradition to meet the challenges of everyday life on the goldfields, to help define the cultural contours of an 'extreme antipodes' in which the old divisions and hierarchies were irrelevant.[136] Her story demonstrates not only the importance of religious practice and belief for many migrants, whether Protestant or Catholic, but also the dynamism and variety of Irish experiences in the region.

Similar points can be made about Mai O'Farrell, the colonial-born daughter of Irish parents who married in Temuka, on the east coast of New Zealand's South Island, in 1881. We do not know why the family returned to her father's home in Borrisokane during Mai's childhood, but it is clear that most of her formative experiences took place in the church-oriented world of the local Tipperary parish. It was here that Mai received her education from the Sisters of Mercy, with whom she became a pupil-teacher and, by the age of 17, a member of the Apostleship of Prayer, the Sacred Heart of Jesus and the Arch-confraternity of the Blessed Sacrament.[137] She brought these complex devotions back to New Zealand in 1914, accompanied on the voyage by her sister, Chris, and an inscribed version of *Selections from the Publications of the Catholic Truth Society of Ireland*, a farewell gift from her parish priest in Borrisokane.[138] The circumstances surrounding their departure from Ireland remain obscure, but their immediate destination, South Canterbury, suggests that kinship networks were involved, a plausible assumption given the existence of family connections and friends in the vicinity of Timaru.[139] Similar ties were also important in facilitating the migration of her future husband's immediate family from Ballinderry, a village near Borrisokane. Patrick Farrell's maternal uncle, Peter Byrnes, had emigrated to Willowbridge many years before and employed the Farrell brothers, Jack and Michael, for a brief period after their arrival in 1911. One of their sisters, Hannah, settled in nearby Waimate, where they were joined by Patrick in 1913, and the two remaining siblings, Matt and Madge, seven years later. Although

Mai and Patrick had known each other in Ireland, they did not marry until 1920, at Rangiora, the parish of Father Matthew Fogarty, who was the groom's friend and a hurling team-mate in Tipperary.[140]

After her marriage, Mai left the familiar world of Waimate and travelled across the Southern Alps to Greymouth, where Patrick had been living since 1916. By this time, the chains of correspondence that spanned the oceans between Borrisokane and the distant colony, carrying news of marriages, deaths and other events, had begun to unravel: '[t]he old warmth, the flirting, the giggling at dances, was in the past – casualties of emigration . . . and of war'.[141] In its place, the 'unwelcome egalitarianism', the apparent crudity and the primitive domestic economy of the West Coast left Mai feeling bewildered and deeply distressed, at least initially. It was a reaction intensified by a dangerous pregnancy and the attitudes of some locals, who resented what they interpreted as signs of snobbery and disdain.[142] In response, she turned to the priests and nuns of the Greymouth Catholic church for friendship and understanding. The Sisters of Mercy had established a foundation in the town in 1882 and nuns from Borrisokane and its surrounding districts worked at the convent, including Sister Fabian, the sibling of Patrick's uncle, Peter Byrnes.[143] In the decades that followed, however, Mai's allegiance to Greymouth and the West Coast gradually deepened, becoming a loyalty that led to open acceptance within this remote colonial world. Mai seems to have become less thoroughly colonialised than Patrick, the trade unionist, Labour Party stalwart and Hibernian, who retained 'little respect or affection for the Ireland he had left'.[144] This difference was evident in their reading: Patrick preferred the *New Yorker* or *Punch* to the *Dublin Opinion*, eagerly devoured works by James Fenimore Cooper and enjoyed adventure novels; Mai identified more closely with heroines from an Irish female literary and political tradition, but her main interest was in the romance of these women's lives, 'rather than in their nationalism'.[145] Both felt an 'embarrassed unhappiness' at the intrusions of a young Irish curate who visited their home unexpectedly 'for tea and talk', opening the back door without knocking and yelling, 'in the broadest possible caricature brogue, "How'r ye living"!'[146] It is significant that by the time of Mai's death in 1970, it was 'merely a distant and irrelevant accident that she had come from Ireland long before. Few knew it, nobody cared'; like her daughter, Mary, cruelly taken by meningitis and buried in the Karoro cemetery, she was from Greymouth.[147]

IV

As the lives of these two women suggest, the formation of religion on the mining frontier was a complex phenomenon. Migrants did not simply transport a static set of traditions and practices across the oceans; rather, they made use of these tools in ways that reflected the cultural imperatives at work on the West Coast. Like other newcomers, Irish men and women reshaped older religious traditions to give meaning to their lives and the circumstances they encountered. The emergence of new religious sensibilities on the West Coast owed much to objects, beliefs and languages from the past, but it is hard to envision the splendid wooden churches at Boatman's and Stafford, now long vanished along with their mixed congregations, as part of an Irish spiritual empire.

6   Far from Home?
Diaspora Politics and the
West Coast Irish

Like marriage and religion, ethnic politics has been an important avenue of
inquiry for historians of Irish migration. Nationalist networks spanned the
oceans in all directions and appeared in a variety of forms.[1] The supporters
of moderate constitutionalism favoured the peaceful resolution of Ireland's
political status within existing structures; hard-line republicans rallied around
the flag of violence; powerful forces coalesced to embrace the question of
land reform; and far-flung adherents of Orangeism celebrated the 'Glorious
Twelfth' and raised their glasses to the Empire and the Unionist cause.[2] We
need to evaluate the levels of active interest in Irish nationalist politics and
draw closer to the ways in which 'diasporic sensibilities' varied over time
and space.[3] This chapter explores the textures of 'diaspora ethnicity' on the
West Coast by focusing on those occasions when it would have been most
visible.[4] The first two parts revisit the 'Fenian controversies' of the late 1860s
and assess their impact on the pattern of community relations.[5] The evidence
presented here and in the third section shows that 'diasporic politics' made
sporadic headway on the mining frontier. Some Irish nationalist organisations
were established, enthusiastic crowds gathered to hear touring Irish politicians,
money was raised for patriotic causes and a few noisy partisans voiced more
extreme opinions. Yet such activities were pursued only for short periods and
by scattered factions. As in the Australian colonies, Irish nationalism had a
very 'limited influence' in the region and 'was to be embraced only warily'.[6]

I
On a warm Sunday morning in March 1868, Detective Richard Dyer watched
groups of mourners assemble outside the Hokitika offices of the *New Zealand
Celt.* Two days earlier, he had seen many of them at a public meeting where
plans were made to hold a funeral procession to express sympathy for three

Irish men, Michael O'Brien, William Allen and Philip Larkin, hanged in Salford for the death of police sergeant Brett during an attack on a Manchester police van in 1867.[7] Dyer feared the worst. The town was ablaze with rumours of Fenian activity and, as a child, he had witnessed demonstrations in Ireland that led to terrible violence. He observed the symbolism of the occasion with a keen eye. 'There were 300 people there at the time – all men.' They wore green sashes and 'green rosettes, with black crape round them'. The cavalcade was joined by a band and a hearse carrying three coffins. One of the colourful banners fluttering in the light sea-breeze 'had a small cross on it, with I.R. underneath, with the words – "Tis Treason to love her, and Death to defend." There was another flag with the figure of a woman, a round tower with flag, having I.R on it, a wolf dog in a sitting position, a harp and shamrock. The woman was in chains, and represented as grasping at the flag; on the flag were the names of Emmet, Allen, Larkin and O'Brien.' At the command of their elected captains the men fell into 'rank and file like soldiers' and marched towards the Ahaura. Dyer did not follow their route but made for the cemetery with the last strains of 'Adeste Fideles' fading in the distance.[8]

By the time it returned to Hokitika with a strong contingent of Waimea supporters, the mournful cortege numbered more than 700 men, women and children. They passed solemnly down Revell Street as far as Tancred Street and marched west along Gibson's Quay and Wharf Street before taking the dusty road to the town's cemetery (Plate 25).[9] Dyer had already encountered the advance guard. William Melody and James Clarke – hotelier and storekeeper – rode ahead and removed the cemetery gates from their hinges. After 'about half an hour' the weary column arrived. 'Father [William] Larkin was dressed in his vestments. He was at the head of the procession. He had a green sash when he was coming up close to the gate.' Behind the popular Waimea curate came 'a cross on a trestle, borne by two men. It was about 5 feet long, painted white, with an inscription' to the 'Manchester Martyrs' which read

IHS
ERECTED
By the inhabitants of Waimea and Stafford Town in loving memory
Of the Irish Patriots,
William Allen, Michael O'Brien and Michael Larkin,
who were executed at Manchester and buried in the yard of
the New Bailey Prison, Salford

Nov. 27, 1867.
RESQUIESCAT IN PACE
GOD SAVE IRELAND[10]

Moving closer, the detective saw Melody at work 'with a long-handled shovel' inside the cemetery. Two other Waimea men, Dennis Hannon and Thomas Harron, were busily arranging banners around the place where the white cross was to stand. For the first time, he noticed that there were females and children in the crowd. 'The women', he recalled, 'were fashionably dressed. Some had green ribbons.'[11] Father Larkin strode forward to address the ring of bystanders:

> Beloved Countrymen and Friends, – We are here, and where is the harm we have done? (Applause) . . . We have come to erect a Celtic cross to the memory of our martyred fellow countrymen, William Allen, Michael O'Brien and Michael Larkin, who were executed at Manchester and laughed to scorn as the drop fell. (Groans and hisses.) We love and respect their memory, we respect, too, the sacrifice they have made for their country. We have come here to-day to erect a tribute to their memory. We have been maligned, we have been blackballed, but we have done no harm. At home, the malice of one or two who had tried to prevent the demonstration in honor of their martyred fellow countrymen, would have been successful owing to recent legislation. But here they have so prostituted the law that the law for us has no force. It is a Sunday, and we are bound to thank and worship the Giver of all good. On this day we are simply doing a duty we owe to our martyred fellow countrymen . . . They died, as they lived, in the bosom of the Catholic Church, and their last words were Jesus and Mary – those names by which they who die in the Catholic Church are saved. Let us hope that they will pray for us and for poor, down-trodden Ireland – that they will pray for us and them, that they may bear the mis-government imposed on them, and all the wickedness that results from that mis-government.

As the late afternoon sun passed beneath the trees, the marchers fell to their knees, Larkin offered prayers for the souls of the deceased and women began to weep. The priest farewelled those assembled and reminded them that his 'prophecy' about the peaceful conduct of the procession would shortly be fulfilled. The crowd dispersed quietly. A few men stayed to plant the cross and replace the cemetery gates. Richard Dyer and his small company set out for the police barracks and 'the sacred ground resumed its still and solemn air'.[12]

This remarkable event formed part of a great wave of commemorative processions among the Irish abroad, but it was not the only political demonstration on the West Coast. One month earlier a meeting at the Belle de Union Hotel in Charleston raised money for relatives of the dead patriots and condemned the British government for their 'murderous executions'. These feelings of sympathy and anger were openly expressed in a procession six days later. The crowd that gathered on the circular beach at Constant Bay equalled the size of its Hokitika counterpart and featured similar elements. With military precision, the men were placed into 11 divisions, each led by marshals. At three o'clock the organisers unfurled a large black banner, the band played the 'Dead March' and the cavalcade wound up between the narrow walls of rock to Charleston. 'After marching through the town,' reported the *New Zealand Celt*, 'the sad procession' headed south 'to the Roman Catholic Burial Ground, and there walked around the cemetery. The Rev. Father Hallan [Stephen Hallum] then came out duly robed, and offered up a prayer to the Most High for the repose of the souls of the departed brave, while the assembled hundreds knelt in solemn adoration.' He 'blessed the banner' and Aden Doyle rose to give an incendiary funeral oration. 'While the voice of a nation is disclaiming against tyranny,' the digger warned, 'the hereditary rulers of the British Empire had better refresh their memories with a casual glance at the opening scenes of the French Revolution, and reflect that another bloody revolution may be at hand . . . Do I or any other Irishman owe allegiance to the British Crown? (Loud cries of 'No!') No! The Manchester tragedy has for ever alienated the Irish heart.'[13]

These scenes were repeated once more at Westport on St Patrick's Day, when '600 or 700 men' swathed in black and green marched in a 'quiet and orderly manner' through the streets. As for the Charleston demonstration, most participants had travelled from the Addison's Flat (or 'the Skibbereen') diggings. The procession made its way around the Catholic section of the town's cemetery and halted next to a stage outside the fence. Commissioner Thomas Kynnersley, chief warden of the Nelson South-West Goldfield, reported that several 'inflammatory speeches' were given and considered a proposal to charge two of the 'stump orators' with seditious slander. He decided, however, that such an action 'would do more harm than good'; the men expressed loyalist sentiments at Addison's soon afterwards and Kynnersley surmised that 'if it suited their purpose, they would reverse their opinions every other day'. The commissioner was far less sanguine in his defence of the public demonstration. 'I am not aware that it is illegal to show respect for the memory of any man', he told the Nelson Provincial Secretary, 'whether that man has been hanged or has met his death in any other manner, and I had stated beforehand, that I could see no objection to the procession if it was conducted in an orderly manner, but that I should decidedly object to the cemetery being desecrated by the burial of any empty coffin, as was at first proposed.'[14]

As Kynnersley's comments suggest, the organising committees of the marches needed to find ways to express their sympathy with 'an act of resistance to the British Government' while simultaneously avoiding blatant provocation.[15] The balance was not easily achieved. On one hand, they had to reckon with clerical denunciation. The Irish Revolutionary Brotherhood (IRB) – or 'Fenians' as its members came to be known – was an oath-bound organisation dedicated to the destruction of British rule in Ireland and the formation of an Irish republic.[16] The Catholic church condemned Fenianism for its conspiratorial secrecy and appeal to violence. But the executions at the New Bailey generated 'a consensus of support' for the movement within Ireland and united priests and people in commemorations inspired by the widely publicised stories of the suffering, piety and patriotism of the prisoners during their final days.[17] A sense of injustice over the fate of Allen, Larkin and O'Brien; memories of Fenian attempts to invade Canada in 1866; the easily subdued 1867 uprising in Dublin and Cork; a fatal explosion at Clerkenwell prison in east London the same year which killed more than 20 people; and reports of Fenian recruiting agents in Hokitika – all these ensured that feelings in the colonies were running high.[18] Justice Richmond spoke for many when he said of the town's procession: 'Gentlemen, that funeral *cortege* was, depend upon it, quite in earnest. It was no mere mockery – no holiday tom-foolery. I ask you – under the outward aspect of grief under the ashes – did there not lurk a dangerous fire?'[19]

Few accounts from Charleston and Westport have survived, but the Hokitika evidence suggests that many residents were alarmed in the days leading up to the demonstration. The Inspector of Police, Thomas Broham, a native of County Limerick and veteran of the Victorian and Otago goldfields, feared the assembly of 'so large a number of men wearing party emblems'.[20] His men stayed in the barracks, constables were summoned from outlying stations and proclamations posted in town. On the day of the funeral march, their presence was barely visible and the plain-clothes detectives were ordered to observe proceedings, but 'to offer no opposition'.[21] Like the police, others foresaw bloodshed at the cemetery gates. William Shaw, the Protestant mayor and proprietor of the *West Coast Times*, carried a gun. 'I saw a great many arms that day – not in the procession – many private individuals showed me they had revolvers under their coats in case they should be called upon to use them.'[22] There could be no greater contrast with the discipline and demeanour of the participants. Richard Dyer 'did not see a stick, stave, revolver, or any other weapon' among the marchers, the *West Coast Times* described the event as 'a very orderly one' and James Bonar, the chairman of the Westland County Council, cabled the Colonial Secretary with news that the day had passed very quietly.[23]

The fragile peace was shattered two weeks later by news that Queen Victoria's son Prince Alfred, the Duke of Edinburgh, had been shot in Sydney. Reports that his would-be assassin, Henry James O'Farrell, held Fenian sympathies circulated widely and fuelled existing tensions.[24] Public meetings were held, loyalty processions planned and dozens of special constables mustered.[25] The *West Coast Times* wondered whether O'Farrell's actions were 'the first of a series of contemplated outrages in the colonies' and mentioned rumours of 'an intended Fenian outbreak'.[26] Taking no chances, colonial authorities acted decisively. In a covert night-time operation, police arrested Larkin and Melody in a Hokitika pub; John Manning, vituperative editor of the *New Zealand Celt*, was 'pounced upon' as he entered the back door of his office; and publican John Barrett 'was touched upon the shoulder by Sergeant Hickson and transferred from the back of his bar to the company of his companions in the lock-up'. Inspector Broham sent mounted troopers to apprehend James Clarke at Waimea, while Denis Hannon and Thomas Harron – 'a noted Fenian' – were taken into custody the next day.[27] After a hearing before the resident magistrate, all seven men were committed to the Supreme Court on charges of riot with an additional count of seditious libel against Larkin and Manning for articles that appeared in the *New Zealand Celt*.[28] Their supporters worked hard to raise funds for the defence and secured the services of Richard Ireland QC, a prominent Irish-Australian lawyer.[29]

As the prisoners awaited trial, Lieutenant Colonel Thomas McDonnell led a detachment of Armed Constabulary to Hokitika aboard the *St Kilda* and they received a rapturous welcome in the streets of the goldfields capital.[30] Later that evening, prominent citizens of 'all nationalities and creeds' met to farewell Father John McGirr at the Duke of Edinburgh Theatre, where they presented him with a glowing testimonial: 'During the time of your residence in Westland, your courteous demeanour and Catholic spirit tended greatly to promote the religious harmony which happily prevailed amongst a people whose privilege it was to live under equal laws, and amongst whom no differences ever arose on the grounds of religious faith.'[31]

The worst fears of many local residents seemed to be confirmed by reports of an attack by 'Irish Fenians' on loyalist marchers at Addison's Flat. In marked contrast to his southern counterparts, however, Commissioner Kynnersley refused to panic and rode to the rickety township with several police to assess the situation. They found the inhabitants milling about in 'a very excited state' and established that the loyalists had antagonised Irish Catholics by placing a white horse at the head of the procession and adding an offensive chorus to their rendition of 'Red, White and Blue'. A large crowd was dispersed after reassurances that armed troops had not been called:

There was no doubt a certain incongruity about the whole proceeding, for most of those who cheered for Law and Order were at the same time armed with axes, pick handles, or large stones, and a few with firearms; but at the same time the general tone of the sentiments expressed was satisfactory to me in that there was no opposition to constituted authorities or to the law taking its course, but a decided objection to open insults or to general attack on the town by the Westport Volunteers.

Kynnersley concluded that the affray was no more than 'a miserable street row'. Yet he remained conscious that the 'partisan feelings' aroused by 'two or three disaffected and insulting speeches and a newspaper war' could lead to sectarian violence. In his characteristic style, the popular warden dampened the smouldering embers. He kept the Volunteers in reserve and emphasised the supremacy of the law in his speeches. But he used his formidable skills to undermine fears of 'a secret terrorism' and liaised with various factions at Westport and Addison's Flat. There would be no retrospective action against men who spoke during the commemorative march on St Patrick's Day. 'I have not yet been able to see', he reasoned, why an attempt 'to assassinate H.R.H the Duke of Edinburgh, in Sydney, should cause me to take proceedings against any persons in New Zealand, which I know would not have been taken if that attempt had not been made.'[32]

The fervour generated by Fenianism had waned when the trials of Larkin and his fellow prisoners began in the Supreme Court at Hokitika on 13 May 1868. Of the witnesses, the Dublin-born detective Charles Browne painted the most benign picture of the political demonstration: 'There were women and children; there were no arms, no breach of the peace, no drunkenness . . . it was as orderly a procession as ever I saw.' For the prosecution, the Attorney-General, James Prendergast, closed the case with a concise summary of the evidence: Larkin and Manning were responsible for articles appearing in the *New Zealand Celt*, the town was in a state of alarm and the action of going into the municipal corporation-owned cemetery 'with a multitude' constituted forcible entry. Richard Ireland delivered a gracious, restrained and celebrated speech for the defence, but his 'colonial pepper' was diluted by the intemperate address of an excitable supporting attorney, William Lee Rees. 'For my own part,' Judge Richmond told the grand jury, this procession 'did imply a most solemn and offensive approval of an act condemned by the law of the land and by right reason – an act of armed and defiant resistance to the Government of the country and its laws.' After several hours of deliberation, the jurors brought a verdict of 'guilty' against all the prisoners with a recommendation of mercy for Clarke, Barrett, Melody, Harron and Hannon. The judge fined each of the men £20, a sentence that he considered 'ridiculously light' for such 'a very great offence'. On legal advice, their co-defendants, Father Larkin and John Manning, pleaded 'guilty' to the charge of seditious libel and, in addition to the imposed fine, were imprisoned 'for one calendar month' in the Hokitika Gaol. 'Had your attitude before the court been different – had you not dutifully submitted to the law of the land,' Richmond warned Larkin, 'I must have required from you heavy recognisances for future good behaviour. With them I can now dispense; trusting, as I do, in your present professions, and that you will go out again amongst your fellow-subjects in a truly Catholic spirit – in that spirit of Christian charity which transcends the narrow bounds of mere national and clannish feelings.'[33]

II

No one could have predicted the hysteria that enveloped the West Coast over those few heady months. The gold rush population lived in relative harmony and there were few signs of popular factionalism. Local newspapers reported only two 'Irish rows' before 1868. The first, in Okarito in 1865, combined mob intimidation by 'the Tips', a dispute in a store and a sizeable crowd 'determined to let the combatants "have it out"'; the second, in 1867, involved a street fight between 'English and Irish denizens' at Ahaura, in which 'a great deal of bad language and almost as much bad brandy were freely expended'.[34] Both episodes were quickly defused by authorities and neither provided a platform for continuing conflict. St Patrick's Day was observed as a public holiday and celebrated with race meetings, grand banquets and monster balls that were widely attended.[35] Even Father Larkin underlined the prevailing cosmopolitanism in his last words from the dock: '[h]ere he had enjoyed the confidence of all classes of the community – Protestants, Presbyterians, and Jews – and until the meeting at the Duke of Edinburgh Theatre he did not think he had a single enemy in Hokitika'. The priest was surprised by the reaction to his oratory: 'My speeches, both at the Cemetery and at the Munster were made on the spur of the moment – they were made in haste and *extempore*. If I have offended in them against the Court or against society, I humbly apologise.'[36]

Be that as it may, Larkin and his companions misread the public mood and failed to craft appropriate tactics for the tense circumstances they faced. Many people feared an escalation of global terrorism by the Fenian movement and took exception to manifestations of party feeling. If procession organisers were to succeed in their aims, they needed to work closely with local authorities, maintain the discipline of participants and find ways to heighten the impact of their political views without provoking confrontation. But there were significant differences in approach. Whereas the Celtic Committee at Addison's accepted Kynnersley's strictures, their Hokitika counterparts disregarded the municipal council's majority decision not to allow marchers to erect a memorial cross in the public cemetery. This brazen act of defiance forced the hand of colonial authorities.[37] At the same time, Larkin and his companions showed no respect for the religious sensitivities of others and continued their agitation in more threatening ways after the procession. James Clarke's remarks to the Supreme Court at the end of the trial revealed a deeper failure: 'All that I have to say is, that I don't hold that this jury is a jury of my countrymen'.[38] The claim was badly at odds with the dominant ethos. 'We are living in a free country,' Kynnersley told the Westport Volunteers, 'where no distinctions of party, race or creed whatever are taken notice of, as they are in the old country, and any attempt to engender party feeling should be discountenanced . . . Whatever country we come from we are now New Zealanders.'[39]

The mock funerals and their messy aftermath exposed serious divisions among Catholics and within the region's Irish population. Nowhere were these more apparent than in Hokitika, where Father John McGirr shunned the demonstration, a suspended priest, Patrick Golden, led a small party from Ross, and Father Stephen McDonough accompanied the marchers 'in his ordinary dress', despite the instructions of Bishop Philippe Viard.[40] Many Irish people did not support these events and enthusiasm for the Fenians was highly localised. Given this complexity, do the processions tell us much about the state of Irish migrant opinion? To what extent did participants share the political views of the organisers? What was the significance of the 'Fenian disturbances'? There is no doubting the anger, shock and sympathy expressed by 'stump orators' or the diasporic dimension of these occasions: similar demonstrations in Great Britain, Ireland and the United States featured black and green adornments, as well as the same funerary ritual and military organisation. But the determined mood of the processions was transitory and it never led to enduring ethnic alignments on the goldfields.

The political failure of local commemoration for the hanged rebels discredited its architects and demonstrated a lack of conviction among Irish militants. Within a few months of the trial, the *New Zealand Celt* ceased publication and a disgruntled John Manning left for California, complaining that the colony's new treason laws made his work impossible. His nemesis, William Shaw, whom Richard Ireland noted 'gave as much as he took' in the 'newspaper quarrel', went to the Thames diggings, while Father McDonough was removed from the diocese by Bishop Viard.[41] The chief protagonist in the Fenian spectacle, William Larkin, suffered a similar fate, but he was no 'Irish martyr'.[42] The 'honest and plucky' priest retained strong support at Addison's and in the Waimea district, where his successor, the All Hallows-educated and Armagh-born James McEntegart, struggled to gain acceptance.[43] Catholic miners informed Father Nicholas Binsfeld that Larkin's actions were 'a matter of pardonable patriotism' and petitioned Viard for his reinstatement.[44] Yet his reputation had been tarnished. 'There was no term more held in abhorrence by his countrymen,' he told Justice Richmond, 'than that of a Suspended Priest.'[45]

Perhaps the most revealing account of Larkin's popularity before his fall from grace was penned by Arthur Dobson, the surveyor son of Canterbury's Provincial Engineer. On one occasion, he accompanied the 'big handsome' priest to the coastlands town of Canoe Creek, south of Punakaiki:

When we arrived a lot of Irish diggers were having a spree. They were half drunk and fighting, some in the bar, and some outside. Father Larkin walked into the bar-room, took off his hat, and exclaimed in a loud voice, 'Peace be to all here'. Instantly every man dropped to his knees, and there was dead silence. Father Larkin then pronounced a blessing, and the men rose.

The high evening tide made a river crossing impossible and the two travellers spent a 'boisterous' evening together beneath the towering Paparoa Ranges. 'The weather was remarkably fine,' Dobson later wrote, 'and there was brilliant moonlight. A wrestling match was got up amongst the miners, which was joined by the priest, who easily threw the best of them, and the night passed with singing and a large consumption of spirits.' After a few hours' sleep, the priest and surveyor rode down the treacherous beach route to Greymouth, where they parted for the last time. Aside from Larkin's political views, Dobson considered his companion 'good company, and just the man to influence a lot of rough men. He had personality, the chief element of success, in my opinion, for the management of men.'[46]

Although we can sympathise with Larkin's plight, he was to a large measure the architect of his own misfortune. His activism seemed almost reckless at times and he ignored the sensible advice of Bishop Viard, on one occasion throwing a telegram counselling 'peace and conciliation' back into the face of Father McDonough.[47] Larkin's co-editorship of the immoderate New Zealand Celt and stubborn resolve over the memorial cross showed poor judgment. When presented with the chance to allay the suspicions of colonial authorities at a loyalist meeting, he managed to raise the political temperature with 'an injudicious speech':[48]

It had been said that he was a Fenian, but he could lay his hand on his heart and solemnly say that there was not one drop of Fenian blood in his veins. He could, however, sympathise with Fenianism: for, if such a thing did exist in Ireland, it was a necessity, and arose from misgovernment and tyranny. It arose from the galling yoke, not of the Royal Family, but of Her Majesty's advisers. Her Majesty was a good Queen and a good mother; but the acts of the English Government were not hers. (Cries of 'I thought you were a Fenian,' and confusion.) He could say fearlessly that no Roman Catholic clergyman had ranked with the Fenians, but they felt bound to sympathise with them, well knowing that there was ample reason for the existence of such a body.

The implicit connections he made between the Great Famine, British policy and the Fenian movement echoed the exiled Irish revolutionary leader John Mitchel:

> He had seen people living for weeks together on weeds of the field, not having even potatoes to keep life in them; they go to the workhouse – it is crammed – and they are dying in the hundreds. The dead were huddled together, and put in a common pit which is left open for a week, when a mound of earth may possibly mark the sacred spot. He then asked if any Irishman had not seen the same, and so inquired if there was not reason why Fenianism existed.

The Galway-born priest claimed that the death of Sergeant Brett was 'a mere accident, which might arise similarly to this: – a policeman in taking a digger to the lock-up, and his mate feels called upon to rescue him, even though an infringement be made of the law. That was the kind of murder for which those men at Manchester suffered.'[49] The analogy was entirely unconvincing. Larkin's opinions, mild by the standards of Irish-America, were foolhardy in a colonial society with strong imperial loyalties.

The state trials and the crushing humiliation that followed contained a number of ironic twists. It emerged in court that workers producing the *New Zealand Celt* had taken strike action until they received their pay from the proprietors; and a craftsman sued Larkin for the costs of the memorial cross and additional labour on the priest's house.[50] The episode was also one of the few political events to provoke comment in migrant letters. Writing from Brandy Creek in Victoria, Christopher Fleming told Michael Flanagan that he had noticed

> a great fuss about a Fenian Funeral or mock funeral at Hokikha and that a whole batch of persons have been committed to take their hints for riot in connection with the affair. There seems to be two priests mixed up with it one named Larkins and the other named McDonagh. Archbishop of Sydney referred to these priests in a Pastoral lately in which he seems to have a very poor opinion of Messrs Larkins and McDonagh. I see by the papers that a certain Father McGirr has arrived in Melbourne from New Zealand. I wonder if he is the same Father McGirr who was stationed in Gippsland for some time and who was a very great Bouncer in Church.[51]

He agreed with Flanagan's assessment: 'The whole affair was a stupid farce from beginning to end but I expect Dick Ireland made a good thing of his little part in it'.[52]

III

The energies unleashed by 'diasporic politics' lasted for brief periods, as the Fenian episode made clear. No crowds gathered to pay homage to Father Larkin after his release from prison and he slipped quietly into obscurity. The *New Zealand Celt* struggled financially and collapsed in less than a year; only the fleeting visit in 1875 by Michael Cody, a former Fenian convict, promoted 'advanced' nationalism.[53] The Irish Land War of 1879–82, on the other hand, stimulated greater colonial interest. Local branches of the Irish National Land League, the principal political organisation involved in the agitation, were established in 1881 and later reconstituted as part of the Irish National League when the parent body in Ireland was proclaimed unlawful.[54] A solitary outpost of the 'radical and independent-minded' Ladies' Land League was launched in 'Miss Hannan's school-room' at Kumara, where its members resolved to assist 'Miss Anna Parnell [the organisation's founder and leader], and her associates, in their charitable undertaking, that is, to alleviate the sufferings of unjustly evicted families, and those families of suspected persons imprisoned at the caprice of the Irish Secretary, who appears for the time being in the role of Dictator of Ireland'.[55] These groups were integrated into far-flung nationalist networks that communicated regularly and worked toward the goals of agrarian reform and Irish independence. Yet they never enlisted more than a fraction of the Irish-born population on the Coast and were largely confined to districts around Kumara and the Grey Valley. Nor was their small nucleus of leaders much interested in creating an ethnic community.[56] Despite an initial surge of enthusiasm, nourished by touring Irish politicians and the cautious endorsement of the Catholic church, membership of the leagues had limited appeal.[57]

The parameters of ethnic solidarity were also evident when representatives of the Irish Parliamentary Party in the British House of Commons visited the West Coast to raise funds for the Home Rule movement.[58] These occasions generated a great deal of fervour, as several historians have demonstrated, and they reveal widespread public sympathy for the constitutional campaign.[59] But it is equally clear that the delegations did not increase migrant participation in nationalist movements or ethnic associations. This pattern holds true for John and William Redmond's influential 1883 'mission' to Australia and New Zealand on behalf of the Irish National League.[60] Sent abroad by their leader, the charismatic Protestant landlord Charles Stewart Parnell (1846–91), the brothers travelled far and wide, taking care to frame their demands for Irish self-government in colonial terms. Nevertheless, the presence of the envoys aroused much hostility in the colonies, at least initially. Newspapers lambasted the mission, venues were withdrawn and the more affluent Irish stayed away from their meetings.[61] William Redmond (the MP for Wexford) toured the South Island with John Walshe, while John Redmond went on his honeymoon with the former Johanna Dalton – the 'near relative of the formidable Dalton dynasty of Orange'.[62] Their visit to the West Coast raised more than £1400 for the Irish National League and received sympathetic press coverage.[63] The *Grey River Argus*, for example, which had editorialised about the 'inflammatory harangues' of the league leadership, urged readers to give the men a fair hearing and expressed 'pleasant surprise' at the 'eloquence and pathos' of an impromptu speech made by William Redmond at a Greymouth function.[64] For their part, the delegates articulated a political vision that chimed with local sentiment. Redmond's oration in Hokitika's Corinthian Hall emphasised the inclusive, non-sectarian and 'thoroughly constitutional' character of his nationalism: 'The Land League was neither composed of Protestant, Catholic, Presbyterian, or Methodist, or of rich or poor. It was an organisation of Irishmen all blended together, containing Protestant, Presbyterian, Catholic, and Methodist clergymen, rich and poor, great and small, with one aim and with a determination never to let any little difference in creed stand between them.'[65] This claim was reiterated at Kumara and Greymouth, where the Wexford MP told a packed audience that 'the League would not rest content till they obtained the same right . . . enjoyed by the Australasian colonies, the right to manage their own affairs by a parliament in Ireland'.[66] In proposing a vote of thanks to the visiting politicians in Kumara, local mining advocate and justice of the peace Peter Dungan, from Newbridge in County Kildare, wove together the themes of social justice, self-determination and empire:

> We have only to look to the history of the last forty years, and what a record does it now show? Ireland in 1845 had a population of over eight millions of

people. Ireland of today is reduced to five millions! What has become of her people? There was one answer to the question . . . Throughout the length and breadth of the land during those years of terrible trouble and of tribulation, and under the working of iniquitous land laws, devastation, exile, and death followed the footsteps and was the bitter lot of this unhappy people. Mr. Redmond's mission was to assist in the laudable endeavour of getting a full measure of justice for the tenant farmers of Ireland, in order that they and the labourers may be enabled to feed and clothe themselves, and live in some degree of comfort, and not in wretchedness, misery and rags – that too long have been the beggar's pittance in their native land.

Yet Dungan stressed that Ireland's national aspirations differed little from those already enjoyed by New Zealanders:

The Irish people feel for, and love their country, and from the splendid services rendered by her children to England, and in the name of justice and of right, her wants should receive every consideration, and their grievances be passed home for redress. The Irish people deserve to see their country in a state of comfort, and contentment, and in the possession of those political rights and liberties – a participator in those solid advantages enjoyed by so many countries and which go to make up the greatness of the British Empire. — (Loud Applause.)[67]

Few West Coasters would have quibbled with Dungan's claims. The tour had succeeded in making the cause of Irish independence respectable in colonial eyes; the published lists of subscriptions collected on the West Coast show that contributors to the National League (and some officers) were drawn from various denominations and nationalities.[68] Quite clearly, Home Rule had won support beyond the ranks of the 'patriotic few' as the most appropriate way 'to reconcile Irish national ambition and imperial security'.[69]

The triumphant West Coast visit by John Dillon (Plate 26) six years later took place in the context of electrifying developments in the political evolution of Parnellism.[70] In 1885 British Liberal Prime Minister William Ewart Gladstone (1809–98) announced his conversion to Home Rule and the Catholic episcopate in Ireland cautiously endorsed the demand for self-government. At Westminster, Parnell played off the two main political parties over Ireland and committed the Irish Party to an alliance with the

Liberals. Gladstone's first Home Rule Bill of 1886 was defeated in the House of Commons; and the struggle for tenant power continued in the second phase of the Land War (1886–7), when Parnell's lieutenants John Dillon (1851–1927) and William O'Brien (1852–1928) orchestrated the 'Plan of Campaign'.[71] Against this background and among a sympathetic citizenry, it was small wonder that the mission by such an eminent Irish politician turned into 'a prolonged ovation'.[72] At Little Grey Junction, for example, 'nearly all the inhabitants' of the district turned out to meet Dillon, who was escorted by an enormous cavalcade of riders and vehicles.[73] Enthusiastic crowds lined the narrow streets of Wallsend, Dobson and Brunnerton as the spirited procession wound its way through the Grey Valley.[74] By the time it reached Greymouth, the procession included some of the town's 'best known citizens and their wives and daughters', while the delegation 'brought in men from the back gullies who rarely come to town at all, either at Christmas or race time; and a goodly number of old miners came to town to hear John Dillon and contribute to the cause to which he has devoted himself who had not been in town for ten or a dozen years before'.[75]

The Mayo East MP was taken aback by his rapturous reception which 'made him feel at times as if he were in the heart of Tipperary itself, or some other equally hot corner of Ireland. He felt some little embarrassment in facing the task of addressing a mixed audience' at the river-port's public hall 'on the affairs of Ireland, or rather the system under which it was governed'.[76] Yet Dillon's anxiety was misplaced in a region where sectarian nettles withered amidst the corn. The nationalist leader must have been surprised by the 'active sympathy' of many colonial-born residents and the breadth of local support for Home Rule.[77] The cosmopolitan flavour was certainly evident when Dillon and his colleague Sir Thomas Esmonde confronted Hokitika's reception party in Goldsborough, which comprised the French priest Father Phillipe Martin, Cornelius Horgan (the Irish National League) and H. Northcroft (Executive Committee of Citizens). Later that evening in the crowded Duke of Edinburgh Theatre, the mayor, New South Welshman and freemason Henry Michel, read an address of welcome to the delegates, which echoed the sentiments expressed at the other West Coast meetings:

Home Rule to many of us is a thing quite unknown from the fact of our having lived all, or nearly all, our lives in this, or the neighbouring colonies where the utmost freedom is enjoyed and hence we can scarcely understand the many aspects of the political questions which are debated with so much acrimony at Home or the necessity and bearing of the tyrannical laws, which, in our opinion interfere so materially with the personal liberty we have a right to enjoy as British subjects.

The 'grant of legislative functions' to Ireland, the citizens concluded, would cement its bonds to the rest of the British Empire much 'more strongly'.[78]

Colonial enthusiasm for Irish independence was dampened by the fratricidal conflict that accompanied the Parliamentary Party 'Split' (1890–91), the tragic death of Parnell in 1891 and the defeat of Gladstone's second Home Rule Bill in 1893.[79] The dazzling Parnellite machine fragmented thereafter 'along a complex of old cleavages and resentments'.[80] Among the array of competing nationalist organisations, only the anti-Parnellite Irish National Federation made an appearance on the West Coast, its 1894 cameo notable for its brevity, localised membership and lack of support.[81] This body won support from P.J. O'Regan, the MHR for Inangahua, who famously told a Denniston branch meeting that only 'a Hide-bound Tory' would oppose 'the granting of Home Rule to Ireland'.[82] But the diminished profile of the Irish question received a much-needed boost when Michael Davitt (1846–1906), the legendary nationalist and land reformer, visited the region in 1895. The local receptions were relatively subdued affairs compared with the excited scenes that accompanied Dillon's mission, although they shared a similar organisational structure: the pivotal role played by local mayors and councils, the formation of ecumenical 'executive committees', the active presence of Catholic clergy and the presentation of citizens' addresses.[83] O'Regan's 'Tories', it seems, were conspicuous by their absence.

The tours of 1907 and 1911 by envoys from an Irish Party reunified under the leadership of John Redmond were as much a swansong as 'a new peak' for colonial interest in Irish political issues.[84] During John Donovan's 1907 visit, the *West Coast Times* commented on his 'pleasant Irish accent' and declared that he had given fresh meaning to 'a more or less hackneyed' topic:

He put the subject in a light that certainly must appeal to free and enlightened colonists, who have always possessed the freedom and liberty under a constitution of their own which the delegate claims for his country. His insistence on one aspect of the question was most satisfactory to all who heard him, being new to most of them. This was as to the coalition of all

parties in Ireland now in their struggle for their rights as an integral portion
of the Empire . . . Their cause of discontent and unhappiness is but the same
as ours would be were we deprived of constitutional government, and had
the control of our affairs moved to London. For these reasons most colonials
must sympathise with the demands of the Irish Party and wish them speedy
success in their self-sacrificing and earnest efforts to secure the same rights,
liberties and privileges which we possess ourselves.[85]

The same reasoning was applied by speakers on Donovan's West Coast
platforms. At Hokitika, the indomitable Henry Michel recalled earlier
delegations to the region and observed how 'strange' it would be 'if the
people of New Zealand did not generally sympathise with such a movement,
they having had Home Rule themselves for over forty years.' In seconding
the mayor's motion, T.E.Y. Seddon, the local MHR, told the Princess
Theatre audience that the appeal 'touched the hearts of West Coasters',
while the County engineer, T.V. Byrne, speaking as 'a New Zealander',
thought it was 'an extraordinary thing that people should have to labour
so long for right and justice, liberty and progress against what he would
term a close corporation of inflated aristocrats (Laughter and applause)'.[86]
These occasions were no longer fiercely 'Irish' affairs, as reports from the
delegate's Kumara meeting made clear: 'Mr Jorgensen in speaking on the
Home Rule question said he hoped that Ireland would have the same freedom
as his native country, Norway, had recently got. Motion carried.'[87]

The goodwill generated by John Donovan yielded a fine pecuniary harvest
when he returned to the region with William Archer Redmond (the son of
John Redmond) in 1911. In Westport, for example, the delegation collected
£250, almost three times the amount Donovan had worked hard to achieve
in 1907.[88] Both men were overwhelmed by the 'boundless hospitality' they
encountered and the valuable assistance their mission received from the 'old
West Coasters'.[89] The envoys enjoyed a 'hearty reception' at Kumara: 'It
was a pleasure to see so many ladies come 4½ miles to meet them. All
women should be home rulers, said Mr Redmond with a twinkle in his
eye.'[90] Such was the enthusiasm at Ross that the delegates delivered eight
speeches in one day and Otira tunnel workers 'from different parts of the
Empire' stopped the travellers to donate over £40 to the cause.[91] The Mayor
of Greymouth, A.C. Russell, presided over a large meeting held at the
public hall, where Redmond outlined Home Rule in language that struck a

chord with his audience: 'All they wanted was the government of their own country. They did not want separation from the Empire; that was a wrong impression. Ireland would occupy a position under the Empire similar to that of each self-governing dominion.' Russell won a bet with Father Carew for 'a silk hat' that the collection, £460, would surpass the £380 made in Christchurch. The *Grey River Argus* was effusive in its praise of 'the people of the town':

A stranger might well have imagined that Greymouth is a peculiarly Irish town, so cordial and generous was the reception accorded to Messrs Donovan and Redmond. We are glad to believe that the demonstration was due far more to the principle that the delegates are advocating than to the fact they are Irishmen. There was a time a few years back when the Irish element of this district was far greater than it is now, and when the enthusiasm of the reception would have caused no great surprise. But as that condition no longer obtains, it is only fair to attribute the cordiality of the reception extended to those Irish gentlemen more to the justice of the cause they advocate and the liberal instincts of the people of Greymouth than to any other reason. Hence its political value. The reception of the delegates to some extent at least is indicative of the growing influence of the political and economic thought of the overseas dominions on the public of the Home country . . .
Ireland has been the Cinderella of Empire for many generations; and although many grievances have been removed, and very much done for the benefit of the Irish people, the most burning grievance of all that the country has suffered from – the absence of the right of managing her own affairs by her own people and in her own way – has been hitherto denied to her. Had that boon been granted, all other minor blessings would have arrived in the ordinary course.[92]

The hopes expressed in the editorial were dashed by subsequent events: the outbreak of the First World War in August 1914; the 1916 Easter Rising in Dublin; the collapse of Home Rule and the consolidation of popular support by Sinn Féin; the relentless slide toward vicious armed conflict in 1919–21; and, with partition, the formation of the newly independent Irish Free State and civil war in 1922–3.[93] Colonial interest in Irish political affairs evaporated, even among New Zealand Hibernians.[94] There were still active nationalists – the anti-conscriptionist Donellan circle at Nelson Creek, the

Doyle brothers of Greymouth or the second-generation 'diasporan' P.J. O'Regan[95] – but these cases were atypical. It would be more accurate to depict the West Coast Irish as 'empire loyalists', a commitment drenched in the blood of their descendants and inscribed on solemn war memorials scattered around the region.[96]

IV

The critical perspective that emerges from the West Coast evidence provides a useful corrective to historical writings that have assumed an automatic connection between 'Irishness' and support for ethnic politics. Like their counterparts elsewhere, the men and women who made their way to the mining frontier did not bring a static blueprint of ideas and traditions; nor did they give universal assent to the various Irish political models on offer. There was real enthusiasm for Home Rule on occasions, and the cause attracted a wide range of local sympathisers, but most migrants did not awake each day to contemplate Irish political affairs: they were faced with much more immediate concerns such as making a living, the price of dietary staples, illness, birth and death, religion, kinship obligations and local issues. Without an Orange-Green dynamic or anti-Irish prejudice, nationalist politics failed to provide an adequate foundation for a durable ethnicity. Instead, migrants fashioned a sense of community on the West Coast by celebrating their loyalty to the empire, their attachment to the region and their common bonds as New Zealanders.

7   Washing Up

In a moving letter written from Goldsborough, a widowed Ellen Piezzi contrasted her own situation with that of her brother-in-law in California: 'I am quite glad to here of you bene so comforted and have good home for your self. Even if I never saw you I like to here from you. I was glad to here that youre sister is nere you. You are great Compny to echoder [*each other*] but poor me I got no none neder of mey one of Julius near me but black strangers to spake to god help me.' The burden of child-rearing and running the Helvetia Hotel was compounded by the vicissitudes of the local economy. 'This pleas is gone to the bad', she told Victer, 'not*h*ing dooing. I think i will try and sell out after crismes and go sumere wher or aother while i am abel to go. I dont know what I will the time is so dull god derect me to best'.[1] Yet the district's prospects must have improved sufficiently for her to open a second 'astableshed' at Rimu:

> I am dooing prity fare traid at present. I got 10 borders and good many coming in and out but if cores [*of course*] it take along time to peell [*pile*] thing up the things is so derr and every move is money. I am dooing as Well as any one les and if the betie [*often better*] but I got to ceep 2 girls one to cook and one to other work foitin beds and I got a new billiard tabel . . . I will be in time if any thing brake out nere and I have no dout but sum New ground will be opened up yet. The are plenty of ground that never Was tuched yet. It Will be opened up yet We live in hopes. I got my brothe*r*s minding the other plase for me and i go home oust Week for cupel of dayes setel up overthing for them and go back again.[2]

Despite her struggles, there is nothing in the surviving letters to suggest that Ellen made extensive use of Irish ethnic networks, and other evidence partially confirms this. According to family tradition, she was known as 'a great communicator' who wrote to her brother, Patrick, and other kinsfolk at home, kept in contact with her husband's relatives in Swiss villages and in the United States, and made many friends among her fellow West Coasters.[3] Ellen's attachment to 'Ireland' did not appear to extend far beyond a particular locality in County Kilkenny and her immediate family in New Zealand. Indeed the only reference to the Old World in the correspondence with her husband's brother is quite ambiguous: 'I reseved a letter from home and the Money last mail. The amount it was three pounds Eighteen shillings . . . in which I am very thankful to for all the trobel you got With it and also your unkel. I return thanks to him.'[4] When Ellen asked Victer to pass on 'her best respects' to his sister, she revealed the cosmopolitan outlook of a seasoned colonial: 'Tell her to rite a fu lines in her own langesh. I will get one of the men to reed it. Send it in your letter to me if not to much trobel.'[5]

Ellen Piezzi's story points toward some of the main themes of this book: the wider trans-Tasman dimension, the role of transnational networks, the companionship of relatives and friends and the importance of religious practice and belief (Plates 27 and 28). Her letters also remind us that a narrow focus on 'ethnic communities' cannot always capture the multiplicity and dynamism of Irish identities abroad. As we have seen, the Irish men and women who came to the West Coast adapted older cultural resources to meet their immediate needs and give meaning to the world around them. But they were never an undifferentiated whole and their experiences defy easy categorisation. The fluidity of social identities on the mining frontier was evident in the biographies of women like Harriette Coates or Mai O'Farrell, in personal correspondence, newspaper obituaries, marriage records and, especially, in family memory.[6] It was equally apparent within local Catholicism, which did not become the distant outpost of an Irish spiritual empire. Nor does this kind of characterisation seem appropriate to describe Catholic Greymouth in the early twentieth century, largely though not exclusively working-class, an amalgam of various influences, but rooted firmly in *colonial* soil.[7] As they drew on materials and practices from the past, ordinary migrants remade themselves and the world, though not entirely on their own terms or in ways they wholly intended. These findings underline the significance of historical and material conditions in shaping local patterns of adaptation and the distinctive tonalities of people's everyday lives.

Irish men and women were always strongly represented on the crowded vessels that thronged busy West Coast ports after the discovery of payable gold. Scattered far and wide across a mining frontier that ran from Karamea to Jackson's Bay, the Irish-born and their descendants made up about a quarter of the total population in the nineteenth and early twentieth centuries. Predictably, single men like Michael Flanagan and John O'Regan – searching for 'the elusive pile' – dominated the seaborne invasion in absolute numbers. But Irish women, along with those of other nationalities, flocked toward the towns where many worked as domestic servants, just as Ellen Piezzi had done before her own marriage. Aside from gender, Irish goldfields migration was complicated by the axes of age, class, county origin, religion, parenthood and marital status. In terms of direction, an overwhelming majority were two- or three-stage migrants who sailed to the region from Dunedin and Melbourne after serving colonial apprenticeships in Victoria and Otago. The Irish regional origins of the movement reflected this general trend and turned upon the key centres of Australian emigration such as Tipperary, Clare and Limerick in Munster, and King's and Kilkenny in Leinster. Newcomers to the West Coast were considerably older on arrival than their compatriots venturing abroad between the Famine and the First World War and more than half of the women had married, three-fifths forming unions in the Australian colonies. The balance of religious denominations among the West Coast's Irish intake matched that of Victoria and the migration featured a sizeable group from well-heeled rural backgrounds. We can find Irish migrants in all sectors of the region's social structure and they matched local patterns of wealth-holding and occupational attainment.

The same mechanisms that bound Killinchy to Ellesmere County in Canterbury, and Clonoulty to Boorowa in New South Wales, also connected Burawn with Charleston, Kilrush with Kumara and Skibbereen with Addison's Flat.[8] As the surviving evidence makes clear, most of the region's Irish were not the atomised or alienated individuals depicted by some scholars of migration.[9] Rather, kinship and neighbourhood connections were crucial to facilitating mobility and providing migrants with information, advice, companionship and material assistance. The reach of personal networks was extraordinary, spanning the oceans in all directions from the West Coast to Australia, North America and distant rural homesteads in Ireland. These complexities show that their migration was not a simple linear journey from a particular homeland to permanent settlement in New Zealand. The movement formed part of a much broader trans-Tasman interchange, which was in turn related to the evolution of world capitalism and the massive outflows of emigrants from Europe between 1815 and 1930.[10] The best vantage point for studying their mobility is therefore to be found 'in the meeting of the extremes: of global forces and local conditions, of the world and the village'.[11]

Because the Irish who settled on the West Coast of New Zealand's South Island lacked the necessary prerequisites for the development and long-term survival of ethnic networks, most did not make the transition from identification with an ethnic category to higher levels of ethnic incorporation.[12] This finding confirms Patrick O'Farrell's view that the attachment of Irish migrants to 'home' was seldom

> nationalist or ideological, or related to Ireland as a whole. It was quite a particular affection for, and loyalty to, a small group of people – immediate family and close friends – and a certain limited area or specific place – in my family's case a group of villages and towns in central Tipperary: Ballinderry, Borrisokane, Nenagh, Birr. Dublin or Cork or Limerick or Belfast were irrelevant to this commitment: they were virtually foreign places, some of them totally unknown.[13]

Irish migrants on the mining frontier never endured the terrible poverty suffered by many of their compatriots in British cities such as Glasgow or Manchester during the nineteenth century, nor the opprobrium heaped on them by hostile native-born Protestants. As active participants in colonisation and British imperialism, they were part of a diverse and numerically strong 'charter group' whose members were heavily involved in the wider social life of their respective local communities.[14] Even the Roman Catholic church, so often considered the main vehicle for the expression of 'Irishness', was at best ambivalent about the maintenance of ethnic boundaries. With one or two exceptions, ethnic exclusiveness was never a concern for Catholic clergy, teaching brothers and nuns on the West Coast: their spiritual labours were aimed primarily at getting their flocks to heaven. In this environment, where a host of factors inhibited the emergence of Irish ethnic networks, the social and cultural distinctiveness of the migrant generation was soon eroded, new social formations developed and ethnicity was overtaken by more pressing loyalties such as religion, family, class and locality.

Bibliography

This bibliography is arranged under the following headings:

PRIMARY SOURCES
I.   Unpublished Official Papers
II. Manuscripts
III. Published Papers
IV. Contemporary Newspapers
V.   Contemporary Books, Pamphlets and Articles

SECONDARY SOURCES
VI. Books
VII. Articles
VIII.Theses and Other Papers

PRIMARY SOURCES

I   UNPUBLISHED OFFICIAL PAPERS
1. Archives New Zealand, Christchurch
      Probate and Letters of Administration Files
      Official Assignee in Bankruptcy Files
      Canterbury Provincial Government Archives
      Testamentary Registers (Inland Revenue Department)
2. Archives New Zealand, Wellington
      Canterbury Archives, Immigration Department
      General Government, Immigration Department
      Probate and Letters of Administration Files
3. Registrar-General of Births, Deaths and Marriages, Lower Hutt (now Wellington)

II   MANUSCRIPTS
1. Alexander Turnbull Library, Wellington
      O'Farrell Family Letters (1911–20), MS-Papers 77–127
      Mother Mary Clare Molony, Diary, 15 October 1878, MS-Papers 1918
2. Christchurch Roman Catholic Diocesan Archives
3. Marist Archives, Wellington

4. Private Collections
    James Noonan Callinan (Brian Nolan, Levin)
    Cecilia Colgan (John Coghlan, Nelson)
    Mary Ann Devery and Thomas Tymons (Ted Matthews, Christchurch)
    Flanagan Letters (Donald Murphy, Termonfeckin, County Louth)
    Patrick and Sarah Gillin (Ted Matthews, Christchurch)
    Samuel and William Gilmer (Juann Ryan, Auckland)
    Susan and Patrick Hogan, Catherine O'Toole (Ted Matthews, Christchurch)
    David McCullough (Moore Fisher Johnston and Sandra Gilpin, Comber, Newtownards,
        County Down)
    Johanna O'Leary and Edward, Jeremiah and Mary O'Connor (Mary O'Connor,
        London)
    Ann O'Donnell (Peter Kerridge, Greymouth)
    John O'Regan (Dennis Regan, Washington, USA)
    Kate Phelan (Brian Nolan, Levin)
    Ellen Piezzi (Teresa O'Connor, Nelson)
4. Wellington Roman Catholic Archdiocesan Archives
5. West Coast Historical Museum

III Published Official Papers
Appendices to the Journal of the House of Representatives
Census of New Zealand, 1867–1921
Commission on Emigration and Other Population Problems, 1948–1954. Dublin, 1954.

IV Contemporary Newspapers, Directories and Periodicals
Grey River Argus
Hokitika Evening Star
Kumara Times
New Zealand Celt
New Zealand Tablet
West Coast Times
Westport News
Westport Times

V Contemporary Books and Pamphlets
Dobson, Arthur Dudley. *Reminiscences of Arthur Dudley Dobson, Engineer, 1841–1930*.
    Christchurch, 1930.
Faris, Irwin. *Charleston: Its Rise and Decline*. Wellington and Dunedin, 1941.
Matthews, Ella. *Yesterdays in Golden Buller*. Christchurch, 1957.
Redwood, Francis. *Reminiscences of Early Days in New Zealand*. Wellington, 1922.
Redwood, Francis. *Sketch of the Work of the Catholic Church for the last-half century in the
    Archdiocese of Wellington, New Zealand*. Wellington, 1887.
The Cyclopedia of New Zealand: Volume 5. Christchurch, 1906.

SECONDARY SOURCES

VI BOOKS

Akenson, Donald Harman. *Half the World From Home: Perspectives on the Irish in New Zealand, 1860–1950.* Ontario, 1985.

Akenson, Donald Harman. 'No Petty People: Pakeha History and the Historiography of the Irish Diaspora', in Lyndon Fraser, ed. *A Distant Shore: Irish Migration and New Zealand Settlement.* Dunedin, 2000, pp. 22–3.

Akenson, Donald Harman. *Small Differences: Irish Catholics and Irish Protestants, 1815–1922: An International Perspective.* Kingston and Montreal, 1988.

Akenson, Donald Harman. *The Irish Diaspora: A Primer*, Toronto, 1996.

Anderson, Michael. *Approaches to the History of the Western Family, 1500–1914.* Cambridge, 1995.

Bailyn, Bernard. *Voyagers to the West: A Passage in the Peopling of America on the Eve of the Revolution.* New York, 1987.

Baines, Dudley. *Emigration from Europe, 1815–1930.* Cambridge, 1995.

Bayor, Ronald and Meagher, Timothy, eds. *The New York Irish.* Baltimore, 1996

Bielenberg, Andy, ed. *The Irish Diaspora.* Harlow, 2000.

Birdwell-Pheasant, Donna.'The Early Twentieth-Century Stem Family: A Case Study from County Kerry', in Marilyn Silverman and P.H. Gulliver, eds. *Approaching the Past: Historical Anthropology Through Irish Case Studies.* New York, 1992, 205–35.

Bodnar, John E. *The Transplanted: A History of Immigrants in Urban America.* Bloomington, 1985.

Bourke, Joanna. *Husbandry to Housewifery: Women, Economic Change, and Housework in Ireland, 1890–1914*, Oxford, 1993.

Brah, Avtar. *Cartographies of Diaspora: Contesting Identities.* London, 1996.

Brooking, Tom and Coleman, Jennie, eds. *The Heather and the Fern: Scottish Migration and New Zealand Settlement.* Dunedin, 2003, pp. 67–85

Byron, Reginald. *Irish America.* Oxford, 1999.

Campbell, Malcolm. *The Kingdom of the Ryans: The Irish in Southwest New South Wales, 1816–1890.* Sydney, 1997.

Clark, Samuel L. *Social Origins of the Irish Land War.* Princeton, 1979.

Cohen, Abner. *Custom and Politics in Urban Africa: A Study of Hausa Migrants in Yoruba Towns.* Berkeley, 1969

Cohn, Bernard S. *An Anthropologist Among the Historians and Other Essays.* Delhi, 1987.

Connell, Kenneth H. *Irish Peasant Society: Four Historical Essays.* Oxford, 1968.

Connolly, S.J. 'Marriage in Pre-Famine Ireland', in Art Cosgrove, ed. *Marriage in Ireland.* Dublin, 1985, pp. 78–98

Connolly, S.J. *Priests and People in Pre-Famine Ireland, 1780-1845.* Dublin, 1982.

Connolly, S.J. *Religion and Society in Nineteenth-Century Ireland.* Dublin, 1985.

Corish, Patrick. *The Irish Catholic Experience: A Historical Survey.* Dublin, 1985.

Cott, Nancy F. *Public Vows: A History of Marriage and the Nation.* Cambridge, Mass., and London, 2000.

Cronin, Mike and Adair, Daryl. *The Wearing of the Green: A History of St. Patrick's Day.* London and New York, 2002.

Davis, Richard. *Irish Issues in New Zealand Politics, 1869–1922.* Dunedin, 1974

Davison, Yvonne and Mills, Frankie, eds. *Women of Westland and Their Families.* Greymouth, 1998.

Diner, Hasia. *Erin's Daughter's in America: Irish Immigrant Women in the Nineteenth Century.* Baltimore, 1983.

Donnelly, James S., Jr. *The Land and the People of Nineteenth-Century Cork: The Rural Economy and the Land Question*. London and Boston, 1975.

Dwyer, Sarah and Fraser, Lyndon. '"We are all here like so many on the cockle beds": Towards a History of Ulster Migrants in Nineteenth–Century Canterbury', in Brad Patterson, ed., *The Hidden Irish: Ulster-New Zealand Migration and Cultural Transfers*. Dublin, 2005, pp. 115–30.

Elliot, Marianne. *The Catholics of Ulster: A History*. London, 2000.

Eriksen, Thomas Hylland. *Ethnicity and Nationalism*. London and Sterling, VA., 2002.

Fairburn, Miles. *The Ideal Society and Its Enemies: The Foundations of Modern New Zealand Society, 1850–1900*. Auckland, 1989.

Fitzpatrick, David. 'Emigration, 1801–1870', in W.E. Vaughan, ed. *A New History of Ireland: Vol. V: Ireland Under the Union, I, 1801–1870*. Oxford, 1989, pp. 562–616.

Fitzpatrick, David. 'Emigration, 1871–1921', in W.E. Vaughan, ed. *A New History of Ireland: Vol. VI: Ireland Under the Union, II, 1871–1921*. Oxford, 1989, pp. 602–42.

Fitzpatrick, David. *Oceans of Consolation: Personal Accounts of Irish Migration to Australia*. Melbourne, 1995.

Fitzpatrick, David. 'Ireland Since 1870', in Roy F. Foster, ed., *The Oxford History of Ireland*. Oxford, 1989, pp. 174–229.

Fitzpatrick, David. 'Marriage in Post-Famine Ireland', in Art Cosgrove, ed. *Marriage in Ireland*. Dublin, 1985, pp. 116–31

Fitzpatrick, David. *Irish Emigration, 1801–1921*. Dublin, 1985.

Foster, R.F. 'Ascendancy and Union', in R.F. Foster, ed., *The Oxford History of Ireland*. Oxford, 1989, pp. 162–73

Foster, R.F. *Modern Ireland, 1600–1972*. London, 1988.

Lyndon Fraser and Katie Pickles, eds. *Shifting Centres: Women and Migration in New Zealand History*. Dunedin, 2002.

Fraser, Lyndon. *To Tara via Holyhead: Irish Catholic Immigrants in Nineteenth-Century Christchurch*. Auckland, 1997.

Gilley, Sheridan. 'Roman Catholicism and the Irish in England', in Donald M. MacRaild, ed. *The Great Famine and Beyond: Irish Migrants in Britain in the Nineteenth and Twentieth Centuries*. Dublin and Portland, 2000.

Griffin, Patrick. *The People with No Name: Ireland's Ulster Scots, America's Scots-Irish and the Creation of a British Atlantic World, 1689–1764*. Princeton and Oxford, 2001.

Guinnane, Timothy W. *The Vanishing Irish: Households, Migration and the Rural Economy in Ireland, 1850–1914*. Princeton, 1997.

Haines, Robin. '"The priest made a bother about it": The travails of that "unhappy sisterhood" bound for colonial Australia', in Trevor McClaughlin, ed. *Irish Women in Colonial Australia*. St. Leonard's, 1998, pp. 43–63.

Hearn, Terry. 'Mining the Quarry', in Eric Pawson and Tom Brooking, eds. *Environmental Histories of New Zealand*. Melbourne, 2002, pp. 84–99.

Hearn, Terry. 'The Irish on the Otago Goldfields', in Lyndon Fraser, ed., *A Distant Shore: Irish Migration and New Zealand Settlement*. Dunedin, 2000, pp. 75–85.

Hearn, Terry. 'Irish Migration to New Zealand to 1915', in Lyndon Fraser, ed., *A Distant Shore: Irish Migration and New Zealand Settlement*. Dunedin, 2000, pp. 55–74.

Hearn, Terry. 'The Origins of New Zealand's Irish Settlers, 1840–1945', in Brad Patterson, ed. *The Irish in New Zealand: Historical Contexts and Perspectives*. Wellington, 2002, pp. 15–34.

Hearn, Terry. 'Scots Miners on the Goldfields, 1861–1870', in Tom Brooking and Jennie Coleman, eds. *The Heather and the Fern: Scottish Migration and New Zealand Settlement*. Dunedin, 2003.

Heimann, Mary. *Catholic Devotion in Victorian England*. Oxford, 1995.

Hajnal, John. 'European Marriage Patterns in Perspective', in D.V. Glass and D.E.C. Eversley, eds. *Population in History: Essays in Historical Demography*. London, 1965, pp. 101–43.

Hobsbawm, Eric. *Nations and Nationalism since the 1780s: Programme, Myth, Reality*. Cambridge, 1990.

Hoppen, K. Theodore. *Ireland Since 1800: Conflict and Conformity*. London and New York, 1999.

Hoskins, Robert. *Goldfield Balladeer: The Life and Times of the celebrated Charles R. Thatcher*. Auckland and London, 1977.

Hutchison, John. 'Irish Nationalism', in D. George Boyce and Alan O'Day, eds. *The Making of Modern Irish History: Revisionism and the Revisionist Controversy*. London and New York, 1996, pp. 100–19.

Jackson, Alvin. *Ireland: 1798–1998: Politics and War*. Oxford, 1999.

Jordan, Donald E., Jr. *Land and Popular Politics in Ireland: County Mayo from the Plantation to the Land War*. Cambridge, 1994.

Keenan, Desmond. *The Catholic Church in Nineteenth-Century Ireland: A Sociological Study*. Dublin, 1983.

Keneally, Thomas. *The Great Shame: A Story of the Irish in the Old World and the New*. London, 1998.

Kennedy, Robert E. Jr. *The Irish: Emigration, Marriage and Fertility*. Berkeley, 1973.

Kenny, Kevin. *The American Irish: A History*. New York, 2000.

King, Michael. *The Penguin History of New Zealand*. Auckland, 2003

Keys, Lillian G. *Philip Viard: Bishop of Wellington*. Christchurch, 1968.

Larkin, Emmet. 'Before the Devotional Revolution', in James H. Murphy, ed. *Evangelicals and Catholics in Nineteenth-Century Ireland*. Dublin, 2005, pp. 15–37.

Larkin, Emmet. *The Historical Dimensions of Irish Catholicism*. Dublin, 1997.

McLeod, Hugh. *Religion and the People of Western Europe, 1789–1970*. Oxford, 1981.

May, Philip Ross. *Hokitika: Goldfields Capital*. Christchurch, 1964.

May, Philip Ross. *Miners and Militants*. Christchurch, 1975.

May, Philip Ross. *The West Coast Gold Rushes*. Christchurch, 1962.

McAloon, Jim. *No Idle Rich: The Wealthy in Canterbury and Otago, 1840–1914*. Dunedin, 2002.

McAloon Jim. 'Resource Frontiers, Environment and Settler Capitalism, 1769–1860', in Eric Pawson and Tom Brooking, eds. *Environmental Histories of New Zealand*. Melbourne, 2002, pp. 84–99.

McCarthy, Angela. *Irish Migrants in New Zealand, 1840–1937: 'The Desired Haven'*. Woodbridge, 2005.

McGill, David. *The Lion and the Wolfhound: The Irish Rebellion on the New Zealand Goldfields*. Wellington, 1990.

MacRaild, Donald M. *Culture, Conflict and Migration: The Irish in Victorian Cumbria*, Liverpool, 1998, and *Irish Migrants in Modern Britain, 1750–1922*. Basingstoke, 1999.

MacRaild, Donald M. *Faith, Fraternity and Fighting: The Orange Order and Irish Migrants in Northern England, c. 1850–1920*. Liverpool, 2005.

MacRaild, Donald M. ed. *The Great Famine and Beyond: Irish Migrants in Britain in the Nineteenth and Twentieth Centuries*. Dublin and Portland, Or., 2000.

Matthews, Betty and Matthews, Ted. *They Shaped Our Lives: West Coast Pioneers*. Christchurch, 2004.

Miller, Kerby A. 'Class, Culture and Immigrant Group Identity in the United States:

The Case of Irish-American Ethnicity', in Virginia Yans-McLaughlin, ed. *Immigration Reconsidered: History, Sociology, and Politics*. New York, 1990, pp. 96–129

Miller, Kerby A. *Emigrants and Exiles: Ireland and the Irish Exodus to North America*. New York, 1985.

Miller, Kerby A. with Doyle, David N. and Kelleher, Patricia. '"For Love and Liberty": Irish Women, Migration and Domesticity in Ireland and America, 1815-1920', in Patrick O'Sullivan, ed., *Irish Women and Irish Migration*, vol. 4, *The Irish Worldwide: History, Heritage, Identity*. Leicester, 1995, pp. 47–52.

Morawksa, Ewa. 'Immigrants, Transnationalism, and Ethnicisation: A Comparison of This Great Wave and the Last', in Garry Gerstle and John Mollenkopf, eds. *E Pluribus Unum? Contemporary and Historical Perspectives on Immigrant Political Incorporation*. New York, 2001, pp. 175–212

Moya, Jose C. *Cousins and Strangers: Spanish Immigrants in Buenos Aires, 1850–1930*. Berkeley, 1998.

Nolan, Janet. *Ourselves Alone: Women's Emigration from Ireland, 1885–1920*. Lexington, Ky., 1989.

O'Day, Alan. 'Irish Diaspora Politics in Perspective: The United Irish Leagues of Great Britain and America, 1900–14', in Donald M. MacRaild, ed. *The Great Famine and Beyond: Irish Migrants in Britain in the Nineteenth and Twentieth Centuries*. Dublin and Portland, Or., 2000, pp. 214–39.

O'Day, Alan. *Irish Home Rule, 1867–1921*. Manchester, 1998.

O'Day, Alan. 'Revising the Diaspora', in D. George Boyce and Alan O'Day, eds. *The Making of Modern Irish History: Revisionism and the Revisionist Controversy*. London and New York, 1996, pp. 188–215.

O'Farrell, Patrick. 'Landscapes of the Irish Immigrant Mind', in John Hardy, ed. *Stories of Australian Migration*. Kensington, 1988, pp. 34–5.

O'Farrell, Patrick. *The Catholic Church and Community: An Australian History*. Sydney, 1992.

O'Farrell, Patrick. *The Irish in Australia*. Sydney, 1993.

O'Farrell, Patrick. *Through Irish Eyes: Australian and New Zealand Images of the Irish, 1788–1948*. Richmond, 1994.

O'Farrell, Patrick. *Vanished Kingdoms: Irish in Australia and New Zealand: A Personal Excursion*. Kensington, 1990.

Ó Gráda, Cormac. 'Some Aspects of Nineteenth-Century Irish Emigration Statistics', in L.M. Cullen and T.C. Smout, eds. *Comparative Aspects of Irish Economic and Social History*. Edinburgh, 1977, pp. 65–73.

Ó Gráda, Cormac. *The Great Irish Famine*. Cambridge, 1989.

Olssen, Erik. 'Families and the Gendering of European New Zealand in the Colonial period, 1840–80', in Caroline Daley and Deborah Montgomerie, eds *The Gendered Kiwi*. Auckland, 1999, pp. 37–62.

O'Meeghan, Michael. *Held Firm by Faith: A History of the Catholic Diocese of Christchurch, 1840-1897*. Christchurch, 1988.

Patterson, Brad, ed. *From Ulster to New Ulster: The 2003 Ulster–New Zealand Lectures*. Wellington, 2004.

Patterson, Brad, ed. *The Irish in New Zealand: Historical Contexts and Perspectives*. Wellington, 2002.

Reynolds, Henry. *Frontier: Aborigines, Settlers and Land*. Sydney, 1987.

Richards, Eric. *Britannia's Children: Emigration from England, Scotland, Wales and Ireland since 1600*. London and New York, 2004.

Richards, Eric, Reid, Richard, and Fitzpatrick, David. *Visible Immigrants: Neglected Sources for the History of Australian Immigration*. Canberra, 1989.

Richardson, Len. *Coal, Class and Community: The United Mineworkers of New Zealand, 1880–1960*. Auckland, 1995.

Rogers, Anna. *A Lucky Landing: The Story of the Irish in New Zealand*. Auckland, 1996.

Scholefield, G.H. *Newpapers in New Zealand*. Wellington, 1958.

Schrier, Arnold. *Ireland and the American Emigration, 1850–1900*. Minneapolis, 1958.

Solow, Barbara. *The Land Question and the Irish Economy*. Cambridge, Mass., 1971.

Sweetman, Rory. *Faith and Fraternalism: A History of the Hibernian Society in New Zealand, 1869–2000*. Wellington, 2002.

Sweetman, Rory. '"How to behave among Protestants": Varieties of Irish Catholic Leadership in Colonial New Zealand', in Brad Patterson, ed. *The Irish in New Zealand: Historical Contexts and Perspectives*. Wellington, 2002, pp. 89–101

Sweetman, Rory. '"The Importance of Being Irish": Hibernianism in New Zealand, 1869–1969', in Lyndon Fraser, ed. *A Distant Shore: Irish Migration and New Zealand Settlement*. Dunedin, 2000, pp. 135–54.

Taylor, Lawrence J. *Occasions of Faith: An Anthropology of Irish Catholics*. Philadelphia, 1995.

Van Hear, Nicholas. *New Diasporas: The Mass Exodus, Dispersal and Regrouping of Migrant Communities*. Oxford, 1998.

Vaughan, W.E. and Fitzpatrick, A.J, eds. *Irish Historical Statistics: Population, 1821–1971*. Dublin, 1978.

Walter, Bronwen. *Outsiders Inside: Whiteness, Place and Irish Women*. London and New York, 2001.

Whelan, Kevin. 'The Catholic Church in County Tipperary', in William J. Nolan, ed. *Tipperary: History and Society*. Dublin, 1985, pp. 213–55.

VII ARTICLES

Akenson, Donald Harman. 'Reading the Texts of Rural Immigrants: Letters from the Irish in Australia, New Zealand, and North America', *Canadian Papers in Rural History* 7 (1990): 387–406.

Arnold, Rollo. 'The Dynamics and Quality of Trans-Tasman Migration, 1885–1910', *Australian Economic History Review* 26 (1986): 1–20.

Birdwell-Pheasant, Donna. 'Irish Households in the Early Twentieth Century: Culture, Class and Historical Contingency', *Journal of Family History* 18 (1993): 19–38.

Bourke, Joanna. '"The Best of All Home Rulers": The Economic Power of Women in Ireland, 1880–1914', *Irish Economic and Social History* 18 (1991): 34–41.

Boyd, Monica. 'Family and Personal Networks in International Migration: Recent Developments and New Agendas', *International Migration Review* 32 (1989): 638–70.

Breton, Raymond. 'Institutional Completeness of Ethnic Communities and the Personal Relations of Immigrants', *American Journal of Sociology* 70 (1964): 193–205.

Brubaker, Roger. 'The "Diaspora" Diaspora', *Ethnic and Racial Studies* 28 (2005): 1–19.

Busteed, Mervyn. 'Parading the Green – Procession as Subaltern Resistance in Manchester in 1867', *Political Geography* 24 (2005): 903–33.

Campbell Malcolm. 'Irish Nationalism and Immigrant Assimilation: Comparing the United States and Australia', *Australasian Journal of American Studies* 16 (1996): 24–43.

Campbell, Malcolm. 'John Redmond and the Irish National League in Australia and New Zealand, 1883', *History* 86 (2001): 348–62.

Campbell, Malcolm. 'The Other Immigrants: Comparing the Irish in Australia and the United States', *Journal of American Ethnic History* 14 (1995): 3–22.

Clifford, James. 'Diasporas', *Cultural Anthropology* 9 (1994): 302–38.

Cohen, Anthony P. 'Culture as Identity: An Anthropologist's View', *New Literary History* 24 (1993): 195–209.

Connell, Kenneth H. 'Peasant Marriage in Ireland After the Great Famine', *Past and Present* 12 (1957): 76–91.

Conzen, Kathleen Neils; Gerber, David A.; Morawska, Ewa; Pozetta, George E.; and Vecoli, Rudolph J. 'The Invention of Ethnicity', *Journal of American Ethnic History* 12 (1992): 3–41.

Donnelly, Jr., James S. 'The Irish Agricultural Depression of 1859–64, *Irish Economic and Social History* 3 (1976): 33–54.

Doyle, David Noel. 'Review Article: Cohesion and Diversity in the Irish Diaspora', *Irish Historical Studies* 31 (1999): 411–34.

Fitzpatrick, David. 'Irish Emigration in the later Nineteenth Century', *Irish Historical Studies* 22 (1980): 126–43.

Fitzpatrick, David. 'Irish Farming Families before the First World War', *Comparative Studies in Society and History* 25 (1983): 339–74.

Fitzpatrick, David. '"That beloved country, that no place else resembles": connotations of Irishness in Irish-Australian Letters, 1841–1915', *Irish Historical Studies* 27 (1991): 324–51.

Foley, Mark C. and Guinnane, Timothy W. 'Did Irish Marriage Patterns Survive the Emigrant Voyage? Irish-American Nuptiality, 1880–1920', *Irish Economic and Social History* 26 (1999): 15–34.

Fraser, Lyndon. 'Irish Migration to the West Coast, 1864–1900', *New Zealand Journal of History* 34 (2000): 197–225.

Fraser, Lyndon. '"To Tara via Holyhead": The Emergence of Irish Catholic Ethnicity in Nineteenth-Century Christchurch, New Zealand', *Journal of Social History* 35 (2002): 431–58.

Gerber, David A. 'The Immigrant Letter Between Positivism and Populism: The Uses of Immigrant Personal Correspondence in Twentieth-century American Scholarship', *Journal of American Ethnic History* 16 (1997): 3–34.

Gibbon, Peter and Curtin, Chris. 'The Stem Family in Ireland', *Comparative Studies in Society and History* 20 (1978): 429–53.

Gilley, Sheridan. 'The Roman Catholic Church and the Nineteenth-Century Irish Diaspora', *Journal of Ecclesiastical History* 35 (1984): 188–207.

Hareven, Tamara K. 'The History of the Family and the Complexity of Social Change', *American Historical Review* 96 (1991): 95–124.

Handleman, Don. 'The Organisation of Ethnicity', *Ethnic Groups* 1 (1977): 187–200.

Jackson, Hugh. 'Churchgoing in Nineteenth-Century New Zealand', *New Zealand Journal of History* 17 (1983): 43–59.

Kenny, Kevin. 'Diaspora and Comparison: The Global Irish as a Case Study', *Journal of American History* 90 (2003): 134–62.

Larkin, Emmet. 'Church, State and Nation in Modern Ireland', *American Historical Review* 80 (1975): 1244–77.

Larkin, Emmet. 'The Devotional Revolution in Ireland, 1850–75', *American Historical Review* 77 (1972): 625–52.

Mageean, Deidre M. 'Emigration from Irish Ports', *Journal of American Ethnic History* 13 (1993): 6–30.

McCaskill, Murray. 'The Goldrush Population of Westland', *New Zealand Geographer* 12 (1956): 31–50.

McCarthy, Angela. '"A Good Idea of Colonial Life": Personal Letters and Irish Migration to New Zealand', *New Zealand Journal of History* 35 (2001): 1–21.

McCarthy, Angela. 'Personal Letters and the Organisation of Irish Migration to and from New Zealand, 1848–1925', *Irish Historical Studies* 33 (2003): 297–319.

Macdonald, John and Shlomowitz, Ralph. 'Passenger Fares on Sailing Vessels to Australia in the Nineteenth Century', *Explorations in Economic History* 28 (1991): 192–207.

McNamara, Heather. 'The *New Zealand Tablet* and the Irish Catholic Press Worldwide, 1898–1923', *New Zealand Journal of History* 37 (2003): 153–67.

Miller, David W. 'Irish Catholicism and the Great Famine', *Journal of Social History* 9 (1975): 81–98.

O'Farrell, Patrick. 'St Patrick's Day in Australia', *Journal of the Royal Australasian Society* 81 (1995): 1–16.

Ó Gráda, Cormac. 'A Note on Nineteenth–Century Emigration Statistics', *Population Studies* 29 (1975): 143–9.

Patterson, Tiffany Ruby and Kelley, Robin D.G. 'Unfinished Migrations: Reflections on the African Diaspora and the Making of the Modern World', *African Studies Review* 43 (2000):11–45.

Pedraza-Bailey, Sylvia. 'Immigration Research: A Conceptual Map', *Social Science History* 14 (1990): 43–67.

Poletti, Alan. 'Italian Censuses in Nineteenth Century New Zealand', *Italian Historical Society Journal* 9 (2001): 26–34.

Richards, Eric 'Irish Life and Progress in Colonial South Australia', *Irish Historical Studies* 27 (1991): 214–36.

Safran, William. 'Diasporas in Modern Societies: Myths of Homeland and Return', *Diaspora* 1 (1991): 83–99.

Stenhouse, John. 'God's Own Silence: Secular Nationalism, Christianity and the Writing of New Zealand History', *New Zealand Journal of History* 38 (2004): 52–71.

Tilly, Louise A. 'Connections', *American Historical Review* 99, (1994): 1–20.

Walsh, Brendan M. 'Marriage Rates and Population Pressure: Ireland, 1871 and 1911', *Economic History Review*, 2nd series, 23 (1970): 148–62.

Yancey, William L.; Eriksen, Eugene P.; and Juliani, Richard N. 'Emergent Ethnicity: A Review and Reformulation', *American Sociological Review* 41 (1976): 391–403.

VIII THESES

Conradson. B.J. 'The County of Westland'. MA thesis, University of Canterbury, 1971.

Laracy, Hugh. M. 'The Life and Context of Bishop Patrick Moran'. MA thesis, Victoria University of Wellington, 1964.

McCarthy, Angela. '"Seas May Divide": Irish Migration to New Zealand as Portrayed in Personal Correspondence, 1840–1937'. PhD thesis, 2 vols, Trinity College, Dublin, 2000.

McCaskill, M. 'The Historical Geography of Westland Before 1914'. PhD thesis, University of Canterbury, 1960.

Macdonald, Charlotte. 'Single Women as Immigrant Settlers in New Zealand, 1853–1871'. PhD thesis, University of Auckland, 1986.

Pickens, K.A. 'Canterbury, 1851–1881: Demography and Mobility. A Comparative Study'. PhD thesis, Washington University, St Louis, 1976.

Sweetman, Rory Matthew. 'New Zealand Catholicism, War, Politics and the Irish Issue, 1912–1922'. PhD thesis, University of Cambridge, 1990.

Vaney, Neil Patrick. 'The Dual Tradition: Irish Catholics and French Priests in New Zealand – the West Coast Experience, 1865–1910'. MA thesis, University of Canterbury, 1976

Notes

ABBREVIATIONS
ANZ–CH   Archives New Zealand, Christchurch
ANZ–W   Archives New Zealand, Wellington
ATL   Alexander Turnbull Library, Wellington
CDA   Christchurch Roman Catholic Diocesan Archives
MAW   Marist Archives, Wellington
RG   Registrar General's Office, Lower Hutt (now Wellington)
WAA   Wellington Roman Catholic Archdiocesan Archives
WCHM   West Coast Historical Museum, Hokitika

ACKNOWLEDGEMENTS
1   Philip Ross May, *The West Coast Gold Rushes*, Christchurch, 1962, pp. 477, 480.

CHAPTER 1
1   Philip Ross May, *Hokitika: Goldfields Capital*, Christchurch, 1964, p. 35.
2   H.F. von Haast, *The Life and Times of Sir Julius von Haast*, 1948, p. 34.
3   John O'Regan to Ellen O'Regan, 26 January 1899, courtesy of Angela McCarthy.
4   Ellen Piezzi to Victer Piezzi, undated (c. 1880), courtesy of Teresa O'Connor. Hard times were worsened by the climate: 'The Weder is very dry just a Now and this is very bad for the digers canot doo Noting When the have Now Water'.
5   I am indebted here to Ron Burnett, *Cultures of Vision: Images, Media and the Imaginary*, Bloomington and Indianapolis, 1995, p. 54 and *passim*.
6   Terry Hearn, 'Mining the Quarry', in Eric Pawson and Tom Brooking, eds, *Environmental Histories of New Zealand*, Melbourne, 2002, pp. 84–99.
7   Francis Redwood, *Reminiscences of Early Days in New Zealand*, Wellington, 1922, p. 26.
8   John O'Regan to Ellen O'Regan, 26 January 1899.
9   Henry Reynolds, *Frontier: Aborigines, Settlers and Land*, Sydney, 1987, pp. 193–4; May, *The West Coast Gold Rushes*, Christchurch, 1962, ch. 17; Jim McAloon, 'Resource Frontiers, Environment and Settler Capitalism, 1769–1860', in Pawson and Brooking, eds, pp. 52–83.
10 Donald Harman Akenson, 'No Petty People: Pakeha History and the Historiography of the Irish Diaspora', in Lyndon Fraser, ed., *A Distant Shore: Irish Migration and New Zealand Settlement*, Dunedin, 2000, pp. 22–3.

170   Castles of Gold

11   David Fitzpatrick, *Irish Emigration, 1801–1921*, Dublin, 1985, p. 30.
12   Dudley Baines, *Emigration from Europe, 1815–1930*, Cambridge, 1995, Table 3, p. 4.
13   R.F. Foster, *Modern Ireland, 1600–1972*, London, 1988, p. 345; Fitzpatrick, *Irish Emigration*, p. 3; Cormac Ó Gráda, *The Great Irish Famine*, Cambridge, 1989, pp. 8, 48–9.
14   W.E. Vaughan and A.J. Fitzpatrick, eds, *Irish Historical Statistics: Population, 1821–1971*, Dublin, 1978, p. 3.
15   Cormac Ó Gráda, 'A Note on Nineteenth-Century Emigration Statistics', *Population Studies*, 29, 1975, pp. 143–9; David Fitzpatrick, 'Irish Emigration in the later Nineteenth Century', *Irish Historical Studies*, 22, 1980, pp. 131–4, 142.
16   David Fitzpatrick, 'Ireland Since 1870', in Roy F. Foster, ed., *The Oxford History of Ireland*, Oxford, 1989, p. 175.
17   *New Zealand Tablet*, 23 August 1889.
18   Deidre M. Mageean, 'Emigration from Irish Ports', *Journal of American Ethnic History*, 13, 1993, pp. 6–30.
19   Kevin Kenny, *The American Irish: A History*, New York, 2000, ch. 2.
20   Ó Gráda, *The Great Irish Famine*, pp. 48–9.
21   For an excellent overview of this process, see Kerby A. Miller, *Emigrants and Exiles: Ireland and the Irish Exodus to North America*, New York, 1985, ch. 8.
22   Fitzpatrick, *Irish Emigration*, pp. 7–8.
23   *Commission on Emigration and Other Problems*, Dublin, 1954, pp. 122, 320; Kelly Family Reunion, 24–26 October 1986, unpublished manuscript, WCHM; Stafford Cemetery, Plot References and Transcript of Inscriptions, WCHM.
24   David Fitzpatrick, *Oceans of Consolation: Personal Accounts of Irish Migration to Australia*, Melbourne, 1995, p. 13.
25   Robert E. Kennedy, Jr., *The Irish: Emigration, Marriage and Fertility*, Berkeley, 1973, p. 119; Donald Harman Akenson, *The Irish Diaspora: A Primer*, Toronto, 1996, pp. 49–52.
26   Cecelia Coghlan to Ellen Anne Edwards, 24 June 1890, courtesy of John Coghlan.
27   Fitzpatrick, *Irish Emigration*, p. 1; Fitzpatrick, *Oceans of Consolation*, p. 534.
28   Vaughan and Fitzpatrick, eds, pp. 261–353; Miller, Table 2, pp. 570–71; K. Theodore Hoppen, *Ireland Since 1800: Conflict and Conformity*, London and New York, 1999, pp. 45–6.
29   Cormac Ó Gráda, 'Some Aspects of Nineteenth-Century Irish Emigration Statistics', in L.M. Cullen and T.C. Smout, eds, *Comparative Aspects of Irish Economic and Social History*, Edinburgh, 1977, pp. 65–73; Fitzpatrick, 'Irish Emigration in the Later Nineteenth Century', pp. 127–28.
30   Donald E. Jordan, Jr., *Land and Popular Politics in Ireland: County Mayo from the Plantation to the Land War*, Cambridge, 1994, pp. 1–9, 103–69. County Mayo suffered a net population loss of 27 per cent between 1851 and 1901.
31   *Kumara Times*, 25 October 1888; *West Coast Times*, 7 March 1906; *The Cyclopedia of New Zealand, Vol. 5*, Christchurch, 1906, p. 526.
32   *Kumara Times*, 5 May, 26 and 29 November 1888.
33   Peter Ewen, 'Ann's "house rules" had their moments in the early Coast pub game', *The Coaster*, May 26 1999, p. 2; Antoinette O'Brien, 'The MacNamara family of Co. Clare', unpublished report, Clare Heritage Centre, September 1998; descendant information, Peter Kerridge.
34   Baines, ch. 1. The United States was the most important destination for migrants in absolute numbers (33 million), followed by Argentina (6.4), Canada (4.7), Brazil

(4.3) and Australia (3.5). For the Irish background, see Timothy W. Guinnane, *The Vanishing Irish: Households, Migration and the Rural Economy in Ireland, 1850–1914*, Princeton, 1997.

35   John E. Bodnar, *The Transplanted: A History of Immigrants in Urban America*, Bloomington, 1985, pp. xv–xxi; Jose C. Moya, *Cousins and Strangers: Spanish Immigrants in Buenos Aires, 1850–1930*, Berkeley, 1998, pp. 1–10.

36   The best vantage point for studying their mobility is therefore to be found 'in the meeting of the extremes: of global forces and local conditions, of the world and the village'. See Moya, p. 4.

37   David Fitzpatrick, *Oceans of Consolation*, p. 534 and *passim*; Angela McCarthy, *Irish Migrants in New Zealand, 1840–1937: 'The Desired Haven'*, Woodbridge, 2005.

38   Louise A. Tilly, 'Connections', *American Historical Review*, 99, 1994, pp. 1–20.

39   Recent works in Irish New Zealand history include Anna Rogers, *A Lucky Landing: The Story of the Irish in New Zealand*, Auckland, 1996; Fraser, ed., *A Distant Shore*; Angela McCarthy, '"A Good Idea of Colonial Life": Personal Letters and Irish Migration to New Zealand', *New Zealand Journal of History*, 35, 2001, pp. 1–21; Lyndon Fraser, '"To Tara via Holyhead": The Emergence of Irish Catholic Ethnicity in Nineteenth-Century Christchurch, New Zealand', *Journal of Social History*, 35, 2002, pp. 431–58; Brad Patterson, ed., *The Irish in New Zealand: Historical Contexts and Perspectives*, Wellington, 2002; Angela McCarthy, 'Personal Letters and the Organisation of Irish Migration to and from New Zealand, 1848–1925', *Irish Historical Studies*, 33, 2003, pp. 297–319; Brad Patterson, ed., *From Ulster to New Ulster: The 2003 Ulster–New Zealand Lectures*, Wellington, 2004; McCarthy, *Irish Migrants in New Zealand*; and Brad Patterson, ed., *The Hidden Irish: Ulster-New Zealand Migration and Cultural Transfers*, Dublin, 2005.

40   Akenson, in Fraser, ed., p. 22. The best introductions to Irish global migration are Fitzpatrick, *Irish Emigration*; Miller, *Emigrants and Exiles*; Donald Harman Akenson, *The Irish Diaspora: A Primer*, Belfast and Toronto, 1993; and Andy Bielenberg, ed., *The Irish Diaspora*, Harlow, 2000. For a valuable compilation of recent work, see especially the multi-volume *Irish World Wide: History, Heritage, Identity* series edited by Patrick O'Sullivan: Volume 1, *Patterns of Migration*; Volume 2, *The Irish in the New Communities*; Volume 3, *The Creative Migrant*; Volume 4, *Irish Women and Irish Migration*; Volume 5, *Religion and Identity*; Volume 6, *The Meaning of the Famine*. For surveys of the current state of scholarship, see Alan O'Day, 'Revising the Diaspora', in D. George Boyce and Alan O'Day, eds, *The Making of Modern Irish History: Revisionism and the Revisionist Controversy*, London and New York, 1996, pp. 188–215; David Noel Doyle, 'Review Article: Cohesion and Diversity in the Irish Diaspora', *Irish Historical Studies*, 31, 1999, pp. 411–34; Kevin Kenny, 'Diaspora and Comparison: The Global Irish as a case study,' *Journal of American History*, 90 2003, pp. 134–62.
     Standard works on the Irish abroad include Hasia Diner, *Erin's Daughter's in America: Irish Immigrant Women in the Nineteenth Century*, Baltimore, 1983; Kerby A. Miller, *Emigrants and Exiles: Ireland and the Irish Exodus to North America*, New York, 1985; Janet Nolan, *Ourselves Alone: Women's Emigration from Ireland, 1885–1920*, Lexington, Ky., 1989; David M. Emmons, *The Butte Irish: Class and Ethnicity in an American Mining Town, 1875–1925*, Urbana, 1989; Kenny, *The American Irish*; David T. Gleeson, *The Irish in the South, 1815–1877*, Chapel Hill and London, 2001; Donald M. MacRaild, *Culture, Conflict and Migration: The Irish in Victorian Cumbria*, Liverpool, 1998, and *Irish Migrants in Modern Britain, 1750–1922*, Basingstoke, 1999; Enda Delaney, *Demography, State and Society: Irish Migration*

172   Castles of Gold

to *Britain, 1921–1971*, Liverpool, 2000; Paul O'Leary, *Immigration and Integration: The Irish in Wales, 1798–1922*, Cardiff, 2000; Patrick O'Farrell, *The Irish in Australia*, Sydney, 1993; Fitzpatrick, *Oceans of Consolation*; Malcolm Campbell, *The Kingdom of the Ryans: The Irish in Southwest New South Wales, 1816–1890*, Sydney, 1997; Cecil J. Houston and William J. Smyth, *Irish Emigration and Canadian Settlement: Patterns, Links and Letters*, Buffalo, 1990; Robert M. Scally, *The End of Hidden Ireland: Rebellion, Famine and Emigration*, New York, 1995; J. Matthew Gallman, *Receiving Erin's Children: Philadelphia, Liverpool and the Irish Famine, 1845–55*, Chapel Hill, 2000; Bronwen Walter, *Outsiders Inside: Whiteness, Place and Irish Women*, London and New York, 2001.

41   Many anthropologists have demonstrated that ethnic boundaries and cultural ones are not necessarily identical. For a superb introduction, see Thomas Hylland Eriksen, *Ethnicity and Nationalism*, London and Sterling, VA., 2002, ch. 3. My own understanding owes a considerable debt to Abner Cohen's *Custom and Politics in Urban Africa: A Study of Hausa Migrants in Yoruba Towns*, Berkeley, 1969.

42   See, in particular, Ronald Bayor and Timothy Meagher, eds, *The New York Irish*, Baltimore, 1996; John Belchem, 'The Liverpool Irish Enclave', in Donald M. MacRaild, ed., *The Great Famine and Beyond: Irish Migrants in Britain in the Nineteenth and Twentieth Centuries*, Dublin and Portland, Or., 2000, pp. 128–46; Eric Richards, 'Irish Life and Progress in Colonial South Australia', *Irish Historical Studies*, 27, 1991, pp. 214–36.

43   This scenario is vividly illustrated in Rory Sweetman's study of Irish Catholic leadership styles in colonial New Zealand. See Rory Sweetman, '"How to behave among Protestants": Varieties of Irish Catholic Leadership in Colonial New Zealand', in Patterson, ed., *The Irish in New Zealand*, pp. 89–101.

44   Fitzpatrick, *Irish Emigration*, pp. 35–6.

45   Don Handelman, 'The Organisation of Ethnicity', *Ethnic Groups*, 1, 1977, pp. 187–200.

46   See Alan O'Day, 'Irish Diaspora Politics in Perspective: The United Irish Leagues of Great Britain and America, 1900–14', in MacRaild, ed., pp. 40–44.

47   Patrick O'Farrell, 'Catholicism on the West Coast: Just How Irish Is It?', *New Zealand Tablet*, 3 May 1973, pp. 53–6.

48   Eriksen, pp. 41–2.

49   Lyndon Fraser, *To Tara via Holyhead: Irish Catholic Immigrants in Nineteenth-Century Christchurch*, Auckland, 1997; Terry Hearn, 'Irish Migration to New Zealand to 1915', in Fraser, ed., pp. 55–74; 'The Irish on the Otago Goldfields', in Fraser, ed., pp. 75–85; 'The Origins of New Zealand's Irish Settlers, 1840–1945', in Patterson, ed., *The Irish in New Zealand*, pp. 15–34; and 'Scots Miners in the Goldfields, 1861–70', in Tom Brooking and Jennie Coleman, eds, *The Heather and the Fern: Scottish Migration and New Zealand Settlement*, Dunedin, 2003, pp. 67–85; Sarah Dwyer and Lyndon Fraser, '"We are all here like so many on the cockle beds": Towards a History of Ulster Migrants in Nineteenth–Century Canterbury', in Patterson, ed., *The Hidden Irish*, pp. 115–30.

50   Patricia Nelson Limerick, 'Has Minority History Transformed the Historical Discourse?', *Perspectives*, 35, 1997, p. 36.

51   On the historical study of Irish migrant letters, see Arnold Schrier, *Ireland and the American Emigration, 1850–1900*, Minneapolis, 1958; Miller, *Emigrants and Exiles*; Donald Harman Akenson, 'Reading the Texts of Rural Immigrants: Letters from the Irish in Australia, New Zealand, and North America', *Canadian Papers in Rural History*, 7, 1990, pp. 387–406; Fitzpatrick, *Oceans of Consolation*; McCarthy, *Irish Migrants in New Zealand*.

52   E.P. Thompson, *The Poverty of Theory and Other Essays*, New York, 1978, p. 88, quoted in Fraser, *To Tara via Holyhead*, p. 10.
53   Bernard S. Cohn, *An Anthropologist Among the Historians and Other Essays*, Delhi, 1987, p. 49.

CHAPTER 2
1   Philip Ross May, *The West Coast Gold Rushes*, Christchurch, 1962, p. 13.
2   *Ibid.*, p. 314.
3   Bernard Bailyn, *Voyagers to the West: A Passage in the Peopling of America on the Eve of the Revolution*, New York, 1987, p. 239.
4   Lyndon Fraser, 'Irish Migration to the West Coast, 1864–1900', *New Zealand Journal of History*, 34, 2000, p. 200.
5   Bailyn, p. 239.
6   See, for example, Lyndon Fraser, *To Tara via Holyhead: Irish Catholic Immigrants in Nineteenth-Century Christchurch*, Auckland, 1997.
7   May, p. 480.
8   *Commission on Emigration and Other Population Problems*, 1948–1954, Dublin, 1954.
9   Terry Hearn, 'The Irish on the Otago Goldfields', in Lyndon Fraser, ed., *A Distant Shore: Irish Migration and New Zealand Settlement*, Dunedin, 2000, p. 82.
10   *Ibid.*, p. 82.
11   *Ibid.*, p. 77.
12   Donald Harman Akenson, *The Irish Diaspora: A Primer*, Toronto, 1993, p. 169.
13   See Kerby Miller, *Emigrants and Exiles: Ireland and the Irish Exodus to North America*, New York, 1985, pp. 350, 376–8, and W.E. Vaughan and A.E. Fitzpatrick, eds, *Irish Historical Statistics: Population, 1821–1971*, Dublin, 1978, *passim*.
14   Miller, pp. 369–80.
15   Hearn, p. 83.
16   May, p. 285.
17   David Fitzpatrick, *Oceans of Consolation: Personal Accounts of Irish Migration to Australia*, Melbourne, 1995, pp 10–11. Yet the Victorian returns for 1852–4 show that only one-ninth of all Irish female arrivals were unassisted, compared with half of their male counterparts. Fitzpatrick also identifies a 'gross Anglo-Irish disparity' that is illustrated by 'the contrast between the Irish component of unassisted migration (5%) and of assisted immigration (29%)', p. 11, fn. 19. On Irish women's government-assisted migration, see Robin Haines, '"The priest made a bother about it": The travails of that "unhappy sisterhood' bound for colonial Australia', in Trevor McClaughlin, ed., *Irish Women in Colonial Australia*, St. Leonard's, 1998, pp. 43–63.
18   See John Macdonald and Ralph Shlomowitz, 'Passenger Fares on Sailing Vessels to Australia in the Nineteenth Century', *Explorations in Economic History*, 28, 1991, pp. 192–207.
19   Descendant information, Teresa O'Connor and Ted Matthews.
20   Joanna Bourke has convincingly argued that many unmarried rural women in Irish society enhanced their status during the late nineteenth and early twentieth centuries by choosing to perform housework for widowed or unmarried male relatives. See "The Best of All Home Rulers": The Economic Power of Women in Ireland, 1880–1914', *Irish Economic and Social History*, 18, 1991, pp. 34–41; *Husbandry to Housewifery: Women, Economic Change, and Housework in Ireland, 1890–1914*, Oxford, 1993.
21   David Noel Doyle, 'Review Article: Cohesion and Diversity in the Irish Diaspora',

Irish Historical Studies, 31, 1999, p. 419.

22   Descendant information, Ron Patterson and Brian Nolan.

23   See Lyndon Fraser, *To Tara via Holyhead: Irish Catholic Immigrants in Nineteenth Century Christchurch*, Auckland, 1997, pp. 32–49.

24   Patrick O'Farrell, *The Irish in Australia*, Sydney, 1993, pp. 85–8.

25   See Ted Matthews, 'Sugar Annie (Bell Hill)', in Yvonne Davison and Frankie Mills, eds, *Women of Westland and Their Families*, Greymouth, 1998, p. 194; Kathleen W. Orr, 'Bridget Goodwin', *A People's History: Illustrated Biographies from the Dictionary of New Zealand Biography, Volume I, 1769–1869*, Wellington, 1992, pp. 88–90.

26   Descendant information, Ted Matthews.

27   Gale Davidson Gibb, 'Memories of Red Jacks: Johanna Shanahan Weir', in Davison and Mills, eds, pp. 185–6.

28   *Ibid.*, p. 186.

29   Descendant information, Mary O'Connor.

30   A substantial body of scholarship in international migration studies emphasises the importance of personal networks in explaining the origins, composition and dynamics of migrant flows. For a useful introduction to the literature, see Monica Boyd, 'Family and Personal Networks in International Migration: Recent Developments and New Agendas', *International Migration Review*, 23, 1989, pp 638–70; Stephen Castles and Mark Miller, *The Age of Migration: International Population Movements in the Modern World*, London, 1998.

31   Gibb, p. 187; descendant information, Ted Matthews.

32   Ellen Piezzi to her brother-in-law Victer Piezzi, undated.

33   There are three surviving letters in this sequence, written between 1926 and 1927. I am indebted to Brian Nolan for access to the Phelan correspondence.

34   Kate Phelan to Cecilia Horan, 19 January 1926.

35   *Ibid.*

36   Fitzpatrick, *Oceans of Consolation*, p. 503 and *passim*.

37   A similar pattern is evident in Irish-Australian correspondence. See David Fitzpatrick, '"An Ocean of Consolation": Letters and Irish Immigration to Australia', in Eric Richards, Richard Reid and David Fitzpatrick, *Visible Immigrants: Neglected Sources for the History of Australian Immigration*, Canberra, 1989, p. 69.

38   Catherine O'Toole to Susan Hogan, 30 July 1890, courtesy of Ted Matthews.

39   Patrick Hogan to Michael Hogan, 10 November 1871.

40   O'Toole to Susan Hogan, 18 October 1887.

41   *Ibid.*

42   This view has been advanced by Miles Fairburn, *The Ideal Society and Its Enemies: The Foundations of Modern New Zealand Society, 1850–1900*, Auckland, 1989, pp. 165–7.

43   Fitzpatrick, 'An Ocean of Consolation', *passim*; Angela McCarthy, '"A Good Idea of Colonial Life": Personal Letters and Irish Migration to New Zealand', *New Zealand Journal of History*, 35, 2001, pp. 1–21.

44   Michael Flanagan to Richard Flanagan, 10 August 1867, courtesy of Donald Murphy.

45   Richard Flanagan to Michael Flanagan, 1 June 1868.

46   *Ibid.*

47   Fitzpatrick, *Oceans of Consolation*, pp. 469–72.

48   The accession number for this file is CH A474/1865, ANZ–CH.

49   Alexander Mitchell to James Mitchell, 1 August 1847, CH A474/1865, ANZ–CH.

50 Alexander Mitchell to James Mitchell, 1 September 1850, CH A474/1865, ANZ–CH.

51 *Ibid.*; Alexander Mitchell to James Mitchell, 24 January 1850, CH A474/1865, ANZ–CH.

52 Richard Megaffin to his parents, 3 September 1857, CH A474/1865, ANZ–CH.

53 Andrew Burns to Michael Flanagan, 8 June 1890.

54 Samuel Gilmer to William Gilmer, 29 June 1886, courtesy of Angela McCarthy.

55 William Gilmer to Robert Gilmer, 11 September 1886.

56 Fitzpatrick, *Oceans of Consolation*, pp. 482–4.

57 Andrew Burns to Michael Flanagan, 8 June 1890.

58 This paragraph is based on Chris Rabey, *A Southland in Westland: 120 Years on the Coast, 1865–1985: Centennial of the O'Connor Family Ownership*, Hokitika, 1985, and descendant information provided by Bill and Mary O'Connor.

59 James O'Connor to the Agent-General, 6 November 1882, courtesy of Mary O'Connor.

60 Jeremiah O'Connor to Edward O'Connor, 1 December 1885, courtesy of Mary O'Connor.

61 Mary O'Connor and Johanna O'Leary to William O'Connor, *c*. 1900.

62 Terry Hearn, 'Scots Miners on the Goldfields, 1861–1870', in Tom Brooking and Jennie Coleman, eds, *The Heather and the Fern: Scottish Migration and New Zealand Settlement*, Dunedin, 2003, p. 77.

Chapter 3

1 Philip Ross May, *The West Coast Gold Rushes*, Christchurch, 1962, p. 501.

2 William Pember Reeves, *The Long White Cloud: Ao Tea Roa*, London, 1899, p. 400.

3 May, *The West Coast Gold Rushes*, p. 313.

4 See Angela McCarthy, '"Seas May Divide": Irish Migration to New Zealand as Portrayed in Personal Correspondence, 1840–1937', PhD thesis, 2 vols, Trinity College, Dublin, 2000.

5 I am indebted to Angela McCarthy for this information.

6 Descendant information, Donald Murphy.

7 Michael Flanagan to John Flanagan, 20 May 1890, courtesy of Donald Murphy.

8 Michael Flanagan to Reverend Richard Flanagan, 18 February 1865.

9 *Ibid.*, 18 February 1865.

10 May, p. 286.

11 Michael Flanagan to Richard Flanagan, 10 August 1867.

12 Patrick Flanagan to Michael Flanagan, 8 September 1869.

13 Patrick Flanagan to Michael Flanagan, 18 October 1869.

14 Patrick Flanagan to Michael Flanagan, 6 December 1869.

15 Richard Flanagan to Michael Flanagan, 20 August 1870.

16 Nicholas Flanagan to Richard Flanagan, 5 January 1869.

17 Jeremiah O'Connor to Edward O'Connor, 1 December 1885, courtesy of Mary O'Connor

18 *New Zealand Herald*, 29 November 1869, p. 3; *New Zealand Herald*, 11 December 1869, p. 5; *Nelson Evening Mail*, 2 and 3 December 1869. Two of the accused, Henry Michael O'Brien and Patrick O'Sullivan, were 'discharged with a severe warning from the Judge'. The third, John McLoughlin, was found guilty by the jury and 'sentenced to two years imprisonment with hard labour'.

19 Richard Flanagan to Michael Flanagan, 20 August 1870.

20 Bridget Kirk to Michael Flanagan, 10 May 1870.

21 *Ibid.*, 10 May 1870; Bridget Kirk to Michael Flanagan, 5 December 1871.

22 For a different interpretation of this correspondence, see David Fitzpatrick, "'An Ocean of Consolation": Letters and Irish Immigration to Australia', in Eric Richards, Richard Reid and David Fitzpatrick, *Visible Immigrants: Neglected Sources for the History of Australian Immigration*, Canberra, 1989, p. 71.

23 Reverend Richard Flanagan to Michael and Patrick Flanagan, 12 May 1870. This delicate task was not completed until 20 years later, when Michael wrote to the New Zealand authorities from Tobertoby and finally obtained the estate money for Kirk's family.

24 Fitzpatrick in Richards et al., p. 71.

25 Patrick Flanagan to Michael Flanagan, 6 December 1869; Patrick Flanagan to Kate O'Brien, 14 December 1869; descendant information, Donald Murphy. The details of Michael's estate were kindly provided by Angela McCarthy.

26 Andrew Burns to Michael Flanagan, 8 June 1890.

27 Philip McCarthy to Michael Flanagan, 23 May 1884.

28 Will of Hamilton Gilmer, AAOM 27056/1919, Will of Samuel Gilmer, AAOM 36375a/1925, ANZ–W.

29 *Grey River Argus*, 17 March 1881.

30 Will of Martin Kennedy, AAOM 19266/1916, ANZ–W; *New Zealand Times*, 26 August 1916. I am indebted to Brain Wood for additional information on the career of Martin Kennedy.

31 May, p. 480.

32 Jim McAloon, *No Idle Rich: The Wealthy in Canterbury and Otago, 1840–1914*, Dunedin, 2002, p. 174 and *passim*.

33 *Ibid.*, p. 75.

34 Descendant information, Ian Cameron.

35 McAloon, pp. 27, 181.

36 May, p. 255.

37 *Ibid.*, p. 311.

38 McAloon, p. 168.

39 Peter Ewen, 'Wealthy early Coaster was also generous', *The Coaster*, 10 March 1999, p. 2.

40 Will of Felix Campbell, GM 365/1922, ANZ–CH.

41 Will of Patrick Michael Griffen, GM 130/1913, ANZ–CH; Peter Ewen, 'Griffen and Smith survives throughout the year', *The Coaster*, 4 August 1999, p. 2.

42 Will of Daniel Sheedy, HK 16/1909, ANZ–CH.

43 *The Cyclopedia of New Zealand, Vol. 5*, Christchurch, 1906, p. 549.

44 *Ibid.*, p. 152.

45 *Ibid.*, p. 258; Will of Robert Patterson, RN 145/03, ANZ–CH. Patterson died intestate leaving a widow, Catherine, and 12 children, four of whom were minors.

46 *The Cyclopedia of New Zealand, Vol. 5*, Christchurch, 1906, pp. 580, 491, 544; GM 298/1904, HK 104/1913 and HK 2101/1907, ANZ–CH.

47 McAloon, p. 147.

48 Will of James William Fair, WP 122/1913, ANZ–CH.

49 McAloon, pp. 47–9; Will of Myles McPadden, WP 119/1913, Will of Thomas McKee, HK 2088/1906, ANZ–CH.

50 Will of Patrick Michael Griffen, GM 130/1913, Will of William Glenn, HK 674/1897, Will of Hubert Dolphin, WP 46/1910; ANZ–CH.

51 As I have suggested elsewhere, this kind of data has limitations, but it does provide one

indication of how well newcomers fared in the local economy. See Lyndon Fraser, *To Tara via Holyhead: Irish Catholic Immigrants in Nineteenth-Century Christchurch*, Auckland, 1997, ch. 5.

52   Will of John Shanahan, GM 292/1905, Will of Richard Cox, WP 14/1901, ANZ–CH.
53   May, p. 287.
54   *Ibid.*, p. 291. Drowning made up 47 per cent of the 239 sudden deaths known to police that occurred on the West Canterbury Goldfield between 5 November 1864 and 31 December 1867. Mining accidents accounted for 20 per cent and 'cause uncertain' was returned in 12 per cent of these cases. Only 14 per cent of the deaths were due to natural causes or 'Visitation of God', p. 292.
55   *Kumara Times*, 18 and 19 October 1886.
56   *Kumara Times*, 21 May 1889.
57   Robert Moorhead, intestate, HK 82/1872, John Kane, intestate, HK 69/1869, Michael Clune, intestate, HK 12/1866, ANZ–CH.
58   Patrick Martin, intestate, CH A52/1866, ANZ–CH.
59   Jeremiah McGrath, intestate, HK D5/1868 and HK 59/1868, ANZ–CH.
60   May, p. 286.
61   *Ibid.*, pp. 250–1.
62   Patrick Donovan, intestate, WP 3/1892, ANZ–CH.
63   Descendant information, Angela McCarthy.
64   David McCullough to his parents and sisters, 4 June 1875, courtesy of Angela McCarthy.
65   David McCullough to his parents and sisters, 21 December 1875.
66   David McCullough to his parents, 1 June 1898.
67   David McCullough to his parents, 2 July 1899.
68   *Ibid.*
69   *Westport News*, 19 December 1934.
70   John O'Regan to his grand-niece, Ellen, 26 January 1899.
71   May, p. 287.
72   Jack Minehan, 'The Pioneers', unpublished manuscript in possession of Brian Wood, n.d.; 'McDavitt: From County Donegal to New Zealand', unpublished manuscript, n.d., WCHM; Mary, Michael, Paul and Nicola Rooney, 'From Ireland to Westland: A Record of the Descendants of James Rooney and Annie Gunning', unpublished manuscript, 1998, WCHM; Helen Booth, 'The McKeogh Family', unpublished manuscript, 1998, WCHM.
73   Without housework, consumption could not take place as it 'transform[ed] income into disposable goods'. Housework, she argues, is best viewed as production. [p. 16] also 276.
74   *Nelson Examiner*, 17 February 1866, from the *Hokitika Evening Star*, 9 February 1866, quoted in May, p. 310.
75   On the perpetual shortage of domestic servants in Westland, see, for example, J.A. Bonar to Minister for Immigration, 22 January 1876, Im 3/1, ANZ–W.
76   See Fraser, *To Tara via Holyhead*, pp. 60–61.
77   Kevin Kenny, *The American Irish: A History*, New York, 2000, pp. 153–4.
78   See May, pp. 323–4.
79   Catherine Flaherty left her position at Orwell Creek in 1882 because she was not getting paid. Despite this setback, she quickly found work at Mrs Johnston's Star Hotel in Ahaura, where she met her future husband, Anton Anderson. See Mary P. Anderson, 'The Anderson Family', unpublished manuscript, WCHM.

80   Kenny, pp. 151–4; Bronwen Walter, *Outsiders Inside: Whiteness, Place and Irish Women*, New York, 2001, pp. 53–7, 100–05, 143–8.

81   Gayle Davidson Gibb, 'Memories of Red Jacks: Johanna Shanahan Weir', in Yvonne Davison and Frankie Mills, eds, *Women of Westland and Their Families*, omnibus edition, Greymouth, 1998, p. 187.

82   Will of John Cronin, HK 124/1914, ANZ–CH.

83   Mark Wallace, 'Recollections of Early Years in South Westland: Catherine Wallace (Markey)', in Davison and Mills, eds, pp. 276–83.

84   *Kumara Times*, 8 February 1889; Andrew Searight, intestate, RN 47/1889, ANZ–CH.

85   Will of Lucy Searight, RN 93/1896, ANZ–CH.

86   Ted Matthews, 'The Deverys and the Gillins: A Brief History', unpublished manuscript, n.d., WCHM.

87   Descendant information, Bill Nolan.

88   Descendant information, Ted Matthews.

89   Anne Hutchison, 'Barbara Weldon', *The Dictionary of New Zealand Biography*, *Volume One, 1769–1869*, Wellington, 1990, p. 581.

90   Wallace, p. 282.

91   *West Coast Times*, 17 September 1894.

92   *Ibid.*, 18, 24, 25 and 26 September 1894; Peter Ewen, 'Ann's "house rules" had their moments in the early Coast pub game', *The Coaster*, 26 May 1999, p. 2.

93   Descendant information, Peter Kerridge; Gerard Morris, ed., *Waiuta, 1906–1951: The gold mine, the town, the people*, Reefton, 1986, pp. 81–5.

94   Peter Graham, 'Mrs Isabell Kathleen Graham', in Davison and Mills, eds, p. 273.

95   Ellen Piezzi to Victer Piezzi, 8 October 1881, courtesy of O'Connor.

96   Magee Family, MS Papers 116, ATL; 'Notes from Journal of Pat Magee', in Davison and Mills, eds, p. 174.

97   Will of Michael Scanlon, WP 1/1894, ANZ–CH.

98   For example, 98 Irish testators (71.5 per cent) transferred the residuary interest in their estates to their spouses absolutely between 1865 and 1915 (n = 137), while another two bequeathed most of their property to their wives (1.5 per cent). Fifteen wills created life-interests in an estate (10.9 per cent), 18 provided an income dependent on continuing widowhood (13.1 per cent) and four documents left widows with little or nothing (2.9 per cent). These patterns differ markedly from those found in Christchurch. See Fraser, *To Tara via Holyhead*, ch. 6.

99   Will of Daniel Falvey, HK 227/1884, Will of James McInroe, GM 153/1890, Will of James Corbett, HK 2172/1908, Will of Bernard Rogers, RN 153/1904, and Will of Patrick Healey, HK 23/1910, ANZ–CH.

100   Donald Harman Akenson, 'Reading the Texts of Rural Immigrants: Letters from the Irish in Australia, New Zealand and America', in Donald Harman Akenson, ed., *Canadian Papers in Rural History, Volume VII*, Ontario, 1990, pp. 395–6.

101   Bridget Scanlon, intestate, WP 185/1915, ANZ–CH.

102   Will of Ellen Harold, WP 159/1914, Will of Mary Hannan, GM 156/1914, Will of Sarah Taylor, GM 96/1912, and Will of Mary Enright, WP 197/1915, ANZ–CH.

103   Will of Ellen Kennedy, WP 9/1902, ANZ–CH.

104   May, p. 310.

105   See Patrick O'Farrell, 'Catholicism on the West Coast: Just How Irish Is It?', *New Zealand Tablet*, 3 May 1973, pp. 53–6.

106   Kevin Kenny, 'Diaspora and Comparison: The Global Irish as a Case Study', *Journal of American History*, 90, 2003, p. 152.

CHAPTER 4

1   Nancy F. Cott, *Public Vows: A History of Marriage and the Nation*, Cambridge, Mass., and London, 2000, p. 1.
2   See Patrick Corish, *The Irish Catholic Experience: A Historical Survey*, Dublin, 1985, pp. 219–22; Donald Harman Akenson, *Small Differences: Irish Catholics and Irish Protestants, 1815–1922: An International Perspective*, Kingston and Montreal, 1988, pp. 109–15.
3   Kerby A. Miller with David N. Doyle and Patricia Kelleher, '"For Love and Liberty": Irish Women, Migration and Domesticity in Ireland and America, 1815–1920', in Patrick O'Sullivan, ed., *Irish Women and Irish Migration*, vol. 4, *The Irish Worldwide: History, Heritage, Identity*, Leicester, 1995, pp. 47–52.
4   Bronwen Walter, *Outsiders Inside: Whiteness, Place and Irish Women*, London and New York, 2001, pp. 15–18.
5   Cott, pp. 2–3.
6   *Ibid.*, p. 4-5 and *passim*; Akenson, *Small Differences*, ch. 5.
7   Cott, p. 1.
8   *Ibid.*, p. 5.
9   My views on the relationship between marriage and ethnicity have been decisively shaped by Abner Cohen, *Custom and Politics in Urban Africa: A Study of Hausa Migrants in Yoruba Towns*, Berkeley, 1969, pp. 183–214.
10 See especially Miller with Doyle and Kelleher, in O'Sullivan, ed., pp. 41–65. There is a rich historiography on marriage patterns in Ireland. See, for example, Kenneth H. Connell, 'Peasant Marriage in Ireland After the Great Famine', *Past and Present*, 12, 1957, pp. 76–91, and 'Catholicism and Marriage in the Century After the Famine', in *Irish Peasant Society: Four Historical Essays*, Oxford, 1968; Brendan M. Walsh, 'Marriage Rates and Population Pressure: Ireland, 1871 and 1911', *Economic History Review*, 2nd series, 23, 1970, pp. 148–62; Robert E. Kennedy, Jr., *The Irish: Emigration, Marriage, and Fertility*, Berkeley and Los Angeles, 1973; S.J. Connolly, 'Marriage in Pre-Famine Ireland', in Art Cosgrove, ed., *Marriage in Ireland*, Dublin, 1985, pp. 78–98; David Fitzpatrick, 'Marriage in Post-Famine Ireland', in Cosgrove, ed., pp. 116–31; Timothy M. Guinnane, *The Vanishing Irish: Households, Migration, and the Rural Economy in Ireland, 1850–1914*, Princeton, 1997.
11 Mark C. Foley and Timothy W. Guinnane, 'Did Irish Marriage Patterns Survive the Emigrant Voyage? Irish-American Nuptiality, 1880–1920', *Irish Economic and Social History*, 26, 1999, pp. 15–34.
12 Guinnane, *The Vanishing Irish*, pp. 6–7 and *passim*.
13 *Ibid.*, ch. 7.
14 David Fitzpatrick, 'The Modernisation of the Irish Female', in Patrick O'Flanagan, Paul Ferguson, and Kevin Whelan, eds, *Rural Ireland, 1600–1900: Modernisation and Change*, Cork, 1987, Table 8.6, p. 168; Foley and Guinnane, p. 16.
15 John Hajnal, 'European Marriage Patterns in Perspective', in D.V. Glass and D.E.C. Eversley, eds, *Population in History: Essays in Historical Demography*, London, 1965, pp. 101–43. For critical overviews, see Tamara K. Hareven, 'The History of the Family and the Complexity of Social Change', *American Historical Review*, 96, 1991, pp. 95–124; Michael Anderson, *Approaches to the History of the Western Family, 1500–1914*, Cambridge, 1995.
16 Anderson, p. 5; Lawrence Stone, *The Family, Sex and Marriage in England, 1500–1800*, London, 1977, ch. 2.
17 Fitzpatrick in Cosgrove, ed., p. 120.
18 Conrad M. Arensberg and Solon T. Kimball, *Family and Community in Ireland*,

Gloucester, Mass., 1961, p. 109.

19   Emmet Larkin, 'Church, State and Nation in Modern Ireland', *American Historical Review*, 80, 1975, pp. 1244–77; Kennedy, *The Irish*, pp. 86–109, 139–72; Connell, *Irish Peasant Society*, ch. 4; Fitzpatrick in Cosgrove, ed., pp. 116–31; Miller, *Emigrants and Exiles*, pp. 402–09.

20   James S. Donnelly, Jr., 'The Irish Agricultural Depression of 1859–64', *Irish Economic and Social History*, 3, 1976, pp. 33–54.

21   For Callinan's property holdings, see *General Valuation of Rateable Property in Ireland, Union of Ballyvaughan*, Dublin, 1855, p. 49. Although the precise details have been lost, oral evidence suggests that Michael Callinan married twice in the district. His second marriage, to Mary Noonan of Lismacteige, took place in 1834 and produced eight surviving children. Descendant information, Brian Nolan.

22   Descendant information, Brian Nolan and Barrie Lynn Callinan.

23   On the stem-family model, see Donna Birdwell-Pheasant, 'The Early Twentieth-Century Stem Family: A Case Study from County Kerry', in Marilyn Silverman and P.H. Gulliver, eds, *Approaching the Past: Historical Anthropology Through Irish Case Studies*, New York, 1992, pp. 205–35.

24   See especially Peter Gibbon and Chris Curtin, 'The Stem Family in Ireland', *Comparative Studies in Society and History*, 20, 1978, pp. 429–53; David Fitzpatrick, 'Irish Farming Families Before the First World War', *Comparative Studies in Society and History*, 25, 1983, pp. 339–74. There is an excellent overview of the issues by Birdwell-Pheasant in Silverman and Gulliver, eds.

25   Guinnane, *The Vanishing Irish, passim*; Birdwell-Pheasant, in Silverman and Gulliver, eds, pp. 205–35; Donna Birdwell-Pheasant, 'Irish Households in the Early Twentieth Century: Culture, Class and Historical Contingency', *Journal of Family History*, 18, 1993, pp. 19–38.

26   Birdwell-Pheasant, in Silverman and Gulliver, eds, p. 228.

27   *Ibid.*, p. 230.

28   Hasia R. Diner, *Erin's Daughters in America: Irish Immigrant Women in the Nineteenth Century*, Baltimore, 1983, pp. 43–54.

29   See, for example, Miller, Doyle and Kelleher, in O'Sullivan, ed, pp. 41–65; Akenson, *The Irish Diaspora*, ch. 7.

30   Foley and Guinnane, pp. 15–34.

31   *Ibid.*, p. 33.

32   Bernard Bailyn, *Voyagers to the West: A Passage in the Peopling of America on the Eve of the Revolution*, New York, 1987, p. 239.

33   See, for example, Lyndon Fraser, *To Tara via Holyhead: Irish Catholic Immigrants in Nineteenth-Century Christchurch*, Auckland, 1997.

34   Charlotte Macdonald, 'Single Women as Immigrant Settlers in New Zealand, 1853–1871', PhD thesis, University of Auckland, 1986, pp. 211–17.

35   Chris McConville, 'The Victorian Irish: Emigrants and Families, 1851–1891', in Patricia Grimshaw, Chris McConville and Ellen McEwen, eds, *Families in Colonial Australia*, Sydney, 1985, p. 5, cited in Akenson, *The Irish Diaspora*, p. 183.

36   See Guinnane and Foley, Table 1, p. 18.

37   The Will of Johanna Moretti, GM 34/1910, ANZ–CH; descendant information, Mary Rooney. Johanna Noonan, who died in 1906, was buried with her first husband, Edmund Trehey.

38   Pauline Rule, '"Tell father and mother not to be unhappy for I am very comfortable": A Sketch of Irish Women's Experiences in Colonial Victoria', in Trevor McClaughlin, ed., *Irish Women in Colonial Australia*, St Leonard's, 1998, p. 131.

39   The Will of Mary Frances Deehan, HK 766/1899, ANZ–CH.

40   I am indebted to Ted Matthews for this story.

41   See Ted Matthews, 'Sugar Annie (Bell Hill)', in Yvonne Davison and Frankie Mills, eds, *Women of Westland and Their Families*, omnibus edition, Greymouth, 1998, p. 194. Kathleen W. Orr, 'Bridget Goodwin', *A People's History: Illustrated Biographies from the Dictionary of the New Zealand Biography, Volume I, 1769–1869*, Wellington, 1990, pp. 88–90.

42   'Morresey: From Ireland to New Zealand', unpublished manuscript, n.d., WCHM.

43   John McLean, 'Fount of Gold: History of the Quinn Family in New Zealand', unpublished manuscript, n.d., WCHM.

44   Descendant information, Brian Nolan and Ron Patterson.

45   John Edward Oliver, 'The Speer Family Tree in New Zealand, 1866–1980', unpublished manuscript, n.d., WCHM.

46   For an excellent introduction to the Irish system of arranged marriages, see Fitzpatrick, 'Marriage in Post-Famine Ireland', in Cosgrove, ed., *passim*.

47   Peter Conaghan, 'The Mangos Family of the Lyell', unpublished manuscript, 1978, WCHM.

48   Descendant information, Ted Matthews. See also Ted Matthews, 'Memories of Kamaka: Sarah Mary Gillin (Devery)', in Davison and Mills, eds, pp. 162-7.

49   Descendant information, Ted Matthews.

50   Thomas Tymons to Mary Devery, 10 November 1868, courtesy of Ted Matthews.

51   *Ibid.*

52   Mary Ann Devery to Thomas Tymons, 23 December 1868.

53   See Macdonald, 'Single Women as Immigrant Settlers', ch. 6.

54   The median age at first marriage for Irish-born men during the 1880s was 33.3, compared with 32.1 for their Scottish-born counterparts and 29.6 for the English-born group.

55   Register of Marriages, 440/1882, RG; Phelan died four years later, leaving Ellen with two young children. See Register of Deaths, 12/1886, Charleston, RG.

56   Register of Marriages, 3411/1886 and 460/1887, RG; Register of Deaths, 61/1902, Greymouth, and 32/1899, Reefton, RG.

57   *Ibid.*, 481/1887, RG. Beatty's bride, Margaret Watson, was born in Scotland. It seems likely that he came originally from County Cavan. See Register of Deaths, 23/1897, Hokitika, RG.

58   See, for example, Report of the Christchurch Diocesan Synod, 16 February 1897, CDA.

59   Report of the Christchurch Diocesan Synod, 11 October 1892, CDA. The original document was handwritten in Latin by Father Le Menant des Chesnais, a French Marist priest.

60   Ellen Piezzi to her sister-in-law Mrs Victer Piezzi, 12 August 1878, courtesy of Teresa O'Connor.

61   Register of Marriages, 2494/1886, RG; descendant information, Peter Dillon.

62   Among the English-born, a group that had a similar rate of endogamy to the Irish (56.3 per cent), more than one-third of all marriages took place in registry offices (35.0 per cent), an experience shared by an almost identical proportion of the Scottish-born (34.5 per cent).

63   See Patrick O'Farrell, 'Varieties of New Zealand Irishness: A Meditation', in Lyndon Fraser, ed., *A Distant Shore: Irish Migration and New Zealand Settlement*, 2000, pp. 25–35.

64   O'Hallahan to Grimes, April 1892, CDA.

182   Castles of Gold

65   Carew to Grimes, 28 March 1895, CDA.
66   Pastoral Letter of the Archbishop and Bishops of New Zealand in Provincial Council
      Assembled to the Clergy and Laity of Their Charge, 29 January 1899, p. 9.
67   *Ibid.*, p. 10.
68   Archbishop Francis Redwood to the New Zealand Catholic clergy, 28 March 1908.
69   On Australia, see Patrick O'Farrell, *The Catholic Church and Community: An
      Australian History*, Kensington, 1992, pp. 349–53.
70   Register of Marriages, 335/1881, RG.
71   *Ibid.*, 432/1888, 458/1888 and 2347/1888, RG.
72   Mary O'Connor, County Kerry, to William O'Connor, c. 1900, courtesy of Mary
      O'Connor (Christchurch). Johanna O'Leary acted as an amanuensis for her mother,
      Mary O'Connor (*née* Myers), in writing this letter. Although the transcript is
      incomplete, the eight surviving pages take the form of a collective narrative in which
      the voices of both women can be clearly detected.
73   Mark Wallace, 'Recollections of Early Years in South Westland: Catherine Wallace
      (Markey)', in Davison and Mills, eds, pp. 276–83.
74   Gale Davidson Gibb, 'Memories of Red Jacks: Johanna Shanahan Weir', in *Ibid.*,
      pp.185–9; descendant information, Ted Matthews.
75   Raymond Breton, 'Institutional Completeness of Ethnic Communities and the
      Personal Relations of Immigrants', *American Journal of Sociology*, 70, 1964, pp.
      193–205.
76   Ellen Piezzi to her sister-in-law Mrs Victer Piezzi, 12 August 1878, courtesy of Teresa
      O'Connor.
77   Ellen Piezzi to her sister-in-law Mrs Victer Piezzi, 6 June 1879.
78   Ellen Piezzi to her sister-in-law Mrs Victer Piezzi, 12 August 1878.
79   *Ibid.*
80   Ellen Piezzi to her brother-in-law Mr Victer Piezzi, 3 June 1879.
81   Ellen Piezzi to her sister-in-law Mrs Victer Piezzi, 6 June 1879.
82   Ellen Piezzi to her brother-in-law Mr Victer Piezzi, 3 June 1879.
83   *Ibid.*

CHAPTER 5
1   Sheridan Gilley, 'Roman Catholicism and the Irish in England', in Donald M.
     MacRaild, ed., *The Great Famine and Beyond: Irish Migrants in Britain in the
     Nineteenth and Twentieth Centuries*, Dublin and Portland, 2000, p. 149.
2   Sheridan Gilley, 'The Roman Catholic Church and the Nineteenth-Century Irish
     Diaspora', *Journal of Ecclesiastical History*, 35, 1984, p. 189.
3   Gilley, in MacRaild, ed., p. 148.
4   *Ibid.*, p. 148. There is considerable support for these claims in historical writing on the
     Irish in New Zealand. Michael King, for example, contends that the rapid expansion of
     the Irish-born population in the colony during the 1860s fuelled demand for Irish clergy
     and transformed the Catholic church 'from a French institution to a largely Irish one'.
     This transition looms large in my own work on nineteenth-century Christchurch, where I
     maintain that religious institutions played a crucial role in mobilising and sustaining Irish
     Catholic ethnicity. See Michael King, *The Penguin History of New Zealand*, Auckland,
     2003, p. 208; Lyndon Fraser, *To Tara via Holyhead: Irish Catholic Immigrants in
     Nineteenth-Century Christchurch*, Auckland, 1997. More recently, Heather McNamara has
     argued that the Catholic weekly, the *New Zealand Tablet*, 'was enjoined with a host of other
     Irish, immigrant and Roman Catholic newspapers in a complex circuit that linked the Irish
     homeland with millions of men and women of Irish birth or descent'. These institutional

and personal networks, she maintains, facilitated an exchange of news and information between the different places Irish people settled and shaped diaspora communities as much as the migrants themselves. See Heather McNamara, 'The *New Zealand Tablet* and the Irish Catholic Press Worldwide, 1898–1923', *New Zealand Journal of History*, 37, 2003, p. 167.

5   The phrase is borrowed from Kevin Kenny, 'Diaspora and Comparison: The Global Irish as a Case Study', *Journal of American History*, 90, 2003, p. 162.

6   Mother Mary Clare Molony, Diary, 15 October 1878, MS-Papers 1918, ATL.

7   See *Mercy in Westland*, centenary booklet, Hokitika, 1978; Greymouth Sisters of Mercy Centennial newspaper, Greymouth, 1982.

8   Molony, Diary, 11 August 1878, ATL.

9   *Ibid.*, 13 and 18 August 1878.

10 *Ibid.*, 22 and 23 August 1878.

11 *Ibid.*, 18 September 1878.

12 *Ibid.*, 2 October 1878.

13 Gilley, in MacRaild, ed., p. 149.

14 *Mercy in Westland*, pp. 16–17; *New Zealand Tablet*, 1 November 1878. Fifty years later, as her funeral cortege made its way to the Karoro cemetery and the red flushes of spring coloured the rugged hillside forests of Westland, Ngai Tahu Poutini of the Arahura Pa sent a message of sympathy which read '[t]he rata has fallen at last, and we grieve for her'.

15 James Clifford, 'Diasporas', *Cultural Anthropology*, 9, 1994, pp. 302–38.

16 Emmet Larkin, 'The Devotional Revolution in Ireland, 1850–75', *American Historical Review*, 77, 1972, pp. 625–52.

17 The term has been much debated by historians. See David W. Miller, 'Irish Catholicism and the Great Famine', *Journal of Social History*, 9, 1975, pp. 81–98; Desmond Keenan, *The Catholic Church in Nineteenth-Century Ireland: A Sociological Study*, Dublin, 1983; S.J. Connolly, *Priests and People in Pre-Famine Ireland, 1780-1845*, Dublin, 1982; S.J. Connolly, *Religion and Society in Nineteenth-Century Ireland*, Dublin, 1985, pp. 7–14, 42–60; Patrick Corish, *The Irish Catholic Experience: A Historical Survey*, Dublin, 1987; Gilley, in MacRaild, ed., pp. 147–67.

18 Emmet Larkin has recently revisited and added further weight to this statement in 'Before the Devotional Revolution', in James H. Murphy, ed., *Evangelicals and Catholics in Nineteenth-Century Ireland*, Dublin, 2005, pp. 15–37.

19 Hugh McLeod, *Religion and the People of Western Europe, 1789–1970*, Oxford, 1981, p. 47.

20 Mary Heimann, *Catholic Devotion in Victorian England*, Oxford, 1995, p. 30.

21 See, especially, Miller, 'Irish Catholicism'; Corish, pp. 166–7, 186–88, 233.

22 In 1850 there was approximately one priest for every 2000 people in Ireland, but by 1870 there was one for every 1250, a level of expansion that was more than matched by the explosion in the numbers of nuns and teaching brothers. See Larkin, p. 644.

23 *Ibid.*, pp. 644–5; Heimann, ch. 2.

24 For some examples from Ulster, see Marianne Elliot, *The Catholics of Ulster: A History*, London, 2000, pp. 286–90; Lawrence J. Taylor, *Occasions of Faith: An Anthropology of Irish Catholics*, Philadelphia, 1995, ch. 2.

25 Elliot, pp. 289–90.

26 On these processes, see especially Barbara Solow, *The Land Question and the Irish Economy*, Cambridge, Mass., 1971, pp. 98–114 and *passim*; James S. Donnelly, Jr., *The Land and the People of Nineteenth-Century Cork: The Rural Economy and the Land Question*, London and Boston, 1975, chs 3 and 5; Samuel L. Clark, *Social Origins of the*

Irish Land War, Princeton, 1979, ch. 4; Kerby M. Miller, *Emigrants and Exiles: Ireland and the Irish Exodus to North America*, New York and Oxford, 1985, ch. 8; R.F. Foster, *Modern Ireland, 1600–1914*, London, 1988, chs 14–16; R.F. Foster, 'Ascendancy and Union', in R.F. Foster, ed., *The Oxford History of Ireland*, Oxford, 1989, pp. 162–73; David Fitzpatrick, 'Ireland since 1870', in Foster, ed., pp. 174–93; Kerby M. Miller, 'Class, Culture and Immigrant Group Identity in the United States: The Case of Irish-American Ethnicity', in Virginia Yans-McLaughlin, ed., *Immigration Reconsidered: History, Sociology, and Politics*, New York, 1990, pp. 96–129; Donald E. Jordan, Jr., *Land and Popular Politics in County Mayo from the Plantation to the Land War*, Cambridge, 1994, ch. 4; Timothy W. Guinnane, *The Vanishing Irish: Households, Migration and the Rural Economy in Ireland*, Princeton, 1997.

27   Elliot, p. 285.
28   *Ibid.*
29   On the great church-building boom before the Famine, see Keenan, *passim*.
30   See, for example, Kevin Whelan, 'The Catholic Church in County Tipperary', in William J. Nolan, ed., *Tipperary: History and Society*, Dublin, 1985, pp. 213–55.
31   'In the guise of its various elements, acting separately or even in concert with the Protestant state, the Catholic Church has . . . done much to reform the local culture and even transform the landscape'. See Taylor, pp. 25, 58, 64–7. Ultramontanism was an ecclesiastical movement that came to dominate Catholicism in the nineteenth century; its proponents 'looked for inspiration "beyond the mountains" to Rome'. See McLeod, p. 47.
32   Donald Harman Akenson, *Small Differences: Irish Catholics and Irish Protestants, 1852–1922: An International Perspective*, Kingston and Montreal, 1988, pp. 141–2.
33   *Ibid.*, pp. 140–1; Connolly, *Religion and Society*, pp. 43–4.
34   See David W. Miller, 'Did Ulster Presbyterians have a Devotional Revolution?', in Murphy, ed., pp. 38–54.
35   K. Theodore Hoppen, *Ireland Since 1800: Conflict and Conformity*, London and New York, 1999, p. 167; Connolly, *Religion and Society*, pp. 45–6.
36   McLeod, pp. 36–43.
37   Hoppen, p. 168.
38   *Ibid.*, pp. 169–70; Elliot, ch. 10.
39   *Ibid.*, pp. 156–70; Corish, ch. 7; Elliot, pp. 280–3.
40   Taylor, pp. 86–7.
41   *Ibid.*, p. 118.
42   Miller, in Murphy, ed., pp. 44–5, 52–4.
43   Emmet Larkin, *The Historical Dimensions of Irish Catholicism*, Dublin, 1997, p. 92.
44   Descendant information, Ted Matthews.
45   Charles R. Thatcher, 'Our Own Correspondent', reprinted in Robert Hoskins, *Goldfield Balladeer: The Life and Times of the celebrated Charles R. Thatcher*, Auckland and London, 1977, pp. 167–9.
46   *Lyttelton Times*, 11 May 1865, quoted in Philip Ross May, *The West Coast Gold Rushes*, Christchurch, 1962, p. 315.
47   See May, pp. 315–17.
48   Henry W. Harper *Letters from New Zealand, 1857–1911: Being Some Account of Life and Work in the Province of Canterbury, South Island*, London, 1914.
49   *Ibid.*, p. 316; 'St Patrick's Church, Greymouth, 1888-1978', Centennial Pamphlet, Greymouth, 1978.
50   Bishop Viard and his Vicar-General, J.J.P. O'Reily, an Irish-born Capuchin, stayed at Gillin's Kamaka homestead on their visit to the West Coast in 1865. Kevin J. Clark,

Grey River Parish Centennial, Greymouth, 1971, pp. 21–2; descendant information, Ted Matthews.

51   Eddie (Ted) Matthews, 'The Deverys and the Gillins: A Brief History', unpublished paper, n.d., WCHM, p. 7.

52   For Shantytown, see <http://www.shantytown.co.nz>.

53   Diocesan Return for the Parish of Greymouth, 22 July 1895, CDA.

54   Francis Redwood, *Reminiscences of Early Days in New Zealand*, Wellington, 1922, p. 27.

55   On the latter, see Patrick O'Farrell, *Through Irish Eyes: Australian and New Zealand Images of the Irish, 1788–1948*, Richmond, 1994.

56   Diocesan Return for the Parish of Greymouth, 26 July 1892, CDA.

57   Archbishop Francis Redwood's Visitation to the Parish of Westport, 1896, WAA.

58   St Patrick's Church (Greymouth) was erected for £4800 and opened by Bishop John Joseph Grimes on Pentecost Sunday in 1888. Diocesan Return for the Parish of Greymouth, 26 July 1892, CDA.

59   Heimann, p. 59.

60   See Diocesan Returns for the Parishes of Greymouth, 26 July 1892, 22 July 1895 and 5 October 1905; Hokitika, 1 July 1892; Ahaura, 21 April 1896 and 15 October 1905; Kumara 1 July 1892 and 27 November 1905; Ross, 1 July 1892 and 24 June 1895, CDA; Archbishop Francis Redwood's Visitation to the Parish of Westport, 1896, WAA.

61   These questions are fully discussed in an English context by Heimann, ch. 4.

62   Michael Cummins to Father Forest (the Marist Vicar-General), 29 July 1874, MAW.

63   Denis O'Hallahan to Bishop John Joseph Grimes, 3 May 1897, CDA.

64   Diocesan Return for the Parish of Kumara, 1 July 1892, CDA. At Hokitika, parish schools were funded by seat rents and annual fees, while Father Eugene Pertius of Ahaura raised additional money from an Art Union draw. See *New Zealand Tablet*, 18 July 1874.

65   Denis Carew to Bishop John Joseph Grimes, 17 April 1895, CDA. These strategies had a longer history within the parish. See the report on St Patrick's Catholic School, Greymouth, in the *Grey River Argus*, 16 March 1869.

66   See the Diocesan Returns cited above, fn. 59. This view was supported by the annual reports of the Inspectors of Schools. See, for example, *Westport Times*, 13 July 1877.

67   On the education struggle in New Zealand, see Richard Davis, *Irish Issues in New Zealand Politics, 1869–1922*, Dunedin, 1974, ch.4; Donald Harman Akenson, *Half the World from Home: Perspectives on the Irish in New Zealand, 1860–1950*, Wellington, 1990, ch. 6. The intensity of these tensions seems to have been partially ameliorated by 'the experiences of local community' on the West Coast. See Neil Vaney, 'The Dual Tradition: Irish Catholics and French Priests in New Zealand – the West Coast Experience, 1865–1910', MA thesis, University of Canterbury, 1976, pp. 142–4.

68   *The Cyclopedia of New Zealand, Vol. 5*, Christchurch, 1906, p. 502.

69   *Marist Messenger*, 1 November 1962, pp. 12–13; Vaney, pp. 34–5, 242, 249–50.

70   Henry W. Harper, *Letters from New Zealand, 1857–1911: Being Some Account of Life and Work in the Province of Canterbury, South Island*, London, 1914.

71   Nicholas Binsfeld, 'Memoirs', MAW. This view was shared by contemporary visitors to the West Coast goldfields like Julius Haast, the Canterbury Provincial Geologist, who considered the miners at Okarito 'the finest set of men one could meet' and among whom 'neither nationality nor colour, nor non-success' were barriers to 'doing good'. *Lyttelton Times*, 29 September 1865, quoted in May, p. 313.

72   Michael O'Meeghan, *Held Firm by Faith: A History of the Catholic Diocese of*

Christchurch, 1840-1897, Christchurch, 1988, p. 53. Father Colin wanted better spiritual and material care for his men than Pompallier had provided and refused to send more Marist clergy until the situation was resolved.

73   On Viard, see Lillian G. Keys, *Philip Viard: Bishop of Wellington*, Christchurch, 1968.

74   Rory Sweetman, '"How to behave among Protestants": Varieties of Irish Catholic Leadership in Colonial New Zealand', in Brad Patterson, ed., *The Irish in New Zealand: Historical Contexts and Perspectives*, Wellington, 2002, p. 92.

75   Patrick O'Farrell, *The Catholic Church and Community: An Australian History*, Kensington, 1992, chs 2–3.

76   Bishop Patrick Moran to Tobias Kirby, 13 March 1871, Kirby Papers, Irish College Rome, quoted in Sweetman, in Patterson, ed., p. 91.

77   This position can be found in Vaney and Fraser, *To Tara via Holyhead*. Of the 82 priests who served on the West Coast for six months or more between 1865 and 1910, about one-half were Irish-born (43); the rest had come from France (22), the colonies (11) or other places.

78   See, for example, the recollections of J.R. McCormick, who was a pupil at Ahaura from 1875 until 1883, in Kevin J. Clark, *Grey Valley Parish Centennial 1971*, Greymouth, 1971, pp. 11–13.

79   The incident is discussed by Vaney, pp. 150–54.

80   Patrick O'Farrell (Greymouth) to Mai O'Farrell (South Canterbury), c.1920. I am indebted to Angela McCarthy for access to the O'Farrell letters, which are held at the Alexander Turnbull Library, MS 77–127.

81   *Ibid.*, ATL.

82   On All Hallows, see Patrick O'Farrell, *The Catholic Church and Community: An Australian History*, Kensington, 1992, pp. 104–06, and *Vanished Kingdoms: Irish in Australia and New Zealand: A Personal Excursion*, Kensington, 1990, pp. 98–9, 116–19.

83   Denis Carew to Bishop John Joseph Grimes, 16 August 1894 and 13 June 1895, CDA.

84   Vaney, pp. 36–7.

85   Denis Carew to Bishop John Joseph Grimes, 13 June 1895, CDA.

86   Denis Carew to Bishop John Joseph Grimes, 9 November 1911, CDA, quoted in Vaney, p. 197.

87   *The Coaster*, 12 March 1998; O'Farrell, Vanished Kingdoms, pp. 98, 103, and 'Catholicism on the West Coast: Just How Irish Is It?', *New Zealand Tablet*, 3 May 1973, pp. 53–6.

88   Denis Carew to Bishop John Joseph Grimes, 11 September 1893, CDA, quoted in Vaney, p. 193.

89   O'Farrell, *Vanished Kingdoms*, pp. 122–4.

90   *Ibid.*, pp. 125, 154.

91   Diocesan Return for the Parish of Kumara, 27 November 1905, CDA; Denis O'Hallahan to Bishop John Joseph Grimes, 3 May 1895, CDA. For an incisive analysis of Italian settlement on the West Coast, see Alan Poletti, 'Italian Censuses in Nineteenth Century New Zealand', *Italian Historical Society Journal*, 9, 2001, pp. 26–34.

92   Michael Cummins to Father Forest (the Marist Vicar-General), 29 July 1874, MAW.

93   See Fraser, *To Tara via Holyhead*, ch. 2. James Joseph O'Donnell, born in Glenroe, County Limerick, in 1855, was educated at Mount Melleray and All Hallows College and ordained by the Bishop of Cork on 24 June 1880. Le Menant des Chesnais to

Archbishop Francis Redwood, 22 December 1887, CDA; Archbishop Francis Redwood to Bishop John Joseph Grimes, 21 July and 27 October 1887, MAW.

94   Akenson, *Small Differences*, ch. 2.

95   Descendant information, Ted Matthews; Betty Matthews and Ted Matthews, *They Shaped Our Lives: West Coast Pioneers*, Christchurch, 2004, pp. 12–13.

96   See *Kumara Times*, 11–14, 16, 18 and 28 March 1878. On Hennebery, see Vaney, pp. 133–6; Hugh Laracy, 'Patrick Hennebery in Australasia, 1877–1882', in Patterson, ed., pp. 103–16.

97   Vaney, p. 146.

98   *Kumara Times*, 17 and 19 May 1880.

99   I am indebted here to Patrick O'Farrell, 'Varieties of New Zealand Irishness: A Meditation', in Lyndon Fraser, ed., *A Distant Shore: Irish Migration and New Zealand Settlement*, Dunedin, 2000, pp. 26–7.

100 *Kumara Times*, 3 March 1879.

101 Binsfeld, quoted in Vaney, p. 145.

102 *Ibid.*, p. 145. See also Mrs F. Gunn, 'It was a Good Life: Mrs Alex Gunn', and Elizabeth McCormack, 'The Bungi Hut: Eleanor (Lena) Green (Wallace)', in Yvonne Davison and Frankie Mills, eds, *Women of Westland and Their Families*, omnibus edition, Greymouth, 1998, pp. 265–9, 284–7.

103 Harper, *op.cit.*

104 Redwood, *Reminiscences*, pp. 26–7.

105 O'Farrell, 'Catholicism on the West Coast', pp. 55–6.

106 *Ibid.*, p. 56.

107 See Hugh Jackson, 'Churchgoing in Nineteenth-Century New Zealand', *New Zealand Journal of History*, 17, 1983, pp. 51 and *passim*.

108 *Ibid.*, p. 49; *Census of New Zealand*, 1891.

109 Diocesan Return for the Parish of Hokitika, 1 July 1892, CDA.

110 Diocesan Returns for the Parishes of Ross and Ahaura, 1 July 1892, CDA.

111 Sec, for example, Archbishop Francis Redwood's Visitation to the Parish of Westport, 1896, WAA; Diocesan Return for the Parish of Greymouth, 22 July 1895.

112 Diocesan Return for the Parish of Greymouth, 26 July 1892, CDA.

113 David Fitzpatrick, *Oceans of Consolation: Personal Accounts of Irish Migration to Australia*, Melbourne, 1995, p. 601.

114 John O'Regan (Barrytown) to his grandniece Nellie O'Regan (Montana), 26 January 1899. I am indebted to Angela McCarthy for access to the O'Regan correspondence.

115 C.M. Fleming (Victoria) to Michael Flanagan (West Coast), 9 December 1865.

116 C.M. Fleming (Victoria) to Michael Flanagan (West Coast), 21 April 1868.

117 Will of William Glenn, HK 674/1897, ANZ–CH. Glenn was born in Drumbarnett, County Donegal. His estate comprised of property worth £1913 in New Zealand and £34,865 in Britain.

118 Will of Daniel Danahy, WP 3/1904, ANZ–CH.

119 Will of Thomas O'Rourke, 1015/1902, ANZ–CH.

120 Will of John Quillinan, RN 140/1902 and HK 1014/1902, ANZ–CH. Quillinan bequeathed his hut and personal possessions to an old friend, John McCaffrey, and set aside £10 for the benefit of Reefton miner Peter O'Donnell. He devised one-third of the residue upon a niece, Alice Hayes of Ballarat, and instructed his executors to divide the remainder equally between a second niece, his sister and brother-in-law, all of whom lived in Geelong.

121 Will of Edward Ryan, HK 15/1910, ANZ–CH. Ryan gave the residuary interest in his estate to his brother and business partner Maurice.

122   Tyrell was also a founder of the *West Coast Times*. Will of John Tyrell, WP 7/1892, ANZ–CH. He gave an annuity of £25 and the residue of his estate to the 'Home', as well as donations 'to all the charities to which I have been in the habit of contributing to'.

123   Will of John Cummins, WP 164/1914, ANZ–CH.

124   Will of Ann Parsons, GM 157/1914, ANZ–CH.

125   Will of Maria Anderson Pearce, WP 27/1909, ANZ–CH.

126   Will of Elizabeth Biel, HK 905/1901; Will of Ellen Doherty, HK 540/1895; Will of Mary Rollini, HK 615/1896, ANZ–CH.

127   Will of Mary Roche, HK 33/09; Will of Margaret Roche, GM 88/12, ANZ–CH. Mary Roche left all her property to Margaret.

128   Donald Harman Akenson, 'No Petty People: Pakeha History and the Historiography of the Irish Diaspora', in Fraser, ed., *A Distant Shore*, p. 17.

129   Diocesan Return for the Parish of Ahaura, 1 July 1892, CDA.

130   Denis Carew to Bishop John Joseph Grimes, 9 April 1895, CDA.

131   Descendant information, Ted Matthews and Anne Bills.

132   Patrick O'Farrell, "Catholicism on the West Coast: Just How Irish Is It?," *New Zealand Tablet*, 3 May 1973, 53–6.

133   I am indebted to Ted Matthews for this story.

134   Mrs Clem McKay, 'Mrs J. W. Coates of Greymouth', in Davidson and Mills, eds, pp.120–21. I am indebted to Ted Matthews for additional research material used in this paragraph and the next.

135   John Stenhouse, 'God's Own Silence: Secular Nationalism, Christianity and the Writing of New Zealand History', *New Zealand Journal of History*, 38, 2004, p. 55.

136   Patrick O'Farrell, *Vanished Kingdoms: Irish in Australia and New Zealand: A Personal Excursion*, Kensington, 1990, p. 49.

137   O'Farrell, *Vanished Kingdoms*, pp. 74–5, 78–9, 87–8.

138   *Ibid.*, p. 71.

139   O'Farrell, 'Catholicism on the West Coast', p. 53.

140   O'Farrell, *Vanished Kingdoms*, pp. 53–4.

141   *Ibid.*, p. 55.

142   This point was made to me by several West Coast informants.

143   O'Farrell, *Vanished Kingdoms*, p. 80.

144   *Ibid.*, p. 103.

145   *Ibid.*, pp. 135–40.

146   O'Farrell, in Fraser, ed., p. 26.

147   O'Farrell, *Vanished Kingdoms*, p. 300.

CHAPTER 6

1   See, for example, Thomas N. Brown, *Irish–American Nationalism, 1870–1890*, Philadelphia, 1966; Gilbert Osofsky, 'Abolitionists, Irish Immigrants, and the Dilemmas of Romantic Nationalism', *American Historical Review*, 80, 1975, pp. 889-912; Victor A. Walsh, '"A Fanatic Heart": The Cause of Irish–American Nationalism in Pittsburgh During the Gilded Age', *Journal of Social History*, 15, 1981, pp. 187–204; John Belchem, 'Nationalism, Republicanism and Exile: Irish Emigrants and the Revolutions of 1848', *Past and Present*, 146, 1995, pp. 103–35; David O. Wilson, *United Irishmen, United States: Immigrant Radicals in the Early Republic*, Ithaca, 1998; Thomas Keneally, *The Great Shame: A Story of the Irish in the Old World and the New*, London, 1998; Alan O'Day, 'Irish Diaspora Politics in

Perspective: The United Irish Leagues of Great Britain and America, 1900–14', in Donald M. MacRaild, ed., *The Great Famine and Beyond: Irish Migrants in Britain in the Nineteenth and Twentieth Centuries*, Dublin and Portland, Or., 2000, pp. 214–39; Donald M. MacRaild, *Faith, Fraternity and Fighting: The Orange Order and Irish Migrants in Northern England, c. 1850–1920*, Liverpool, 2005. On nationalism, see especially Ernest Gellner, *Nations and Nationalism*, Oxford, 1983; Benedict Anderson, *Imagined Communities: Reflections on the Origin and Spread of Nationalism*, London, 1983; Eric Hobsbawm, *Nations and Nationalism since the 1780s: Programme, Myth, Reality*, Cambridge, 1990.

2   For an excellent introduction, see K. Theodore Hoppen, *Ireland Since 1800: Conflict and Conformity*, ch. 5. See also John Hutchison, 'Irish Nationalism', in D. George Boyce and Alan O'Day, eds, *The Making of Modern Irish History: Revisionism and the Revisionist Controversy*, London and New York, 1996, pp. 100–19.

3   On the notion of diaspora, see Kevin Kenny, 'Diaspora and Comparison: The Global Irish as a Case Study', *Journal of American History*, 90, 2003, pp. 134–62; MacRaild, *Faith, Fraternity and Fighting*, ch. 8. For a sustained attempt to use diaspora as a framework for the study of Irish migration, see Bronwen Walter, *Outsiders Inside: Whiteness, Place and Irish Women*, London and New York, 2001. The diaspora literature is voluminous, but standard works include Stuart Hall, 'Cultural Identity and Diaspora', in Johnathan Rutherford, ed., *Identity: Community, Culture, Difference*, London, 1990, pp. 222–37; William Safran, 'Diasporas in Modern Societies: Myths of Homeland and Return', *Diaspora*, 1, 1991, pp. 83–99; Paul Gilroy, *The Black Atlantic: Modernity and Double Consciousness*, Cambridge, Mass., 1993; Daniel Boyarin and Jonathan Boyarin, 'Diaspora: Generation and the Ground of Jewish Identity', *Critical Inquiry*, 19, 1993, pp. 693–725; James Clifford, 'Diasporas', *Current Anthropology*, 9, 1994, pp. 302–38; Avtar Brah, *Cartographies of Diaspora: Contesting Identities*, London, 1996; Robin Cohen, *Global Diasporas: An Introduction*, Seattle, 1997; Floya Anthias, 'Evaluating "Diaspora": Beyond Ethnicity', *Sociology*, 32, 1998, pp. 557–80; Nicholas Van Hear, *New Diasporas: The Mass Exodus, Dispersal and Regrouping of Migrant Communities*, Oxford, 1998; Tiffany Ruby Patterson and Robin D.G. Kelley, 'Unfinished Migrations: Reflections on the African Diaspora and the Making of the Modern World', *African Studies Review*, 43, 2000, pp. 11–45. The weaknesses of 'diasporic' approaches are discussed by Kenny, pp. 140–45, 158–60; Roger Brubaker, 'The "Diaspora" Diaspora', *Ethnic and Racial Studies*, 28, 2005, pp. 10–13. On the notion of 'transnationalism', see Ewa Morawksa, 'Immigrants, Transnationalism, and Ethnicisation: A Comparison of This Great Wave and the Last', in Garry Gerstle and John Mollenkopf, eds, *E Pluribus Unum? Contemporary and Historical Perspectives on Immigrant Political Incorporation*, New York, 2001, pp. 175–212.

4   I am indebted here to Lawrence J. Taylor, *Occasions of Faith: An Anthropology of Irish Catholics*, Philadelphia, 1995, pp. 33–4.

5   On the West Coast 'Fenian disturbances', see Richard Davis, *Irish Issues in New Zealand Politics, 1868–1922*, Dunedin, 1974, ch. 1; Neil Vaney, 'The Dual Tradition: Irish Catholics and French Priests in New Zealand: The West Coast Experience, 1865–1910, MA thesis, University of Canterbury, 1976, ch. 3. Michael O'Meeghan, *Held Firm By Faith: A History of the Catholic Diocese of Christchurch, 1840–1987*, Christchurch, 1988, ch. 4; David McGill, *The Lion and the Wolfhound: The Irish Rebellion on the New Zealand Goldfields*, Wellington, 1990. McGill's extensive research corrects many of the factual errors contained in earlier accounts.

6   Malcolm Campbell, 'Irish Nationalism and Immigrant Assimilation: Comparing the United States and Australia', *Australasian Journal of American Studies*, 16, 1996, pp. 24–43 See also Malcolm Campbell, 'The Other Immigrants: Comparing the Irish in Australia and the United States', *Journal of American Ethnic History*, 14, 1995, pp. 3–22.
7   For an incisive analysis, see Mervyn Busteed, 'Parading the Green – Procession as Subaltern Resistance in Manchester in 1867', *Political Geography*, 24, 2005, pp. 903–33.
8   *West Coast Times*, 19 May 1868.
9   *Ibid.*, 9 March 1868.
10   *Ibid.*, 9 March, 2 April and 19 May 1868.
11   *Ibid.*, 19 May 1868.
12   *Ibid.*, 9 March 1868.
13   *New Zealand Celt*, 21 February 1868. Few copies of the paper have survived. On the background, see Philip Ross May, *The West Coast Gold Rushes*, Christchurch, 1962, p. 533; G.H. Scholefield, *Newpapers in New Zealand*, Wellington, 1958, pp. 245–6: 'In his journalistic reminiscences, James Browne tells how the Celt was founded by John Manning, an educated Irishman who had contributed to *Chambers's Edinburgh Journal* stories of life in Australia. Browne met him in Geelong, but lost sight of him until he called in Hokitika to seek employment. Browne suggested an Irish paper of light reading, but Manning was deeply moved by events in Ireland and decided to publish a paper through which Irishmen might further the cause of their country'. See also Browne's testimony in the Magistrate's Court at Hokitika, *West Coast Times*, 6 April 1868.
14   'Mr Kynnersley's Report on the Disturbances at Addison's Flat', *Nelson Examiner*, 23 April 1868, reproduced in McGill, pp. 169–73. For varied newspaper reaction to the report, see Vaney, pp. 50–52.
15   Justice Richmond quoted in the *West Coast Times*, 22 May 1868.
16   On Fenianism, see T.W. Moody, ed., *The Fenian Movement*, Cork, 1968; R.V. Comerford, *Charles J. Kickham: A Study in Irish Nationalism and Literature*, Dublin, 1979; 'Patriotism as Pastime: The Appeal of Fenianism in the mid-1860s', *Irish Historical Studies*, 22, 1981, pp. 239–50; and *The Fenians in Context: Irish Politics and Society, 1848–1882*, Dublin, 1985; Keith Amos, *The Fenians in Australia, 1865–1880*, Kensington, 1988.
17   Alvin Jackson, *Ireland: 1798–1998: Politics and War*, Oxford, 1999, p. 103; Hoppen, pp. 174–5.
18   On these events, see R.F. Foster, *Modern Ireland, 1600–1972*, London, 1988, pp. 390–95; Jackson, pp. 93–109; May, p. 308.
19   *West Coast Times*, 22 May 1868.
20   *Ibid.*, 19 May 1868.
21   *Ibid*, 19 May 1868.
22   *West Coast Times*, 19 May 1868.
23   Ibid., 19 May and 9 March 1868; Bonar to the Colonial Secretary, quoted in McGill, p. 33.
24   See Patrick O'Farrell, *The Irish in Australia*, Sydney, 1993.
25   See, for example, *Hokitika Evening Star*, 26 and 27 March 1868.
26   *West Coast Times*, 24 and 27 March 1868.
27   *Ibid.*, 28 and 30 March 1868.
28   *Ibid.*, 30 and 31 March 1868; *Hokitika Evening Star*, 28, 30 and 31 March 1868.
29   Richard Ireland's fee was 600 guineas. Davis, p. 19; McGill, pp. 121–3. Davis

claimed that £11,500 had been raised for the defence, but this figure seems grossly exaggerated. McGill's estimate of £1500 is much more plausible. The treasurer of the defence fund, Cornelius Driscoll, reported £1222 13s 1d in the *New Zealand Celt*, 19 June 1868.

30   *West Coast Times*, 6 April 1868.

31   The priest was presented with 'a handsome gold lever watch' and 'an elegant Albert chain'. At the end of formalities, Hugh Cassidy 'begged Father McGirr to leave him his snuff–box, as his souvenir of his residence amongst them: – a request, which the Rev. gentleman kindly seceded to'. *West Coast Times*, 7, 8 and 9 April 1868.

32   'Kynnersley's Report', in McGill, pp. 169–73.

33   *West Coast Times*, 19, 20, 21, 22 and 30 May 1868. Larkin and Manning were released from prison on 10 June 1868. See *Hokitika Evening Star*, 11 June 1868. According to family tradition, Larkin spent the next 12 months at Mary Ann Devery's hotel in Revell Street. Descendant information, Ted Matthews.

34   *West Coast Times*, 12 December 1865; May, p. 308.

35   See, for example, *West Coast Times*, 17 and 18 March 1868. This pattern continued throughout the nineteenth century, although the festival became more of a Catholic occasion than an Irish one. See *Ibid*., 18 March 1869: 'The ball in honor of the festival of St Patrick – the funds derived from which are to be applied in aid of liquidating the debt on St Mary's church and presbytery – came off last night, and proved a great success. There were a large number of the elite of Hokitika present on the occasion and, dancing, to an excellent band of music, was kept up with untiring zeal until the small hours of the morning.' See also Patrick O'Farrell, 'St Patrick's Day in Australia', *Journal of the Royal Australasian Society*, 81, 1995, pp. 1–16.

36   *Ibid*., 21 May 1868.

37   *Ibid*., 2 April 1868. The move was proclaimed by Father Larkin in a public meeting at the Munster Hotel a few days before the demonstration. Richard Dyer recalled that 'Larkin made a speech. Some one put a note in his hand, the substance of which was that the Municipal Council had refused to allow them to plant the cross in the Cemetery. He said you can go back to the Council, and tell them that the priest at the Waimea would open the gates and allow the procession to enter.'

38   *Ibid*., 20 May 1868.

39   *Westport Times*, 27 March 1868, quoted in Vaney, p. 48.

40   *West Coast Times*, 10 March 1868.

41   *Ibid*., 20 May 1868; May, p. 281; Vaney, pp. 58–61; ch. 16; McGill, p. 146.

42   Davis, p. 21. This view has been reiterated by O'Meeghan, p. 84.

43   *New Zealand Celt*, 19 June 1868; *Wellington Independent*, 24 March 1868; Vaney, pp. 62–5. McEntegart arrived in Hokitika aboard the *Omeo* on 27 March 1868. *West Coast Times*, 29 March 1868.

44   Nicholas Binsfeld, 'Memoirs', 1904, MAW, quoted in McGill, p. 145.

45   *West Coast Times*, 21 May 1868.

46   Arthur Dudley Dobson, *Reminiscences of Arthur Dudley Dobson, Engineer, 1841–1930*, Christchurch, 1930, p. 134.

47   McGill, p. 50.

48   *Ibid*., p. 69.

49   The meeting was held at Owen's Sluicers' Arms Hotel in Stafford Town and chaired by Father Larkin. *West Coast Times*, 27 March 1868.

50   *Ibid*., 6, 7, 8 and 9 April 1868; Vaney, p. 63; McGill, p. 148.

51   C.M Fleming to Michael Flanagan, 21 April 1868.

52   C.M. Fleming to Michael Flanagan, 20 August 1868.

53   On fundraising for the Fenian cause in New Zealand, see Keneally, pp. 531, 560 and 565; Davis, p. 22. Michael Cody was a Sydney hotelier and former Fenian prisoner transported to Western Australia.

54   See Vaney, pp. 84–8; Davis, pp. 100–05.

55   Jackson, p. 124. *Kumara Times*, 28 and 31 May, 4 June 1881. Hannan ran the private Kumara Academy on Main Street. See also Margaret Ward, *Unmanageable Revolutionaries: Women and Irish Nationalism*, London, 1989.

56   Kumara leaders favoured the resolution of the land question 'by strictly constitutional means' and the Ladies' Land League solicited for money from 'all nationalities and creeds'. See *Kumara Times*, 17 and 28 May, 6 June 1881.

57   There were Irish National League branches at Kumara, Boatman's, Notown, Nelson Creek, Paroa and Greymouth. These combined to hold 'annual joint meetings' on four occasions. See Vaney, p. 91; Davis, p. 105; *New Zealand Tablet*, 4 March 1881. Branches were later established at Hokitika and Westport.

58   On Irish Home Rule, see Alan O'Day, *Irish Home Rule, 1867–1921*, Manchester, 1998.

59   For detailed accounts, see Davis, ch. 5; Vancy, ch. 4; Rory Sweetman, '"The Importance of Being Irish": Hibernianism in New Zealand, 1869–1969', in Lyndon Fraser, ed., *A Distant Shore: Irish Migration and New Zealand Settlement*, Dunedin, 2000, pp. 140–6.

60   See Malcolm Campbell, 'John Redmond and the Irish National League in Australia and New Zealand, 1883', *History*, 86, 2001, pp. 348–62.

61   *Ibid.*, pp. 349–55.

62   *Ibid.*, p. 353; *West Coast Times*, 27 September and 2 October 1883.

63   Redmond delivered lectures at Westport, Reefton, Kumara, Boatman's, Greymouth, Hokitika and Ross. See *New Zealand Tablet*, 19 October and 2 November 1883.

64   *Grey River Argus*, June 21 1881 and 1 October 1883; *West Coast Times*, 28 September 1883.

65   *West Coast Times*, 5 October 1883.

66   *Kumara Times*, 2 October 1883, quoted in *New Zealand Tablet*, 19 October 1883; *Grey River Argus*, 29 September 1883.

67   *Ibid.*, 2 October 1883.

68   See, for example, *New Zealand Tablet*, 2 November 1883.

69   *Ibid.*, 5 October 1883; Sweetman, p. 140. The only sour note to an otherwise well-received visit was the Hokitika Borough Council's decision not to permit Redmond and Walshe the use of the Town Hall for 'throwing down the torch of sedition'. *New Zealand Tablet*, 26 October 1883.

70   There is an extensive literature on Charles Stewart Parnell and 'Parnellism', but see especially F.S.L. Lyons, *Charles Stewart Parnell*, London, 1977; R.F. Foster, *Modern Ireland, 1600–1972*, London, 1988, chs 16–17; D. George Boyce and Alan O'Day, eds, *Parnell in Perspective*, London, 1991; Alan O'Day, *Charles Stewart Parnell*, Dublin, 1999.

71   Hoppen, pp. 124–34, 175–80. David Fitzpatrick, 'Ireland Since 1870', in R.F. Foster, ed., *The Oxford History of Ireland*, Oxford, 1989, pp. 180–85.

72   *Grey River Argus*, 25 November 1889.

73   *Ibid.*, 25 November 1889.

74   *Ibid.*, 26 November 1889.

75   *Ibid.*, 25 and 28 November 1889.

76   *Ibid.*, 26 November 1889.

77   *Reefton Guardian* n.d., quoted in *West Coast Times*, 23 November 1889.

78   *West Coast Times*, 28 and 30 November 1889. The address of the Hokitika branch of the Irish National League referred to New Zealand as the 'Britain of the South'.

79   See Jackson, pp. 133–69.

80   Foster, p. 424.

81   There were short-lived branches of the anti-Parnellite Irish National League at Denniston, Addison's Flat, Charleston, Westport and the Lyell. *New Zealand Tablet*, 4, 11 and 18 May 1894.

82   *Ibid.*, 8 June 1894.

83   *Ibid.*, 1, 8, 15 and 29 November, 1895; *West Coast Times*, 12, 13, 19 and 20 November 1895; *Grey River Argus*, 18, 22 and 23 November 1895.

84   Davis, p. 127.

85   *West Coast Times*, 23 January 1907.

86   *Ibid.*, 22 January 1907. In response, Donovan noted the 'proverbial generosity of West Coasters'.

87   *Grey River Argus*, 17 January 1907.

88   *West Coast Times*, 20 June 1911. For a report of the meeting, see *New Zealand Tablet*, 29 June 1911.

89   *Ibid.* 22 and 28 June 1911. *New Zealand Tablet*, 6 July 1911.

90   *Ibid.*, 27 June 1911.

91   *Ibid.*, 24 and 28 June 1911.

92   *Grey River Argus*, 26 June 1911.

93   See Jackson, chs 5 and 6. For reaction to the 1916 Easter Rising, see *Grey River Argus*, 28 and 29 April 1916.

94   Sweetman, pp. 146–52.

95   Patrick O'Farrell, *Vanished Kingdoms: Irish in Australia and New Zealand: A Personal Excursion*, Kensington, 1990, pp. 263–4, 267.

96   There were few signs of the 'intolerance and sectarianism' that Rory Sweetman argues 'scarred' New Zealand during the decade after 1922. See Rory Sweetman, 'New Zealand Catholicism, War, Politics and the Irish Issue, 1912–1922', PhD thesis, University of Cambridge, 1990, p. 1 and *passim*.

CHAPTER 7

1   Ellen Piezzi to Victer Piezzi, 8 October 1881.

2   Ellen Piezzi to Victer Piezzi, undated (probably 1882).

3   Descendant information, Teresa O'Connor.

4   Ellen Piezzi to Victer Piezzi, 24 October 1879.

5   Ellen Piezzi to Victer Piezzi, 8 October 1881.

6   The 'messiness' of their encounter with new realities underlines Patrick Griffin's warning about the limitations of 'identity', a term which sometimes 'obscures the richness and detail of experience, underestimates contingency, and mutes dissonant voices'. See Patrick Griffin, *The People with No Name: Ireland's Ulster Scots, America's Scots-Irish and the Creation of a British Atlantic World, 1689–1764*, Princeton and Oxford, 2001, p. 7.

7   See Patrick O'Farrell, *Vanished Kingdoms: Irish in Australia and New Zealand: A Personal Excursion*, Kensington, 1990.

8   On Irish settlement in Ellesmere County (Canterbury) and Boorowa (New South Wales), see Sarah Dwyer and Lyndon Fraser, '"We are all here like so many on the cockle beds": Towards a History of Ulster Migrants in Nineteenth–Century Canterbury', in Brad Patterson, ed., *The Hidden Irish: Ulster-New Zealand Migration*

and Cultural Transfers, Dublin, 2005; Malcolm Campbell, *The Kingdom of the Ryans: The Irish in Southwest New South Wales, 1816–1890,* Sydney, 1997.

9   See, for example, Kerby A. Miller, *Emigrants and Exiles: Ireland and the Irish Exodus to North America,* New York, 1985; Miles Fairburn, *The Ideal Society and its Enemies: The Foundations of Modern New Zealand Society, 1850–1900,* Auckland, 1989; Frances Porter and Charlotte Macdonald, eds, *'My hand will write what the heart dictates': The Unsettled Lives of Women in Nineteenth-Century New Zealand as Revealed to Sisters, Family, and Friends,* Auckland, 1996. For an alternative view, see Lyndon Fraser, *To Tara via Holyhead: Irish Catholic Immigrants in Nineteenth-Century Christchurch,* Auckland, 1997; Angela McCarthy, '"A Good Idea of Colonial Life": Personal Letters and Irish Migration to New Zealand', *New Zealand Journal of History,* 35, 2001, pp. 1–21; Angela McCarthy, *Irish Migrants in New Zealand, 1840–1937: 'The Desired Haven',* Woodbridge, 2005.

10   I am indebted here to Rollo Arnold's notion of the 'Perennial Interchange'. See Rollo Arnold, 'The Dynamics and Quality of Trans-Tasman Migration, 1885–1910', *Australian Economic History Review,* 26, 1986, pp. 1–20; Philip Ross May, *The West Coast Gold Rushes,* Christchurch, 1962.

11   Jose C. Moya, *Cousins and Strangers: Spanish Immigrants in Buenos Aires, 1850–1930,* Berkeley, 1998, p. 4.

12   Don Handelman, 'The Organisation of Ethnicity', *Ethnic Groups,* 1, 1977, pp. 187–200.

13   Patrick O'Farrell, 'Catholicism on the West Coast: Just How Irish Is It?,' *New Zealand Tablet,* 3 May 1973, p. 54. See also Patrick O'Farrell, 'Landscapes of the Irish Immigrant Mind', in John Hardy, ed., *Stories of Australian Migration,* Kensington, 1988, pp. 34–5.

14   American historian Jack Greene uses the term 'charter group' to describe the powerful influence exerted by the earliest arrivals in new societies, 'who took possession of the land, devised ways to manipulate local resource materials for their own survival and profit, reordered the physical and social landscape, and worked out the political, legal, and other cultural arrangements appropriate to their situation'. See Jack P. Greene, 'Pluribus or Unum? White Ethnicity in the Formation of Colonial American Culture', *History Now/Te Pae Tawhito o Te Wa,* 4, 1998, p. 4.

Index

 Otago History Series

Otago University Press is the proud publisher of the Otago History Series. From Irish migration to the 1951 Waterfront crisis, public heritage to mental health treatment, this vibrant series makes an important contribution to a growing understanding of the rich history of New Zealand, Australia and the Pacific.

Selected titles

Adventures in Democracy: A History of the Vote in New Zealand
Neill Atkinson
paperback, 192 pages, illustrated,
ISBN 1 877276 58 8

Shifting Centres: Women and Migration in New Zealand History
Edited by Lyndon Fraser & Katie Pickles
paperback, 216 pages,
ISBN 1 877726 32 4

Landscape/Community: Perspectives from New Zealand History
Edited by Tony Ballantyne & Judith A. Bennett
paperback, 192 pages,
ISBN 1 877372 06 4

Sexuality Down Under: Social and Historical Perspectives
Edited by Allison Kirkman & Pat Moloney
paperback, 288 pages, illustrated,
ISBN 1 877372 10 2

'Rats and Revolutionaries': The Labour Movement in Australia and New Zealand, 1890–1940
James Bennett
paperback, 216 pages,
ISBN 1877276 49 9

Class and Occupation: The New Zealand Reality
Erik Olssen & Maureen Hickey
paperback, 320 pages,
ISBN 1 877372 03 X

Edward Eyre: Race and Colonial Governance
Julie Evans
paperback, 208 pages,
ISBN 1 877372 07 2

Class, Gender and the Vote: Historical Perspectives from New Zealand
Miles Fairburn & Erik Olssen
paperback, 288 pages,
ISBN 1 877372 02 1

Otago books are available from good booksellers
Further information: www.otago.ac.nz/press

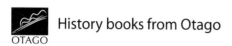 History books from Otago

OTAGO

Disputed Histories: Imagining New Zealand's Pasts
Edited by Tony Ballantyne and Brian Moloughney
Paperback, 240 pages, illustrated, ISBN 1 877372 16 1

The Welcome of Strangers: An Ethnohistory of Southern Maori, 1650–1850
Atholl Anderson
paperback, 252 pages, illustrated, ISBN 1 877133 41 8
hardback, illustrated, ISBN 1 877133 59 0

The Land Girls: In a Man's World, 1939–1946
Dianne Bardsley
paperback, 170 pages, illustrated, ISBN 1 877133 94 9

More than Law and Order: Policing a Changing Society 1946–1992
Susan Butterworth
hardback, 400 pages, illustrated, ISBN 1 877276 99 5

Women and Children Last: The Burning of the Emigrant Ship Cospatrick
Charles R. Clark
paperback, 176 pages, illustrated, ISBN 1 877372 14 5

Infectious Diseases: Colonising The Pacific?
John Miles
paperback, 124 pages, ISBN 1 877133 26 4

Travels in Oceania
Dr Louis Thiercelin, translated by Christiane Mortelier
paperback, 352 pages, illustrated, ISBN 0 908569 71 8

New Zealanders at Home: A Cultural History of Domestic Interiors 1814–1914
Anna K.C. Petersen
paperback, 160 pages, illustrated, ISBN 1 877276 14 6

Otago books are available from good booksellers
Further information: www.otago.ac.nz/press